I, MONSTER

I, MONSTER

SERIAL KILLERS IN THEIR OWN CHILLING WORDS

COLLECTED BY
TOM PHILBIN

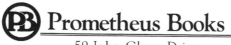 Prometheus Books

59 John Glenn Drive
Amherst, New York 14228–2119

Published 2011 by Prometheus Books

Inquiries should be addressed to
Prometheus Books
59 John Glenn Drive
Amherst, New York 14228–2119
VOICE: 716–691–0133
FAX: 716–691–0137
WWW.PROMETHEUSBOOKS.COM

20 19 18   8 7 6

Library of Congress Cataloging-in-Publication Data

Philbin, Tom, 1934–
    I, monster : serial killers in their own chilling words / by Tom Philbin.
        p. cm.
    Includes bibliographical references and index.
    ISBN 978–1–61614–163–9 (pbk. : alk. paper)
    1. Serial murderers—Case studies. 2. Serial murderers—Interviews. I. Title.

HV6515 .P48 2010
364.152'32—dc22

2010003608

Printed in the United States of America on acid-free paper

Every attempt has been made to trace accurate ownership of copyrighted material in this book. Errors and omissions will be corrected in subsequent editions, provided that notification is sent to the publishers.

CONTENTS

FOREWORD

A CLUB WITH A COST

I f you read this book, then you're joining a club.

It's the club of people who have had conversations with murderers about their crimes.

I'm part of this club. I interviewed Charles Manson for more than four hours. Tom Philbin is also part of this club. By turning these pages you're about to become an associate member. Let's sit and chat at the next meeting.

Most are changed by joining this club.

I don't mean to alarm you, but if you haven't joined this type of tough club before, I should tell you that there is a cost for admission. While reading this book you're experiencing some of the worst of humanity. The killers in these pages are depraved, vile, warped, disgusting people. If this were a medical textbook, these chapters would be about the worst diseases. Spending time with these low people is costly. Your soul may hurt. No normal person could read this book without taking several breaks to get away from these people. You may have to go outside and let the vapors of evil that have attached to you evaporate away from your body, because their spirit of evil will try to infiltrate you. To paraphrase George Lucas, you will never find a more wretched hive of scum and villainy than in these pages.

But, that's not how these serial killers see themselves.

To mention a few, they see themselves as

- *Craftsmen.* Dennis Rader, or BTK, mass murderer and serial killer (see chapter 14). He saw himself as a good student of serial killers and an excellent practitioner. In these pages he tells a judge, "I'm not bragging . . . ," though he was bragging on his skill as a serial killer.
- *Society's protectors.* Gary Ridgway, the Green River Killer (see chapter 16). He thought he was protecting society from prostitutes.
- *Victims.* Prostitute Aileen Wuornos (see chapter 20). When she murdered her johns, it was because of her hatred of them for their "raping" her.

Over more than thirty years, serial killer Dennis Rader read books about serial killers. He studied them, including some of the killers in this book (for example, H. H. Holmes and Jack the Ripper). Rader even earned a university degree with a major in criminal justice and took a class taught by the deputy chief of the Wichita Police Department, who spent portions of several class periods talking about the BTK case. Rader not only studied other serial killers but he also learned from his opponents: the law enforcement community, the mental health community, the spy community, the news media, and all types of sleuths, fictional and nonfiction, amateur and professional.

Similarly, I have no doubt that among the readers of this book will be a few uncaught serial killers. They will study this book as part of their self-education in what they see as their craft. Perhaps Zodiac will read this, or the East Area Rapist murderer, or other uncaught killers not given a public name. Perhaps some will be inspired to begin composing their remarks for the day they either publicly talk about their crimes or privately write their memoirs.

To you law-abiding readers, I say that for journalists, students, scholars, writers looking for a quote, this book is a treasure. For true crime readers, this book will give you an additional perspective on criminals—*creatures* might be a more apt word—with whom you're familiar.

Tom Philbin's service in compiling the interviews in this book is to provide you the opportunity to read these serial killer's words verbatim. You can interpret them yourself without the intermediary of the television talking head or newspaper editor.

I saw one talking head on television claim that in Dennis Rader's courtroom conversation with Judge Greg Waller, Rader never explained his motivation for committing his murders. If that commentator's view was the only thing you heard about Rader's full exchange with Judge Waller, then you might believe that. But here is an exchange from that

transaction, found in the pages in this book, where Rader explains his motivation:

> The Court: All right. And—and why did you have these potential hits? Was this to gratify some sexual interest or—

> The Defendant: Yes, sir.

In context, Dennis Rader said his motivation for murder was sex—perverse, twisted sex—which was the motive for most of these killers.

Is the truth believable?

What if you wanted to talk privately with the most guarded woman in the world, but she doesn't know you? Moreover, you do not want to alert her guards and servants that you are alone with her. She lives in a walled fortress surrounded by soldiers because this important woman has been constantly threatened. To get to her sounds impossible, but you might try to assemble a crack team of experts to plan the caper. Whether it succeeded or failed, it could make a great story.

What would not make a great story is if you simply climbed over the fortress wall and were ignored by the first guard who saw you on his monitor. Then you were ignored by staff and by more guards. You poked all around the six-hundred-room castle because you had never looked at a floor plan and had no idea where your target was. Not finding her on one floor, and being unable to figure out how to get to the next floor from the inside, you went outside, climbed up a drainpipe, and then crawled in an unlocked window. Then, by pure chance, you found her bedroom. This was coincidentally just moments after the woman's personal bodyguard took her dog for a walk and thus was away from her door. Then, when she pressed her bedside panic button, no one came because the guard monitoring the panic button had taken a break.

That's unbelievable and no one would credit that story.

Except that it really happened.

On July 9, 1982, after drinking late at a pub, Michael Fagan boasted that he thought he could get in to see Queen Elizabeth in Buckingham Palace. Everything described happened, and more. There was an investigation. If not for the evidence, no one would believe the story.

The Fagan story is solid gold true, but is it believable? Is fantastic truth believable?

The fantastic true crime stories in these twenty chapters sound unbelievable, but these killers declare this is the truth and objective evidence supports most of what they say.

Most. Some we can never know. We either take the killers' words for these iffy parts or we disbelieve them. There are reasons to disbelieve these killers. For much of their criminal lives they managed to stay out of prison by deceiving others. There's no reason to believe that they had suddenly stopped deceiving others when they made these statements.

In fact, one of these serial killers, Dennis Rader (BTK), has said that when he learned that the police had deceived him about their ability to trace him via a computer floppy disc, he became enraged. You can see the exchange on video. Rader is thumping the disc with his finger and angrily saying, "Why did you lie to me?" The officer responds, "Because I wanted to catch you." Rader sits back. A female author who has conducted hundreds of hours of interviews with Dennis Rader for a forthcoming book told me that at that point Rader said to himself, "Okay. You fucked with me. Now I'm going to fuck with you." Thereafter, everything Rader said in his thirty-three hours of recorded interviews with the police, and everything he said to Judge Waller, was a mixture of truth and fiction. Even after he was under arrest, Rader continued to laugh at and deceive police and society.

The point is, we acknowledge that what Rader did in mixing truth and fiction with his statements is probably true to a greater or lesser extent with all these murderers. They tell some truth. They tell some fiction. They serve their own interests, not ours. Yet, in their telling, and in this sharing, there is value. The key parts of what these killers have said are verifiable. As for the unverifiable parts, from events like the Michael Fagan story, we know that some unbelievable events really happened, so maybe the parts of their stories we don't believe are true. We must be exposed to human history, good and bad, believable and unbelievable, to learn from it. That's one reason why there are true crime books.

This is a true crime book to learn from.

Now you must excuse me. I must go for a walk, or an exorcism, to put some distance between me and these spirits of evil.

Robert Beattie
New York Times bestselling author of
Nightmare in Wichita: The Hunt for the BTK Strangler
and *Language of Evil*

Introduction

A ROUGH RIDE

This book will not be everyone's cup of tea. But for true crime fans who like to take their murder stories straight, it would be hard to think of anything more appealing because it is written by the serial killers themselves, direct quotations from their letters, confessions, trial transcripts, and the like. While a good hunk of the material can be fairly characterized as a rough ride, not all of it is. For example, one thing of particular interest was the questionnaire filled out by John Wayne Gacy, the serial killer who murdered more than thirty young boys in a suburb outside Chicago. His answers to it are utterly oblivious to his homicidal persona.

But the words of some killers are horrific, straight from hell. For example, what could be more horrific than Edmund Kemper describing in his confession to cops how he frenziedly stabbed a sixteen-year-old girl to death one lovely day in California and experienced a "sexual exultation" as he did. Or Westley Allan Dodd and the unspeakable things he did to a four-year-old victim, or Dennis Rader, who wiped out, one by one, an entire family and described the experience with all the interest he might have in blowing his nose.

Each of the chapters start with a background on the particular killer so the reader will be able to put the killer's utterances and deeds into context. Reason: the more you understand the context, the more you'll enjoy—if that is the right word—the book. Unless otherwise noted, the killer quotes come from official sources such as court transcripts and inter-

views with police and district attorneys. The advantage of using this kind of material is that it is more likely to be truthful. When cops and other official investigators probe for the truth, they usually get it.

And though I consider myself a card-carrying ghoul with the requisite cast-iron stomach when it comes to the subject, I had some difficulty making it through some of the material. The reason, I think, is that while this book is about serial killers, it is also about their victims. Never before have I grasped what victims go through then when researching this book. More than once I had to stop reading for a while, and more than once my sense of liberalness, my constant quest to understand why, went away and all I wanted to do was use my bare hands to kill the killers.

A great offshoot of this book, we think, is that it will provide insight into the mind and soul of the serial killer as never before. As you get to see how these people react with their victims, you start to understand that none of them has a conscience, none of them cares at all for their victims. You understand that when they kill, it is a sexual experience. Most will have an erection or experience orgasm as their victims die. And for most if not all, you come to realize that power and control over their victims is paramount. And you will come to understand that they relive the death of their victims by handling parts of their victims or pieces of their property. And you come to understand that one body isn't enough for serial killers. They will never stop killing until someone stops them.

All of the main monsters of the twentieth and twenty-first centuries will be heard from, people like cannibal and child killer Albert Fish; Green River Killer Gary Ridgway, who killed so many women he couldn't remember how many; Ted Bundy, who killed untold numbers of women—estimates vary—including two in one day; Dennis Rader, the BTK (Bind, Torture, Kill) murderer from Topeka, Kansas, who in court testimony described his stomach-churning escapades with a nonchalance, as suggested above, bordering on boredom. And David Parker Ray, who with a coven of diseased cohorts in New Mexico tortured kidnapped teenagers and young women, raping them thirty to forty times before getting down to serious torture. And two nineteenth-century killers, Jack the Ripper and H. H. Holmes, are quoted.

In a few instances, when the material is particularly nasty, we have provided cautionary notes.

Tom Philbin

i.

DAVID BERKOWITZ

BACKGROUND

D avid Berkowitz—who would grow up to become the infamous serial killer "Son of Sam," prowling the streets of New York City, armed with a .44 caliber Bulldog revolver and shooting people at random, mostly young women—was born to two people who were married. But not to each other. They gave the bastard child up for adoption to Nat and Pearl Berkowitz, who raised David in the Coop City complex of apartments in the Bronx.

The exact reasons for his development into a serial killer are not known, but by the age of twenty-two he was, as one cop put it later, "three quarts low." He thought bloodthirsty demons were controlling him, one in particular named "Sam," who was embodied in a neighbor's black Lab dog. (Which, ironically, is one of the most gentle dog breeds there is.) Berkowitz started thinking of himself as a "Son of Sam," the sort of son-of-a-bitch who would follow Sam's orders exactly, and those orders were to send people into the next life.

Following are selections from official court documents or notes and letters he wrote after his conviction.

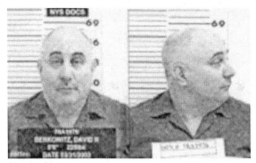

David Berkowitz

PERSONAL WRITINGS

At one point Berkowitz cruised Southampton, Long Island, looking for victims. But he said the demons in him didn't want him to murder that night so they started a storm to stop him. *They had enough force to call these clouds to stop me. . . . They always selected the people I'd shoot. It wasn't up to me.*

I am the demon from the bottomless pit here on earth to create havoc and terror. I am War, I am death and I am destruction.

I am tormented
I cry in my cell
I miss my daddy
I am very uptight
I hear demons
I see demons
I need to talk to someone.
I cannot be left alone
I will have a breakdown
I cannot be understood
I am truthful
I am doomed

I have made myself a promise not to remain locked up behind bars forever. I have debut [sic] to pay to society and one day I will be free to repay it.

I must repay society and now that I am a Christian I will work to help other people find true freedom and eternal life.

In this hospital I found Jesus Christ and it is Him who I am obligated to. I must tell society about the truth and hope.

A LETTER TO DAD

In November 1975 Son of Sam wrote a letter to his adoptive father, Nat, who had moved to Florida and left Berkowitz to fend for himself as, of all things, a security guard. In the letter, Berkowitz more than hinted at the depression he was feeling.

Dear Dad,

It's cold and gloomy here in New York, but that's okay because the weather fits my mood—gloomy. Dad, the world is getting dark now. I can feel it more and more. The people, they are developing a hatred for me. You wouldn't believe how much some people hate me. Many of them want to kill me. I don't even know these people, but they still hate me. Most of them are young. I walk down the street and they spit and kick at me. The girls call me ugly and they bother me the most. The guys just laugh. Anyhow, things will soon change for the better.

On Christmas Eve of that year—a month after he wrote this letter—Berkowitz, his paranoia in full blossom, went on his first hunt and started killing people.

SON OF SAM WRITES TO POLICE AND THE PRESS

In the midst of the Son of Sam killings, Berkowitz got offended by Captain Joseph Borrelli of the NYPD and wrote him the following letter.

Dear Captain Joseph Borrelli,

I am deeply hurt by your calling me a wemon hater. I am not. But I am a monster. I am the "Son of Sam." I am a little brat.

When father Sam gets drunk he gets mean. He beats his family. Sometimes he ties me up to the back of the house. Other times he locks me in the garage. Sam loves to drink blood.

I AM DEEPLY HURT BY YOUR CALLING
ME A WEMON HATER. I AM NOT.
BUT I AM A MONSTER.
I AM THE "SON OF SAM." I AM A LITILE
"BRAT".
    WHEN FATHER SAM GETS DRUNK
HE GETS MEAN. HE BEATS HIS
FAMILY. SOMETIMES HE TIES ME
UP TO THE BACK OF THE HOUSE.
OTHER TIMES HE LOCKS ME
IN THE GARAGE. SAM LOVES TO
DRINK BLOOD.
    "GO OUT AND KILL" COMMANDS
FATHER SAM.
    BEHIND OUR HOUSE SOME
REST. MOSTLY YOUNG - RAPED
AND SLAUGHTERED - THEIR
BLOOD DRAINED - JUST BONES
NOW
    PAPA SAM KEEPS ME LOCKED
IN THE ATTIC, TOO. I CAN'T
GET OUT BUT I LOOK OUT THE
ATTIC WINDOW AND WATCH
THE WORLD GO BY.
    I FEEL LIKE AN OUTSIDER.
I AM ON A DIFFERENT WAVE
LENGTH THEN EVERYBODY

ELSE - PROGRAMMED TOO
KILL
  HOWEVER, TO STOP ME YOU
MUST KILL ME. ATTENTION
ALL POLICE: SHOOT ME FIRST-
SHOOT TO KILL OR ELSE.
KEEP OUT OF MY WAY OR
YOU WILL DIE!

     PAPA SAM IS OLD NOW.
HE NEEDS SOME BLOOD TO
PRESERVE HIS YOUTH.
HE HAS HAD TOO MANY
HEART ATTACKS. TOO MANY
HEART ATTACKS. "UGH ME
HOOT IT URTS. SONNY BOY."

    I MISS MY PRETTY
PRINCESS MOST OF ALL.
SHE'S RESTING IN
  OUR LADIES HOUSE
BUT I'LL SHE HER SOON.

    I AM THE "MONSTER" -
"BEELZEBUB" - THE
"CHUBBY BEHEMOUTH".

"Go out and kill," commands father Sam.

Behind our house some rest. Mostly young—raped and slaughtered—their blood drained—just bones now.

Papa Sam keeps me locked in the attic too. I can't get out but I look out the attic window and watch the world go by.

I feel like an outsider. I am on a different wavelength then everybody else—programmed too kill.

However, to stop me you must kill me. Attention all police: Shoot me first—shoot to kill or else keep out of my way or you will die!

Papa Sam is old now. He needs some blood to preserve his youth. He has had too many heart attacks. "Ugh, me hoot, it urts, sonny boy."

I miss my pretty princess most of all. She's resting in our ladies house. But I'll see her soon.

I am the "Monster"—"Beelzebub"—the chubby behemouth.

I love to hunt. Prowling the streets looking for fair game—tasty meat. The wemon of Queens are prettyist of all. It must be the water they drink. I live for the hunt—my life. Blood for papa.

Mr. Borelli, sir, I don't want to kill anymore. No sir, no more but I must, "honour thy father."

I want to make love to the world. I love people. I don't belong on earth. Return me to yahoos.

To the people of Queens, I love you. And I want to wish all of you a happy Easter.

May God bless you in this life and in the next.

And for now I say goobye and goodnight. Police: Let me haunt you with these words: I'll be back! I'll be back! To be interrpreted as—bang, bang, bang, bang, bang—ugh!!

Yours in murder
Mr. Monster

Below is a letter written to Jimmy Breslin, a reporter for the New York Daily News, who received it on May 30, 1977.

Hello from the gutters of N.Y.C., which are filled with dog manure, vomit, stale wine, urine, and blood. Hello from the sewers of N.Y.C. which swallow up the delicacies when they are washed away by the sweeper trucks. Hello from the cracks in the sidewalks of N.Y.C. and from the ants that dwell in these cracks and feed on the dried blood of the dead that has seeped into these cracks.

J.B., I'm just dropping you a line to let you know that I appreciate your interest in those recent and horrendous .44 killings. I also want to tell you that I read your column daily and I find it quite informative.

I LOVE TO HUNT. PROWLING
THE STREETS LOOKING FOR
FAIR GAME - TASTY MEAT. THE
WEMON OF QUEENS ARE Z
PRETTYIST OF ALL. I MUST
BE THE WATER THEY DRINK.
I LIVE FOR THE HUNT - MY LIFE.
BLOOD FOR PAPA.

MR. BORELLI, SIR,
I DONT WANT TO KILL ANYMORE
NO SIR, NO MORE BUT I
MUST, "HONOUR THY FATHER."

I WANT TO MAKE LOVE TO THE
WORLD. I LOVE PEOPLE.
I DONT BELONG ON EARTH.
RETURN ME TO YAHOOS.

TO THE · PEOPLE OF QUEENS,
I LOVE YOU. AND I
WANT TO WISH ALL OF
YOU A HAPPY EASTER.
MAY GOD BLESS YOU
IN THIS LIFE AND IN
THE NEXT AND FOR NOW

I SAY GOODBYE AND GOODNIGHT.

POLICE- LET ME HAUNT YOU WITH THESE WORDS;

I'LL BE BACK!

I'LL BE BACK!

TO BE INTERRPRETED AS— BANG, BANG, BANG, BANK, BANG — UGH!!

YOURS IN MURDER

MR. MONSTER

Tell me Jim, what will you have for July twenty-ninth? You can forget about me if you like because I don't care for publicity. However you must not foget Donna Lauria and you cannot let the people forget her either. She was a very, very sweet girl but Sam's a thirsty lad and he won't let me stop killing until he gets his fill of blood.

Mr. Breslin, sir, don't think that because you haven't heard from me for a while that I went to sleep. No, rather, I am still here. Like a spirit roaming the night. Thirsty, hungry, seldom stopping to rest; anxious to please Sam. I love my work. Now, the void has been filled.

Perhaps we shall meet face to face someday or perhaps I will be blown away by cops with smoking .38's. Whatever, if I shall be fortunate enough to meet you, I will tell you all about Sam if you like and I will introduce you to him. His name is "Sam the Terrible".

Not knowing what the future holds I shall say farewell and I will see you at the next job. Or should I say you will see my handiwork at the next job? Remember Ms. Lauria. Thank you. In their blood and from the gutter "Sam's Creation" .44

Here are some names to help you along. Forward them to the inspector for use by N.C.I.C: "The Duke of Death" "The Wicked King Wicker" "The Twenty Two Disciples of Hell" "John 'Wheaties'—Rapist and Suffocator of Young Girls"

PS: J.B. Please inform all the detectives working on the slaying to remain.

P.S: J.B., please inform all the detectives working the case that I wish them the best of luck. Keep 'em digging, drive on, think positive, get off your butts, knock on coffins.

Upon my capture I promise to buy all the guys working on the case a new pair of shoes if I can get up the money.

Above material from David Klausner, *Son of Sam: Based on the Authorized Transcription of the Tapes, Official Documents and Diaries of David Berkowitz* (New York: McGraw-Hill, 1981); letter from Berkowitz to Borrelli, Serial Killer Database, http://www.serialkillerdatabase.net (accessed April 22, 2010), and used by permission of Joshua Henderson; letter from Berkowitz to Breslin, *New York Daily News*, June 5, 1977, http://www.nydailynews.com/features/sonofsam/letter.html (accessed May 12, 2010). Photo courtesy of NYS Department of Corrections.

Ted Bundy

2.

TED BUNDY

BACKGROUND

Theodore Robert "Ted" Bundy was born on November 24, 1946, in Burlington, Vermont, in a home for unwed mothers. Some investigators think that his grandfather on his mother's side fathered him.

Bundy spent his early years in Vermont living with his grandparents. At one point his mother took custody of him, remarried, and raised him as her younger brother, not wishing to face the then powerful stigma of having an illegitimate child. He grew up in the north end residential area of Tacoma, Washington. He was a Boy Scout.

He and his stepfather didn't get along well, and for some reason he developed a hatred for his mother. Tellingly, most of the women he killed had their hair parted down the middle—just like his mother.

After he graduated from the University of Washington he attended the university law school while doing charity work and campaigning for the Republican Party. He developed a series of normal relationships with women. At one point Bundy worked in Seattle on a suicide hotline and sat next to Ann Rule, who would later become a best-selling crime writer. She wrote of her experience with Bundy in *The Stranger Beside Me*.

Between 1974 and 1978 Bundy sexually assaulted and murdered young women in Washington, Oregon, Colorado, Utah, and Florida. He confessed to killing thirty women, but there were likely many more.

Following his trial, in 1979 he was sentenced to death for the murder of two college students and the following year he was again sentenced to death, for the rape and murder of a twelve-year-old girl named Kimberly Leach, whom he had beaten badly. Investigators found six of her teeth under her body, as was his habit in murdering people.

Bundy rode the lightning, as they say, on January 24, 1989. It's hard to imagine just what kind of a monster he was because he came disguised as a human being. To help this along, we have included a list of some of his known murder victims. Just note how young they were, most just teenagers.

BUNDY'S VICTIMS

Below is a chronological list of Ted Bundy's known victims. Bundy never made a comprehensive confession before he was executed. He confessed to murdering thirty women, only twenty of which were identified. Bundy also admitted to decapitating at least a dozen of his victims, and many were found with front teeth missing.

1973

May. Unknown hitchhiker, Tumwater, Washington, area. Confessed to Bob Keppel before Bundy's execution. No remains found.

1974

January 4. "Joni Lenz" (pseudonym) (survived). University of Washington first-year student who was bludgeoned in her bed and impaled with a speculum in her vagina as she slept.

February 1. Twenty-one-year-old Lynda Ann Healy was bludgeoned while asleep and abducted from the house she shared with other female University of Washington students.

March 12. Nineteen-year-old Donna Gail Manson was abducted while walking to a jazz concert on the Evergreen State College campus, Olympia, Washington. Bundy confessed to her murder, but her body was never definitively discovered.

April 17. Eighteen-year-old Susan Elaine Rancourt disappeared as she walked across Ellensburg's Central Washington State College campus at night.

May 6. Twenty-two-year-old Roberta Kathleen "Kathy" Parks vanished from Oregon State University in Corvallis, Oregon, while she was walking to another dormitory to have coffee with friends.

June 1. Twenty-two-year-old Brenda Carol Ball disappeared from the Flame Tavern in Burien, Washington.

June 11. Eighteen-year-old Georgeann Hawkins disappeared from behind her sorority house, Kappa Alpha Theta, at the University of Washington.

July 14. Twenty-three-year-old Janice Ann Ott and nineteen-year-old Denise Marie Naslund were abducted several hours apart from Lake Sammamish State Park in Issaquah, Washington.

September 2. Bundy confessed to killing an unknown teenage hitchhiker in Idaho. No remains were found.

October 2. Sixteen-year-old Nancy Wilcox disappeared in Holladay, Utah. Her body was never found.

October 18. Seventeen-year-old Melissa Anne Smith vanished from Midvale, Utah, after leaving a pizza parlor.

October 31. Seventeen-year-old Laura Aime disappeared from a Halloween party at Lehi, Utah.

November 8. Carol DaRonch escaped from Bundy by jumping out of his car in Murray, Utah.

November 8. Seventeen-year-old Debra "Debby" Kent vanished from the parking lot of a school in Bountiful, Utah, hours after Carol DaRonch jumped out of Bundy's car. Shortly before his execution, Bundy confessed to investigators that he dumped Kent at a site near Fairview, Utah. An intense search of the site produced a human patella, which matched the profile for someone of Kent's age and size. DNA testing has not been attempted.

Bundy is a suspect in the murder of Carol Valenzuela, who disappeared from Vancouver, Washington, on August 2, 1974. Her remains were discovered two months later south of Olympia, Washington, along with those of an unidentified female.

1975

January 12. Twenty-three-year-old Caryn Campbell, a nurse from Michigan, vanished between the hotel lounge and her room while on a ski trip with her fiancé in Snowmass, Colorado.

March 15. Twenty-six-year-old Julie Cunningham disappeared while on her way to a nearby tavern in Vail, Colorado. Bundy confessed to investigators he had buried Cunningham's body near Rifle, Colorado, but they found no remains.

April 6. Twenty-five-year-old Denise Oliverson was abducted while bicycling to visit her parents in Grand Junction, Colorado. Bundy provided details of her murder but a body was never found.

May 6. Thirteen-year-old Lynette Culver was snatched from a school playground at Alameda Junior High School in Pocatello, Idaho. Her body was never found.

June 28. Fifteen-year-old Susan Curtis disappeared while walking alone to the dormitories during a youth conference at Brigham Young University in Provo, Utah. Her body was never found.

Bundy is a suspect in the murder of Melanie Suzanne "Suzy" Cooley, who disappeared April 15, 1975, after leaving Nederland High School in Nederland, Colorado. Her bludgeoned and strangled corpse was discovered by road maintenance workers on May 2, 1975, in nearby Coal Creek Canyon. Gas receipts place Bundy in nearby Golden, the day of the Cooley abduction. The Jefferson County, Colorado, Sheriff's Office has classified the Melanie Cooley murder as a cold case.

1978

January 15. Twenty-year-old Lisa Levy and twenty-one-year-old Margaret Bowman died during the Chi Omega killings at Florida State University, Tallahassee, Florida. Karen Chandler and Kathy Kleiner survived.

January 15. Cheryl Thomas was bludgeoned in her bed, eight blocks away from the Chi Omega Sorority house, but survived.

February 9. Twelve-year-old Kimberly Leach was kidnapped from her junior high school in Lake City, Florida. She was raped and murdered. Her body was discarded in Suwannee River State Park, Florida.

BUNDY AND PORNOGRAPHY

Bundy said he began casually reading soft-core pornography when he was twelve or thirteen. His friends found pornographic books in the garbage cans in his neighborhood. "From time to time," he said, "we would come across pornographic books of a harder nature . . . a more graphic, explicit nature than we would encounter at the local grocery store," he told James Dobson, the founder of Focus on the Family, who had the last interview with Bundy before he was executed. "But slowly throughout the years, reading pornography became a compulive habit.

"My experience with pornography," Bundy said, "is (that) once you

become addicted to it (and I look at this as a kind of addiction like other kinds of addiction), I would keep looking for more potent, more explicit, more graphic kinds of material. Like an addiction, you keep craving something that is harder, something which gives you a greater sense of excitement. Until you reach a point where the pornography only goes so far, you reach that jumping off point where you begin to wonder if maybe actually doing it would give you that which is beyond just reading or looking at it."

Although Bundy said he did not blame pornography, he explained that pornographic materials shaped and molded his behavior. He also warned that "the most damaging kinds of pornography . . . are those that involve violence and sexual violence. Because the wedding of those two forces, as I know only too well, brings out the hatred that is just, just too terrible to describe."

DEATH WISH?

"Where are most people likely to be executed now?" Ted Bundy once asked his lawyer. At the time, Bundy was in jail in Silver Springs, Colorado.

"I suppose it might be Georgia . . . no," Bundy's lawyer corrected himself, "it'd probably be Florida now."

"Florida?" repeated Bundy.

A short time later Bundy escaped from prison and fled to Florida, where he killed two women and a twelve-year-old. He was caught, tried, and executed. A number of psychiatrists felt he had a death wish.

AN UNUSUAL REQUEST

One of the chief pursuers of the Green River Killer in Washington State was Detective Robert Keppel, who also pursued and was on the verge of catching Bundy. Indeed, not catching him was a source of great pain to Keppel because a free Bundy was a murdering Bundy. He was in the same situation with the Green River Killer.

Murder victims began to surface in the Seattle area, and they continued to for twenty years. The largest murder task force ever was put together—the Green River Task Force—and they pursued literally thousands of leads, many of which came through the mail.

But a combination of factors—including incompetence—got them nowhere.

Then one day the desperate task force received a letter from Bundy, who was on death row in Starke, Florida. Bundy offered to help them find the Green River Killer.

Keppel wrote the following letter to Bundy, a letter that was vetted by psychiatrists and was careful not to offend Bundy in any way.

Dear Ted:

This is to acknowledge receipt of your letter to the Green River Task Force dated October 1, 1984. Your request that any communications may be kept in "strictest of confidence" is absolutely honored. I, too, am concerned that any comments made by you could be detrimental to the Green River Investigation.

I am interested in what information you have that could prove useful in apprehending the person(s) responsible for the Green River murders. In order to assess the immediacy of your assistance, could you provide just some facts about the nature of your help? I could, tentatively, visit Florida in the middle of November in conjunction with other investigative duties. I have made inquiry to your local FBI to arrange a possible visit. You may hear from them. The sensitivity of this matter was emphasized.

I respect your statement of "playing no games" and, frankly, playing games with you is presumptuous on my part and a waste of my time. I am interested in what is useful in resolving the Green River killings and what your contribution is. We will communicate at your request only about the Green River killings and "nothing else."

In less than two weeks Bundy responded with a twenty-two-page letter detailing how he thought he could contribute to the Green River investigation and the wide variety of areas where thought he could be useful.

Keppel and head of the Green River Task Force, Dave Reichert, traveled to Starke, Florida, to visit Bundy. He speculated about the motive and methods of the Green River Killer, whom Keppel called "The Riverman" and later wrote a book of the same name. Bundy gave extensive opinions of how the Green River Killer operated and revealed some of his own twisted secrets. In the end, Bundy's insights were extremely valuable to Keppel and Reichert in terms of getting to know how a serial killer thinks.

Bundy's help was comprehensive. Here he is, for example, on the method employed by the Riverman. Bundy said, "He had a method that's more generalized to pick up anybody he selects—if he's just selecting prostitutes, now, that's one thing—but maybe later he's going to start selecting runaways or juvenile delinquents or girls that hang out in bars. They are the kinds of people who you don't identify as directly falling into your pro-

file. Let's say he chose those who were not car-date prostitutes, but who are delinquents and runaways—he just shifted his approach to victims a notch to the right. He's not going for prostitutes but prostitute-types, who dress or act or look to him like prostitutes. If you haven't found them yet, he's just disposing of them very well or it would be my guess he may have moved and is no longer operating in the King County area."

At various times in their interactions, Bundy and the two investigators clashed a little. Bundy, in particular, had a large ego—which a psychiatrist will tell you adds up to no ego—and sometimes he threw it right into the investigators' faces.

One time, for example, Dave Reichert casually asked Bundy if it was possible—since after October 1983 there hadn't been any bodies discovered for a while—if he thought the Riverman had stopped killing. As written in *The Riverman*,

> The gleaming smirk on Ted's face was his answer: "No! Not unless he was born again and got filled with the Holy Spirit in a very real way. He's either moved, he's dead, or he's doing something very different." The prospect that the Riverman was murdering in a different way was enlightening. What would he be doing differently? I thought. After pausing for a while as if he were meditating, Bundy announced, "My feelings are this! There's no question in my mind, if he's straightened up, he's changed his victim class just a little, dealing with runaways, generally, rather than prostitutes specifically. He broadened out a little bit more just to deal with runaways and delinquents and was more careful in the way that he disposed of their bodies, and there's no question that this explains the apparent drop-off." As it turned out, Bundy was correct on this assumption. Gary Ridgeway, the GRK, was at one point targeting younger victims, runaways, and delinquents, many of whom were cocaine addicts desperate for money for their score.

DONNA MANSON'S SKULL

Donna Gail Manson was an Evergreen State College student in Olympia, Washington, who disappeared on March 12, 1974. She was last seen on her way to a jazz concert in Olympia, and that same year Bundy admitted to killing her but did not give any details on where her remains were. Remains, of course, are vitally important to family, and since Keppel and Reichert had established a relationship with Bundy, they asked where her remains were. The skeleton of a young female had been found at the foot

of Mount Rainier in Washington by two fishermen, but police were unable to identify them definitively as the remains of Manson.

Here is Keppel questioning Bundy about the girl.

"Okay, how about Donna Manson? Gal from Thurston County, Olympia."

"Where is she? That was different. That was different."

"What was different about it? You told me before that she might be buried."

He grinned sheepishly, and stuttered like he was about to tell a lie, offering that Manson was buried farther up the power line road and slightly inside the tree cover.

But he did not seem to want to discuss her though Keppel told him that if he could be more specific cops might be able to find the remains.

"I won't beat around the bush with you anymore, because I'm just tired, and I just want to get back and go to sleep."

"Okay," Keppel said, waiting expectantly for him to talk.

"So let me just tell you. I know that part of her is buried up there, but nothing identifiable, probably just literally bones. The head, however, the skull, wouldn't be there," Ted said.

"Where is it?"

"It's nowhere."

"It's nowhere?"

"Well, I'm not trying to be flippant. It's just nowhere. It's in a category by itself. Now, I'd just as soon this is something that you just kept. I can see the headlines now. But—"

"Ted there's not going to be any details. What you told me about Georgeann Hawkins isn't going to be known. And I have parents out there that don't even want to know the details. I want to know for my own good."

"Well," Ted said, "it was incinerated. It was just an exception. A strange exception, but it was incinerated."

"Where did you incinerate it?" I asked, shocked.

Laughing, Ted said, "Ahh."

"Come on, partner," Keppel said. "These are things I don't know about you."

"Yeah," Ted said proudly, "this is probably the disposal method of preference among those who get away with it. It's the most bizarre nature I've ever been associated with, and I've been associated with some bizarre shit."

"Right. It's incinerated." Keppel was stunned.

"It's incinerated," Ted repeated.

"Tell me about it. What the hell happened?"

"Well, I don't know the address of the place. I never wanted to tell

this—I promised myself I'd never tell this, because of all the things I did to this woman, this is probably the one she was least likely to forgive me for. Poor Liz. [He was referring to Elizabeth Kendall, his former fiancée.] In her fireplace. That's not really that humorous, but I mean, the fireplace at that house," Ted said with sinister, satisfied laughter in his voice.

"Burn it all up?" Keppel asked, disbelieving.

"Down to the last ash, and in a fit of—you know—paranoia and cleanliness, what have you, just vacuumed down all the ashes. That's the twist. It's a twist. And it's a lot of work and certainly very risky, under the circumstances. I mean, the kids come home from school, there's a roaring fire in the fireplace, and it's warm outside," Ted said. With finality.

THE FINAL NIGHT OF BUNDY'S LIFE

On the final night before he was to die, many people hoped that Bundy would come forth and confess to some uncleared cold case homicides. A list was given to him and he went through it efficiently, with the prison warden doing the questioning.

"January 24, 1989," Bundy began. "For the Utah detective named 'Couch,' there's one more we didn't have time for. It's going to be hard. Between Price and Green River, about ten miles south of Price, a road going south out of Price, maybe five or ten miles, the inside road to the left going toward the mountains, going east. A quarter mile in there's a dirt road to the left. This is not going to work too well," Bundy said, looking at a map he had, "but I'll try to do something with it. A hundred to two hundred yards in on the dirt road, stop and to the left off the dirt road, maybe fifty yards in, there's the remains of a young woman who disappeared from Brigham Young University, June of 1975. That's as close as I can get it from the map that we have here."

"Do you know her name?" the warden asked.

"No, I don't," Bundy answered.

"Is that it?" the warden asked again.

"To Mike Fisher and the Colorado detectives, the last woman they wanted to talk about, Denise Oliverson, I believe. Referring again to Denise Oliverson, or whoever it was out of Grand Junction that Mike Fish wanted to discuss, I believe the date was in April 1975. The young woman's body would have been placed in the Colorado River about five miles west of Grand Junction. It was not buried. That's all the ones that I can help you with. That's all the ones that I know about. There are no missing ones outstanding that we haven't talked about."

"That's all of 'em, Ted?" the warden wanted to know.

"Yeah," Bundy said, then asked if he could "get a smoke off somebody."

"I see we had some inquiries from Illinois and New Jersey," the warden continued.

"Okay," Bundy answered. "Well, let's just deal with whatever is outstanding like that. I can say without any question that there is nothing for instance that I was involved in in Illinois or New Jersey."

"How about Burlington, Vermont?" the warden asked. "Nothing there? Texas?"

"No," Bundy answered.

"Miami?" the warden continued.

Bundy responded no.

"Okay," the warden continued. "No. That's all we've got. Okay, Ted, thank you."

"You're welcome," Bundy said, and that was the end of the final interview he gave to law enforcement about his crimes on the last night of his life.

Victim information from http:wickipedia.org/Ted_Bundy/#victims (accessed July 14, 2010); material from James Dobson interview from http://www.boundless.org/2005/articles/a0001949.cfm (accessed July 14, 2010); other sources: Tom Philbin, *Murder USA* (New York: Warner Books, 1992); Robert Keppel, *The Riverman: How Ted Bundy and I Hunted for the Green River Killer* (New York: Pocketbooks, 2004). Photo courtesy of author.

3.

JEFFREY DAHMER

BACKGROUND

Jeffrey Dahmer was born in Milwaukee in 1960. When he was six years old, his family moved to Ohio. There is not a great body of evidence to hint about or clearly explain what happened to create Jeffrey Dahmer the killer, but it is known that, as a child, he witnessed his mother and father's blistering arguments, which of course would be quite threatening to a child. There were also reports that a male neighbor had sexually molested him. Whatever the confluence of forces, by the age of ten, Jeffrey was clearly showing the signs of a future serial killer—he delighted in violating the bodies of dead animals, such as mounting the head of a dog on a stake, decapitating rats and mice, and bleaching chicken bones.

In June 1978, when he was eighteen years old, he murdered his first human being. His mother and father, who had separated by this time, had gone off somewhere on separate journeys and had left him alone in the house. He had a car and he picked up a hitchhiker named Steven Hicks. He took Hicks home with hopes of having sex with him. But when Hicks wanted to leave, Dahmer prevented him by smashing him in the skull with a barbell. Dahmer then cut him up and buried the parts.

In 1982, Dahmer moved in with his grandmother in West Allis, Wisconsin. In August of that year, he was arrested for exposing himself at a state fair. In September 1986, he was charged again with public exposure after two boys accused him of masturbating in public. This time he was sentenced to a year in prison.

Jeffrey Dahmer

On September 25, 1988, he was arrested for fondling a thirteen-year-old Laotian boy in Milwaukee. On May 23, 1989, Dahmer's lawyer, Gerald Boyle, and assistant district attorney Gale Shelton presented their arguments to Judge William Gardner. Shelton wanted a prison sentence of at least five years. "In my judgment it is absolutely crystal clear that the prognosis for treatment of Mr. Dahmer within the community is extremely bleak. . . . His perception that what he did wrong here was choosing too young a victim—and that that's all he did wrong—is a part of the problem. . . . He appeared to be cooperative and receptive, but anything that goes below the surface indicates the deep-seated anger and deep-seated psychological problems that he is unwilling or incapable of dealing with."

He had a good lawyer in Gerald Boyle, and Dahmer was quite articulate himself and spoke to a judge who wanted to lock him up and throw away the key because he had served time for sex offenses earlier. He got a year, served ten months in a work-release camp, then convinced the judge that he needed therapy. He was released on good behavior with five-year probation. Shortly thereafter, he racked up a string of brutal murders, some of which involved cannibalism, ending with his 1991 arrest.

I think in some way I wanted it to end, even if it meant my own destruction.

CONFESSIONS

To relieve the minds of the parents I mean . . . it's a small, very small thing, but I don't know what else I could do. At least I can do that . . . because I created this horror and it only makes sense that I do everything to put an end to it, a complete end to it.

It's just a nightmare, let's put it that way. It's been a nightmare for a long time, even before I was caught . . . for years now, obviously my mind has been filled with gruesome, horrible thoughts and ideas . . . a nightmare.

I couldn't find any meaning in my life when I was out there. I'm sure as hell not going to find it in here. This is the grand finale of a life poorly spent and the end result is just overwhelmingly depressing . . . it's just a sick, pathetic, wretched, miserable life story, that's all it is. How it can help anyone, I've no idea.

I don't even know if I have the capacity for normal emotions or not because I haven't cried for a long time. You just stifle them for so long that maybe you lose them, partially at least. I don't know.

I don't know why it started. I don't have any definite answers on that myself. If I knew the true, real reasons why all this started, before it ever did, I wouldn't probably have done any of it.

If I'd been thinking rationally I would have stopped. I wasn't thinking rationally because it just increased and increased. It was almost like I wanted to get to a point where it was out of my control and there was no return. I mean, I was very careful for years and years, you know. Very careful, very careful about making sure that nothing incriminating remained, but these last few months, they just went nuts. It just seemed like it went into a frenzy this last month. Everything really came crashing down. The whole thing started falling down around my head. That was the last week I was going to be in that apartment building. I was going to have to move out and find somewhere to put all my possessions. Should I get a chest and put what I wanted to keep in that, and get rid of the rest? Or should I put an end to this, try to stop this and find a better direction for my life? That's what was going through my mind that last week.

One thing I know for sure. It was a definite compulsion because I couldn't quit. I tried, but after the Ambassador, I couldn't quit. It would be nice if someone could give the answer on a silver platter as to why I did all this and what caused it, because I can't come up with an answer.

I felt in complete shock. I just couldn't believe it happened again after all those years when I'd done nothing like this . . . I don't know what was going through my mind. I have no memory of it. I tried to dredge it up, but I have no memory whatsoever.

I didn't want to keep killing people and have nothing left except the skull. . . . This is going to sound bad, but . . . should I say it? . . . I took the drill while he was asleep.

Yes, I do have remorse, but I'm not even sure myself whether it is as profound as it should be. I've always wondered myself why I don't feel more remorse.

After the fear and terror of what I'd done had left, which took about a month or two, I started it all over again. From then on it was a craving, a hunger, I don't know how to describe it, a compulsion, and I just kept doing it, doing it and doing it, whenever the opportunity presented itself.

I knew my grandma would be waking up and I still wanted him to stay with me so I strangled him and I brought him up to the bedroom and pretended he was still alive.

ON THE MURDER OF STEVEN HICKS

That night in Ohio, that one impulsive night. Nothing's been normal since then. It taints your whole life. After it happened I thought that I'd just try to live as normally as possible and bury it, but things like that don't stay buried. I didn't think it would, but it does, it taints your whole life.

DAHMER'S SEXUAL NATURE

At about eleven o'clock at night, when everyone was gone and the store was locked up from the outside, I went out and undressed the mannequin and I had a big sleeping bag cover. I put it in that, zipped it up and carried it out of the store, which was a pretty dangerous thing to do. I never thought of them maybe having security cameras or being locked in the store, but I walked out with it and took it back home. I ended up getting a taxi and brought it back and kept it with me a couple of weeks. I just went through various sexual fantasies with it, pretending it was a real person, pretending that I was having sex with it, masturbating, and undressing it.

ON THE MURDER OF ANTHONY SEARS

I took the knife and the scalp part off and peeled the flesh off the bone and kept the skull and the scalp. . . . If I could have kept him longer, all of him, I would have.

ON GERALDO RIVERA

He just wants to make people feel as guilty and lousy as possible. The guy is such a prick.

ON THE MURDER OF ERNEST MILLER

I separated the joints, the arm joints, the leg joints, and had to do two boilings. I think I used four boxes of Soilex for each one, put in the upper portion of the body and boiled that for about two hours and then the lower portion for another two hours. The Soilex removes all the flesh, turns it into a jellylike substance and it just rinses off. Then I laid the clean bones in a light bleach solution, left them there for a day and spread them out on either newspaper or cloth and let them dry for about a week in the bedroom.

THE MURDERS THAT WEIGHED HEAVIEST ON DAHMER'S MIND

On Steven Hicks: *I wish I hadn't done it.*

On Steven Tuomi: *I had no intention of doing it in the first place.*

On Jeremiah Weinberger: *He was exceptionally affectionate. He was nice to be with.*

ON CONTROL

Something stronger than my conscious will made it happen. I think some higher power got good and fed up with my activity and decided to put an end to it. I don't really think there were any coincidences. The way it ended and whether the close calls were warning to me or what, I don't know. If they were, I sure didn't heed them. If I hadn't been caught or lost my job, I'd still be doing it, I'm quite sure of that. I went on doing it and doing it and doing it, in spite of my anxiety and the lack of lasting satisfaction. How arrogant and stupid of me to think that I could do something like this and just go about my life normally as if nothing ever happened. They say you

reap what you sow, well, it's true, you do, eventually. . . . I've always won-dered, from the time that I committed that first horrid mistake, sin, with Hicks, whether this was sort of predestined and there was no way I could have changed it. I wonder just how much predestination controls a person's life and just how much control they have over themselves.

I was completely swept along with my own compulsion. I don't know how else to put it. It didn't satisfy me completely so maybe I was thinking another one will. Maybe this one will, and the numbers started growing and growing and just got out of control, as you can see.

REFLECTIONS ON DEATH

It's just like a big chunk of me has been ripped out and I'm not quite whole. I don't think I'm overdramatizing it, and I'm certainly deserving of it, but the way I feel now, it's just like you're talking to someone who is terminally ill and facing death. Death would be preferable to what I am facing. I just feel like imploding upon myself, you know? I just want to go somewhere and disappear.

When you've done the types of things I've done, it's easier not to reflect on yourself. When I start thinking about how it's affecting the families of the people, and my family and everything, it doesn't do me any good. It just gets me very upset.

If I was killed in prison. That would be a blessing right now.

All quoted material from Serial Killer Central, http://www.skcentral.com/ articles.php?article_id=25 (accessed July 15, 2010), originally taken from Serial Murder through the Looking Glass, http://serial-killers.virtualave .net, by permission of the Serial Killer Central Web site, Joe Hiles. Photo courtesy of Milwaukee County Sheriff's Department.

Westley Allan Dodd

4.

WESTLEY ALLAN DODD

BACKGROUND

Westley Allan Dodd said that as a child growing up in Washington State he was neglected, and by the age of fourteen he was molesting small children, starting with his cousins. He molested over fifty kids. His fantasies became more and more violent. Finally, molestation led to murder. He tortured and murdered a four-year-old boy named Lee Iseli near Portland, Oregon, and two preteen brothers, Cole and William Neer, in a Vancouver, Washington, park. Dodd was arrested and captured, and at his request dropped out of the legal procedure that would have extended his life. He was hanged, also his choice, in 1993.

In his own small printing and handwriting, Dodd kept what he described as "A Diary of Death." In it he detailed his plans and the results of his murderous molestations.

The material that follows is from that diary. In "Part One," "How It Started Chapter 1," he describes his early forays into molestation. In "No. 2" he describes the Iseli killing, and in "No. 3" he describes how he hunted for victims and how he found the Neer brothers and stabbed them to death.

Warning: These handwritten journals are horrific, and horrific is not exaggerating. Indeed, the author himself had to read the journals in short segments.

PART ONE
How it Started
Chapter 1

9-23-89

370

On the weekend of my 9th birthday, my brothers and sister were in the hospital having tonsils removed (July 3rd). I stayed at my cousin Johnnies. (My Dads-brother-s-kid). John also had a cousin from his mothers side of the family, I think his name was Mike. John was a month older than I, and Mike about a month younger.

The three of us were in John's room getting ready to go swimming in a 1-foot deep pool he had. John and Mike wanted me to watch something. They both pulled down their swim trunks, then touched their penises together. I don't remember what was said, but I ended up doing it with Johnny.

A few days later, at home, I remember pulling my swim trunks to my knees and crawling on my arms around our own little swimming pool. I remember feeling excited about it - "skinny dipping I think is what they call it."

So, I had, at age 9, had one sexual experience with two nine-year-old boys, and one sexual experience while alone.

Also, that same summer, after a bath, I remember rubbing hand lotion over every part of my body. This gave me a warm feeling inside. I do not recall having an erection while rubbing lotion into my groin, crotch, and other things. (At this point I did not know what it was called. I'd never heard any of the terms used; i.e. dick, balls, penis, privates, secret parts, etc.)

At the end of that summer I was very upset, though I didn't show it, because I had to change 2 or 3 pairs of pants in front of mom and 2 or 3 aunts to show them my new school clothes. I didn't like them seeing me in my underwear.

This gave me a good start on the road of sexual

①

deviancy. This started in July of 1970. I had just turned 9

years old, and was preparing for the 4th grade, in Yakima.

With about a month left in the 4th grade, we moved

to Umatilla, OR. I was un-happy at the prospect of moving

again. It had now been 3 years since I completed one

entire school year at one school.

1971

Now between 4th and 5th grade, my 10th birthday in July.

At the end of July some people moved into the empty house

next door. They had two daughters; Vauna, my age (my class

at school), and Darla, 8 or 9 years old.

One day Darla had an idea. It was something she had said

she'd done before. Kathy (my sister, 4 years younger than I) and I

went into Darla's garage.

Back in the corner, Darla went first, Kathy seemed just as in-

terested as I was. Darla pulled up her shirt a little, then pulled her

pants, then her underpants, down to her knees. She

stayed that way for about 5 seconds. That was

just enough for me to ask her to do it again. I

wanted to study her a little longer. - I'd never seen this before. But,

she said it was my turn. I was disapointed and frustrated when

Darla wouldn't look and my sister did. Darla said she'd seen it

before on other boys. This may explain why a lot of my future

victims would be boys.

X X X

I don't recall any other incidents until the end of my 9th

grade year, at the age of 14. I'd been teased by the girls, and

by the boys in the locker room. Later on a counselor told me I may

X

have been trying to "prove" I was a man. He also said that these

incidents just mentioned were 'normal' childhood experimentation.

(2)

2 _____ This is it! _____

Chapter 2.

376 ____ In March or April I remember seeing a picture (no details
actually showing) in National Geographic. There were several
naked men. I "snuck" 5 or 6 peaks at that picture over
3 or 4 days. My parents split up in June. I knew it was
coming, and was relieved. It was about this same time
My deviant behavior began. _____

As you will see, things started out as flashing,
and got progressively worse, until I tried to get ~~~
~~~ a boy to go into an empty building with me 3 days
before his 8th birthday. I ~~intended to~~ hoped he would allow
me to molest him (perform oral on him and crotch fuck him),
but was prepared for a forced rape. Fortunately, he knew
something was up. I was found innocent of the charge
against me, but was offered access to who I believe the
best counselor in this type of business, and have had no
problems since June 13, 1977.

It's quite simple. The junior high I went to was 3
blocks from home, and let out 15 minutes before the grade
school, one block from home.

Mom + Dad both worked. My brother and sister got home
about 10-15 minutes after the grade school kids
walked by our house.

So, at home alone, I'd yell "HEY" as younger kids,
mostly 8-10 yrs. old walked by. They'd look up and see me
exposing myself from an upstairs bedroom window.

This happened 8 or 9 times over about a 3 week period.
I flashed just one boy, or groups of up to 5 or 6 kids, if most
in the group were boys. I never flashed just girls - only ③

when they were with a group of good looking boys between 7-10 years old.

One day I flashed a single boy and he just stared as he SLOWLY walked by. I thought he liked it. That night a cop told mom & dad someone exposed himself to a boy from this house. Mom & Dad wondered if it might be one of my friends. But that stopped the flashing. School was almost over anyway — there wouldn't be any more kids walking by.

I decided to take my flashing on the road. That way if they told, they wouldn't know where I lived.

Around my 15th birthday I'd ride my bike around town. As I'd done 3 or 4 times already, I'd find a good boy or group of boys, then ride around the block. I'd pull my cock and balls out through my fly & hide them by pulling down my T-shirt. When I returned to the boy(s) I'd pull up the shirt and say "HEY!" — exposing myself. This happened 8 or 9 times.

On one occasion there were three 9 yr. olds and one 4 yr. old. A couple of the older ones yelled "do it again!"

Continued Next Page

④

3   ———————————————————   9-26-89

as I passed them. I went back and stopped. I said "I'll do
it again if one of you do first." Right there on the sidewalk
tho 4 year old pulled down the front of his pants. He only
exposed his groin, but wouldn't do it again. They all said "now
you again."

I took them into their yard behind some shrubs and
pulled down the front of my shorts. (I wore no underwear on
these trips.) I said "anyone want to touch it?". The 4
year old did and said "yep - it's real!". They all laughed, and
the 4 year old and two of the 9 year olds agreed to meet
meet me at a vacant field nearby that evening so I could
do it again and show them some tricks (making "it bigger",
"bouncing" it without touching it, and making stuff come out),
and I might even teach them how to do it, but they
never showed.

That was the last time I ever flashed a kid. One
had touched me, and gave me a better feeling than just
showing myself. I now wanted to be touched, not seen.

To put this in categories, Category 1 was flashing -
no contact. I'm now moving to Category 2 - them touching
me.

Chapter 3

My problem was in getting a kid to actually touch me, and
not scare them off. The answer came quickly. I found a group
of six kids (3 boys, 3 girls) in a school playground. I wanted
to be touched badly. That went took out worries of location,
numbers, or whether they were boys or not.

③

I asked them if they wanted to play a game? Yes they did, what? "Line up - your backs to me, and I'll put something in your hand, and you have to guess what it is without looking."

I gave them a rock, then an ink pen. Then I said "I'll have to hold the next one so it doesn't get broke." I reminded them not to look, and let each one wrap their hand around my cock for 2 or 3 seconds. (They're all 8-9 yrs. old.

None of them knew what it was when asked, but one boy said he might know, but he'd try again anyway. They each tried again, but still didn't know. I pointed to my now covered parts and said "this." The one boy said "yeah - I knew it!" I asked and the one said he'd go to a more private area and do it again, if someone else went, even if they didn't play again, but no one agreed.

A couple weeks later, I hadn't found any more boys I could approach, so I settled on 3 girls. I went up to them. One, about 6 or 7, had a shirt on the ground. All were on some swings. I asked the topless one "are you a boy or girl?" She said "girl!" The other 2 were 8 or 9. One said "He just wants to see your Kee-Kaw."

They then, upon being asked, played the same guessing game as the previous kids. They said "yes" when I asked if the wanted to see "it". I said - "I will if one of you will." All 3 girls agreed the youngest would drop her pants. She started to run. I chased and caught her, She fell to the ground on her back. I got down on my knees, straddling her legs, and started to unsnap her pants. She started crying, and I

(6)

let her go.

A school janitor must have seen all this, including the "game". He asked if I wanted to come inside for a while and help him. I didn't. I thought he was going to call police. I learned a few months later a janitor there was fired for raping a 7 year old girl! and an 8 yr. old boy. (He almost had a 15 yr. old boy - me!).

A few days later, then youngest girl was on our doorstep with her father. Dad came from and took me to his apartment for a chat. I gave up on getting strangers to touch me.

Chpt. 4

At this point, it didn't matter if I had boys or girls. I didn't know what you could do with either one, except get them to touch you. (I'm now about 14 years old (remember)

Then one day some cousins were over. Among them, 9 year old Cindy. I played the guessing game with her. She knew what it was, but agreed to go into a closet with me for another guessing game!

In the closet I had her hold my dick for a few seconds, then had her pull on it as hard as she could. I had her feel my balls. Then I had an idea! I could touch a kid, instead of just them touching me!

I was happy when she agreed to pull her pants down as long as I left the closet door closed so I couldn't see her. I put my hands on her hips. I could see her outline. I asked if I could "touch it." She said "Oh God" (Her favorite expression).

I put my lips against her "Koo-Koo", (the only name

I knew it by, thanks to the girls at the school), and blew on it

A few days later we were at her house. Cindy told my sister (10 yrs.) and her 8 year old brother Mike, what we'd done before, but they didn't believe her. I said "let's do it again." Cindy said "where?"

I told Cindy "right here so we can show them so they'll believe us." She pulled down her pants. I said "lay on the end of the bed." She did, pants around her ankles, legs bent at knees over end of bed I helped her spread her legs out and got my first good, close look at a girl

I saw that she didn't wipe very good, as there was a crusty film around her "Kee-Kaw." I almost didn't do it, but decided it was that way when I did it in the dark closet too. Mike and Kathy watched as I again blew out against Cindy's "privates".

Cindy then helped me talk Mike into trying it. This first time, at age 14, I had an 8 year old cock in my mouth, I just blew it right back out.

Later, alone with Mike, I put a hand down the front of his pants as I leaned over his shoulder from behind. I wanted to know what he felt like. He made stop or he'd "tell." I stopped.

About this time I was questioned about some incidents around town (flashing, and asking a 2 or 3 kids to pull down pants with no luck) by the police. This was around my 15th birthday. I missed a band trip

⑧

5

the beginning of my sophomore year because of this.

I did'nt do anything more until about January of 1977, at age 15, because of my police scare. (No charges were filed, because I was a "nice kid." I did go to therapy for about 2 months, then quit.

~~Included~~ CHPT. 5

I started again because I was asked to babysit a 6 year old boy, a 3 yr. old girl, and a 1 yr. old boy. I had a week to p write down what I planned to do to them all. I'd get away with it because I'd do it around midnight to 1:00 A.M., while they slept.

I planned on licking all their butts. My counselor had taught me the "birds & bees", and various ~~tp,~~ ways of having "sex" (new word & ideas!) with men/women, or, ~~better~~ ~~yet~~ men/men. Well—I decided to try men/boys! So, I was going to suck both boys dicks, lick their butts, rest their hands on my privates, and masturbate them.

The 6 yr old woke up when I tried to pull down his PJ's and underwear. I couldn't pull down the one year olds diaper, and didn't want to remove it for fear of not being able to get it back on and being found out by their parents.

I decided to try my plans for the girl. I'd of course lick her "vagina" (new word from my counselor), instead of sucking dick, or "penis" (new word!), and continue with her butt, and her touching me. ~~It also wanted to put my dick between all 35 days to Saintise intercourse (counselor).~~

⑨

6

the next step up. I was preying on, or hunting for
boys, who would pull down their pants when told, without
a fight. Force would not be used. I figured if I didn't
make them do it, they wouldn't tell.

CHPT 6

(11)

No. 2

Plans/ideas Began _ 9-6-89

Hunt start: 10-29-89 _ 10:30A end: 10-29-89 _ 12:50 P.M.

Incident: 10-29-89 _ 12:50 P.M. _ to _ 7:35 P.M. on 10-29-89

INCIDENT #2
FINAL COPY
PLANNING TO COMPLETION

1.a.

1989	Time	
9-6	10:00 P.	For my first incident, knife was best choice as my kill would have to be quick and easy for the chosen location. Decided that this incident would have a cleaner kill - probably choking, to have a clean body for butt fucking (penetration would be too painful for a live child, and thus too noisy - also don't want to torture - just kill as painlessly as possible after use.). I want a better location for this incident, so I feel more comfortable and can take more time for various types of sex before killing the child. Also will be able to fuck the dead instead of running off. Also considering to see how long a boy can live after died amputation.
		One possibility is kidnapping - at home I'd have all the time I need. One thing for certain is for this incident the sex will take longer, and death will be something different than stabbing.
9-8	10:00 A.	Decided to hold off until things from incident #1 cools down somewhat.
9-17	11:00 A.	Thinking of trying Tri-Cities when money & car allows.
9-18	8:15 P.	As in article in today's paper, I've considered kidnapping and keeping a child secretly for the sole purpose of sex. When one gets too old, getting a fresh one and disposing of the first, as I believe was go happening in this article. He/they would be securely locked up, or tied & gagged while I'm at work, shopping, etc.
9-22	11:00 P.	Looking over Vancouver / Portland area maps for possible kidnap sites, and secondary locations to take child to for the kill.
	11:10 P.	"Oaks-Pioneer Park" in Portland appears worth checking out ASAP. Tri-Cities, Yakima, etc., are still possibilities.
9-24	5:20 P.	One possibility - kidnap 10 yr. old, have my way for day or two, kill, and perform "exploratory surgery" to study the reproduction system and practice vasectomy & amputation to later perform on living subjects. My study on this is on page 1.b. I'll need to obtain items to use for these "surgeries."

①

1.b.

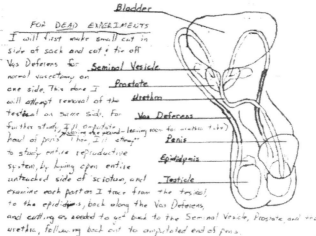

FOR DEAD EXPERIMENTS

I will first make small cut in side of sack and cut & tie off Vas Deferens for normal vasectomy on one side. This done I will attempt removal of the testical on same side. For further study, I'll amputate *(leaving the penis—leaving room for urethra tube)* head of penis. Then, I'll attempt to study entire reproductive system, by laying open entire untouched side of scrotum, and examine each part as I trace from the testical, to the epididymis, back along the Vas Deferens, and cutting as needed to get back to the Seminal Vesicle, Prostate, and the urethra, following back out to amputated end of penis.

On a living subject, I would attempt the amputation, the vasectomy, and the removal of one or both Testicles. If exploratory surgery proves ok, enough, I may even attempt removal of a seminal vesicle, or the prostate on a living subject as well. One subject, depending on physical reactions to operation, may or may not undergo various "operations."

Possible surgery combinations could be a minor one (vasectomy), followed by major (Seminal vesicle or prostate, as these require going deep into the groin). Or it could be two somewhere in between (amputation of the penis head, and removal of a testicle.) Also removal of both testicals one at a time, or together. Could also amputate entire scrotal sac as one major operation. Also try amputation of entire penis; or removal of all outer sex organs (to make him a her!)

Would like to video tape the exploratory, as well as future operations, to use as future reference, to show "patients" what I'll be doing, or to "terrify" victims, if I wish to do so, but at this time (9-24-89 / 8:15 A.M.) I don't think I want to merely "terrify" them.

Labels on diagram:
Bladder
Seminal Vesicle
Prostate
Urethra
Vas Deferens
Penis
Epididymis
Testicle

2a.

9-24 10:30 P. | In surgery on live "patients," with or without "patients" consent, why'll be tied down as Lee demonstrates for me in photo # 5, in the pages to follow.   One thing I could do is cut kids hair and shave entire body completely bald, making a "space alien", or I could have a painted kid (blue maybe?)

I could induce unconsciousness by keeping them up late, then giving several sleeping pills, which would allow me to do things that may otherwise be painful for them.

Ways of killing include stabbing, suffocation (choking, drowning included), bleeding to death (even missing pints of blood could be collected in jars), or ?

9-25 11:00 A. | Poison would also work. (Drugs, poisons, antifreeze, alcohol - also good for anesthetic).

9-30 11:15 P. | Thoughts of getting Jeremy for a period of time, or custody of Ryan - could both be taught Lucifers ways, and be an assistant to Lucifer, through me, until they're able to work on their own, or get too old and are used as a possible sacrifice - but, as they'd grow with me, I may start having sex with boys/men that have hair on genitals - or more likely - share kids with them.

9-30 11:45 P. | The last couple of days I've really been wanting a child. I hope something happens soon.

10-27 10:00 P. | Have been working too much till now to get too excited about kids - also giving time for things to cool down. Bought X-acto knives and tweezers - am now ready for "surgery."

I've asked Satan for a child by writing "I'd like a 6-10 year old boy to make love to, suck & fuck, play with, photograph, kill, and do "exploratory" surgery on." on my legs? got my groin I wrote "I now have needed tools for surgery." and I took a one nap with for 1½ hours this afternoon with this writing.

I now ask Satan that this boy be an easy target; meaning, due to incident #1, I can't do much "hunting" for fear of being "noticed" by a "witness."

2b.

10-27 | 10:20 P. _____ The perfect time to "find" this boy would be on way home from work Saturday (3:30 - 4:00 P.M.) That way I'd have him alive from 4:00 P.M. Saturday to 4:00 P.M. Sunday, at which time he'd be killed for experiments. I want to know if a dead boy can be given an erection by sucking his dick to pull in blood, and if so, will the body maintain the erection. I also want to get pictures of the dead boy hanging by various body parts. Also wanting to do my exploratory surgery.

10-27 | 10:35 P. _____ I intend to have sex with him a time or two, or more if time allows, then kill for dead sex, photos, experiments, and the exploratory - using what I learn to later operate on live boys.

Perfect would be a 3 yr. old to kill and a 6-8 yr. old to help with surgery. I'd later hang the nude 6-8 yr. old and photograph him dying. Just writing this makes me quite erect.

10-28 | 4:30 P. _____ Nothing on way home. If I don't find one today or at movies tonight, I'll try a park in Portland tomorrow, where I hope hunting will as it was at David Douglas in incident #1.

10-28 | 4:52 P. _____ Will go check out Oaks - Pioneer park in Portland now.

10-28 | 7:40 P. _____ Just got home. Will hunt the park tomorrow for a few hours. About 6:40 P.M. on way back I saw movement around a school in a very dark neighborhood - not even lights at the school. Turned out to be teens & adults. On my back to the main street I saw 3 smaller kids. Went back & found 3 7-9 yrs. olds. I circled and intended to approach, telling them one had to come with me and send the other two in opposite directions, so they couldn't see my car. I figured it was dark enough they couldn't get a good description of me. When I circled back they had disappeared, and a 15 minute search was useless.

10-28 | 7:29 P.M. to 10:45 P.M. _____ Watched "The Bear." Followed one boy to bathroom, intending to say "come with me" and take him out of the theater and to my apt., but he was coming out as I went in. I should have known kids would go quick to get back to movie faster. I'll try again Sunday for 2 or 3 movies if I don't get a boy at the park in the morning.

3a.

10-29	10:30 A	Left home.
	10:45 A	Bought film for polaroid camera.
	11:30 R	At the school I found yesterday evening - saw 2 8-9 yr. olds, and a 4-5 yr. old a little ways away. Watched a few minutes + decided not to risk it.
	11:45 P.	Arrived at park.
	12:15 P.	No signs of any children.
	12:43P.	Back at school. 3 8-9 yr. olds and one 4 or maybe 5. Circled school (drove around block) and thought an adult showed up. [with another 3-4 yr. old.] Park on opposite side of school from kids - adult turned out to be only about 13 yrs. old. I stood against a pole. The big kid and his 3-4 yr. old brother left. Two 8-9 yr. olds were playing ball and heading toward the far end of the school. The other 8-9 yr. old was sitting on a post watching them, the backs of the other 3 toward me and the 4-5 years old, playing on a mound 20 feet to my left.

I went up to the little boy and asked him if he wanted to "have some fun and make some money." He seemed unsure, but not scared. I said "come on - this will be fun" and reached out my hand. He took it and walked to the end of the building with me - we got out of sight of the other kids unseen. I told him as we kept walking, hand in hand, "we're going to get in my car." He said "I don't want any money." I picked them up and said - "we're still going - let's go ask your dad if you can go with me." We got to my car, I put him into the drivers side. As we drove away he said "I live the other way." I said "we're going to my house and play some games - just do what I tell you and I promise I won't hurt you."

	12:50P.	A couple blocks from the school, I asked and he said his name was Lee, and he was 4 years old. He started to cry a couple times, but I reached out and held his hand, assuring him he'd be O.K., and that we'd have some fun.
10-29	1:30P.	We got to my house at 1:30 P.M. Both the landlady and the other tenant were gone. Perfect. I started to carry him from the car but he said "I can walk," and I put him down.

10/29/89

1:30 home

(1)   3b.

10-29-89   1:30 P.M.

1 | Lee - 4 yrs. old - as I found him - then showed him nude photo book.
   naked at [crossed out] 1:36
2 | touched 1:42
3 | " 1:44
4 | after 3 2 minutes, oral in att. to gain erection 1:48
4 | after 3 " in bathtub ready for foreplay 1:56   (200 - 225 sec)
5 | for show at 1:52

4:02 P.M. Lee wanted to open birthday - back to pictures - put pictures of him in photo book. 4:10 P.M. Decided to spend night w/me if I buy him a toy and go out for a burger. We did.

5:35 P.M. So returned home - he played with "Robo-cop." Was happy + cheerful and I let him put his clothes back on at [crossed out].

2:30 P.M. Watched Yogi Bear at 3:00.

6:38 Lee's still playing. Will probably wait till morning to kill him. He suspects nothing now, and that way his body will still be fairly fresh for experiments after work. Or I'll suffocate him in his sleep when I wake up for work. [If I sleep].

6:40 Lee spilt hot coffee on him. I let him wear one of my shirts - it made his chest red.

7:00 P.M. started crying because his dad + brothers miss him. I was able to quickly quiet him.

7:48 P.M. He wanted to look at pictures again - he thumbed through album + kept looking up at me.

8:05 P.M. Peeked through crack in door as he was taking a shit.

9:00 P.M. Wants to "look at my pictures one more time" - He wants to see the nude photos, but doesn't want to do any more. Little does he know that in about 20 hours I'll take photos of a dead, 4 yr. old naked boy.

9:35 P.M. bed asleep 9:45 - had him naked by 10:00 - me also.

10:45 P.M. there played w/dick a little + felt out his balls - surgery will be very delicate. Am waiting for 11:00 P.M. news, + trying to decide best way of killing him - kill with the choked strangle or rather what (TIME, PLACE)

3 C

...I dont want to have marks on his neck but it must be quick & quiet.
His body will be hidden in closet behind sleeping bag while I'm at work
(Want 11:00P.M. news as this will be 1st of news broadcast since
he "disappeared").   OK - News says he disappeared from a
store, (not where I got him at school.)

10-30-89   Didn't sleep at all. Sucked him 5 or 6 times, must. 10-15
times, crotch fucked leon 7 times.

10/30/89 (2:00 A.M.) He woke up - didn't seem to mind being nude, I pulled him
up on top of me - his belly to mine - my cock in his navel. We slept
on top of my for 1/2 hour as I rubbed his back & butt. He was off to
quiet long good erection as he slept (3:15 A.M.) Said I going to the bathroom he said no I
said before he didn't   put cock into his butt - he woke & said "whats
on there" when it was 1/2 way in, I put it in again under the covers.
(4:55 A.M.) He woke as I fucked him and I let him watch me put the
rod to his cock - it hurt just a little he said.
(5:30 A.M.) him on his back near his left
side leaning into him. My body pinned his right arm down between
us. I put my right leg over his legs, my left arm under pillow
and his head - holding his left arm up by pillow. Thus totally
pinned, I choked him with my right hand. He got his leg loose,
I had to hold my hand very tight on his neck so I held for about
15 seconds after he quit struggling. He lay motionless. After about
30 seconds I blew into his mouth to see if he was revivable. Decided
not but he started slow gasps about 20 seconds after that. I checked
him for about another minute before he rested again. He started to
gasp again and opened his eyes I grabbed a rope and put around his neck
as he lay breathing slowly but unconscious. I tightened the
rope & picked him up by it pulling him onto my lap (both of us
nude) and holding him upright with the rope. His chest was heaving
but he wasn't getting air. Keeping rope tight with right hand
I picked him up under his butt and carried him to the closet holding
him up by just the rope as I moved clothes aside. I then hold his

4 a

~~butt~~ ... ~~butt up with left hand as I tied rope to the clothes bar and hung~~
him so ~~he~~ wouldn't get tired of a gag and maybe let him breath again.
He hung about 10 minutes as I took (pictures #7) and cleaned
up the room. At 5:45 I cut the rope and lay him on the bed. I
sucked his cock a little and shoved my cock into his mouth to fuck
him that way, but I had a bad angle and gave up. I checked for
heartbeat and breathing, then put him up on a shelf in the closet
10-30 behind some blankets & a sleeping bag. I'll do more after work.
~~Today~~ 4:10 P.M. got home. Saw paper article about missing boy in
Today Oregonian. 4:20 P.M. Caught up this day as I
havent written in it since I watched the 11:00 P.M. news last night
4:50 P.M. Will now go take a break and take the naked
body of 4yr. old Lee Joseph Iseli out of the closet. I'll
tape everything as I go now. (The paper article - labeled
"The Oregonian 1/10/30/84" was on page 5 of section B. Like it was
no mayor dead he's missing. Looks like a perfect kidnapping)
5:05 Talked to them - now getting too out.
     Oh yeah - I knew for sure this morning he was dead. I'd
heard of muscles ~~relax~~ relaxing and its normal to "go potty" after
dying - he peed on me twice as I laid his body in the closet, & once
more on the shelf in the closet.
5:40 P.M. He is rather gross to looking - cold, stiff, and purple. I was going
to try butt fucking him, but now not sure I could if I wanted to -
I'll check. See (photos #8, #9). Will now (5:46 P.M.) try to
loosen him up a little, as well as get his body bag over his butt. These
photos show the position his stood in from being in a small closet one.
     At least he did : balls are ~~hang~~ - I'll all of dead boys' ~~erections~~
erections w/ suction to pull in blood. I wish I had time for this while
he was still warm. Erection not possible (frozen blood?) I was hoping to
keep him a couple days, but I'll have to get rid of him tonight I think.
5:25 P.M. Hes too cold for a normal fever thermometer - wish I had an indoor/out-
door thermometer which the bulb I could stick up his ass.

4b

10/30/89   5:30 P.M.   See (photo #10) how stiff dead little boys are - this is after I loosened up his legs.

5:35 P.M.   I am going to go get some garbage bags & now to put his buddled up body into after I try to get my bag out into his little butt. Then I'll figure out a place to dump the "garbage." I'll wear gloves when handling the bag - no chance for fingerprints if someone discovers contents of the bag. Honey, alloway - I think I'll use a rubber to penetrate his butt.

6:00 P.M.   Have 2 rubbers & trash ___ bags - if I can't get good anal penetration I'll tie off rubber & ___ with full his body. The youth is now out - both are penised together. It stinks anyway. Spent 20 minutes but fucking him - got it about 3/4 way in. Felt good - I went slow and stopped short of climax 3 times - ejaculating on 4th climax (more climaxes). Was wearing gloves (6:50 P.M.) Later showered, the handle trash bags to get him in... real now so dump his.   8:00 P.M.   done.   Dumped 7:35 P.M. 10-30

10/31/89   5:32 P.M.   Put ___ a plate ___ on ___ news of person seen talking to Lee at the school - ___ looks a lot like ___ me.   6:00 O'clk news added: Blue baseball cap, and "person of interest" may have had a german shepard with him and was either driving or dropped off by a white pick-up truck. FBI is entering info into their files. I'll be watching news carefully for about a month now, as ___ well as staying out of sight.

10/31/89   6:40 P.M.   Burnt his socks, shirt, sweater, & pants. Will bury his underwear as souvenier. Will throw away his shoe tomorrow at a Cities.

11/1/89   ___ 4:40 P.M.   Washed his underwear in shower when I took it - they smelled like "P."

11/2/89   7:55 P.M.   Cut his shoes into 4 parts, and divided the sole, and burnt it all, along with newspapers missing articles about him.   5:40 P.M. news said drawing of man seen was discarded so he was seen leaving ___ without Lee.

11/3/89   6:00 P.M.   ch 6 news at 6 said police had talked to man drawn by artist and ___ throwing the picture away - not a suspect and he knew nothing.

No. 3

Plans/ideas Began   11-4-89

Hunt start: end:

Incident:

1

-4-89   11:10 P.M. Victim in #3 will die by suffocation - plastic bag over his head. Bag will be secured after I suck him erect. As he suffocates to death (tied down of course) I'll keep sucking to keep him erect. Thanks to Lee I know I can't make a dead one erect, but will they stay erect if erect at time of death?

1-10-89   10:20 P.M. Instead of the bag, I'll tape his mouth shut, then, when ready, I'll use a clothespin or something to plug his nose. This way I can clearly see his face as he dies, as well as get some pictures of a naked, dying boy. This suffocation also eliminates the neck/rope burns, as Lee had in incident #2.

Electrocution also a good means for a quick death.

-4-89   7:30 P.M. to 10:00 P.M. At the movie "The Bear" (as in incident #2) to find a lone boy in bathroom. Talked to a 7-8 yr. old, who was not as cute in the lighted bathroom as he looked in the dark. He insisted no, I said "O.K. - wait here - I'll leave", then "No - you're coming with me" (changed my mind). I finally decided I couldn't get him out quietly, but at one point almost punched him to knock the wind out of him - but he was too big to carry out pretending my "little boy was sick?" I quickly left the theater. There was nothing on the news.

11-12-89   5:00 PM to 7:00 P.M. Drove around town looking for kids
8:10 P.M. Went to Cameo Theater to watch "Honey, I Shrunk the Kids" - There was only one boy at the 9:00 P.M. show. About 8-9 yrs. old, and Oriental (2 strikes against (too old to get out of the theater easily)) but didn't have

2.

to use the bathroom anyway. However - there were several 4-2o8 yr. old boys that left the 7:00 P.M. showing - I'll try the 7:00 P.M. show tomorrow.

-13-89 4:40 P.M. Have updated log entries. Will now prepare ropes as I had for Incident #2, (tied to bed & kiddies under it - to use on victim as soon as wanted or needed - needing only to tie loose rope ends to the victim, other ends already attached to bed, or - my "rack" & woodframework built for this purpose]).

4:45 P.M. Now ask Satan to guide me, and provide or help me obtain a boy tonight. This one I'd like to keep a while - keeping him awake all night each night, so he'll sleep all day while I'm at work (tied and mouth taped shut to be on safe side.) I may only keep him for 3 days, or even longer if it works out. I'll give him a haircut & buy a new set of clothes for him, to change his appearance, in case I take him out as I did here in #2. I might even get 2 boys (Perhaps a 6 or 7 yr. old taking a 3 or 4 yr. old to the toilet? In the case of two like this - the older (or both?) would decide (when I tired of them) which was to die. Don't know now if survivor (or just a lone boy) would die, or be used to help get another boy here. Will have to wait & see. I also want to do my medical experiments this time, once done with sexual play on the body(ies). Also hoping for more, better pictures. May also play again the "battle" or stripping games. (Especially with 2 boys).

1-13-89 5:25 P.M. Now going to Camas - will check out local parks before movie.

1

9-2-89

Sep. 2, 1989   Located David Douglas Park and did this:

David Douglas Park

Ideal area - South & West sides of park - wooded & gulley.
Isolated areas, especially east end. 1/2 hr. saw 3
together (6:40-6:40 P.M.); and nothing else.

Good for R & M at sight, or K R M.

Mill Plain

stopping
7 artifices

Sun. Sep. 3, 1989   10:40-11:00 A.M.
Checked the same area out. I intend to spend up
to 5 hrs. here this afternoon to obtain what
I want. Depending on circumstances will R & M
at sight, or may K from there, R at home, and
again dep. on areas, will either M at home, or
take to another location and possibly R again before M. If I can
get it home I'll have more time for various types of R., rather
than just one quickie before M.

NOTE: I spent evening of 9-2-89, and evening of 9-3-89, preparing photo
book # P-1.   In my photo books use this key:
      P - photos by other photographers, old & new / scene "art"
      C - photos of children I see nude, or get them to pose for me,
          but I have no sex contact with.
   ● V - photos of children in a more sexual ones relationship,
          who I trust to keep quiet. Some of these photos may
          have me in them also.
      M - photos of children who I forced, or they co-operated,
          either way ending in M.
   In photos ● I just put into P-1, all were taken from a
   series of books from "Life Library of Photography", from two of
   the books in that series - "The Great Themes" & "Photographing Children".
      These photos take up pages 1-11, inclusive, in book P-1.

Sun. 9-3-89
11:45 A.M. All my actions from now on will be logged, & immediately following
each circumstance, and in those boys/stories, I'll refer to proper photo
album and page numbers as they exist for those stories. I hope within
4 months to be using video tape as well as polaroids ~~film~~ for certain
cases.   11:50 A.M. Will get a cup of coffee and head out for
a few hours. Intend to have fun today, or tomorrow at latest,
1:05 [circled] — since tomorrow's a school closed holiday (Labor Day).

2:00 P.M. Returned home for food/drink.

→ 1) 2 boys—approx 9 & 10/11 (oldest trying for teen age—would have taken
       younger (smaller) if alone for R?M.
→ 2) 2 girls 7; 12. Would have R?M younger if alone.
→ 3) 4 boys/ 3 7or8, 1 about 12. ~~~~ If older was not
       there I would have separated younger 3, doing M to first two, then left
       to the last (best looking of 3). ~~~~ They were looking for place to go bathroom and hope
       to catch ~~~~ alone in ~~~~ "I watched them pee"
→ 4) One boy about 4 was wandering away from teenagers playing ball,
       but never got far enough away or out of their sight, else I would have
       gotten him further out of sight for possible KRM or at least RM.

2:15P.M. Lunch, time to go, will be back on hunt by 3:15P.M.

4:00 P.M. Back home. No luck. Were 4 boys & 2 girls, but w/ 2 adult females
          3 boys close—were good, 4th a ways away but poss. 1 girl poss. If only I
          good get 1-3 boys alone (1 up to 10yrs / 2 up to 8 or 9 yrs / 3 up to 7 or 8 y

4:13 P.M. Better equipped (added long shoe string and Ly-ace bandage to the
          knife I've been carrying. Knife will be held by the ace band. to ride
          better. Ace or string also used for tying up, or to use for choking, instead
          of relying on tape, but to choke may not have a start & I may not want
          to use knife)—especially since knife would best be cleaned or (last of any)
          knit(s) — ~~~~ choking may be best. Back to hunt by 4:15 P.M.

2

5:30 P.M. Gave up — went to look around Fred Meyer. There was a 6-7 yr. old boy there with some cute little shorts, and so etc. I had an urge to pull his shorts down right there. I went back to the park.

6:00 P.M. Started walking away from car — after 50 yds 3 boys, all about 7 yrs. old, passed me on bikes. I went back to car for my knife — I intended to separate them, do the two M's, and then the R & M, but they rode off again. I wonder if they'd have stayed if I hadn't gone back for my knife? Will try again tomorrow. Noon to 3 or 3:30 seems best hunting, esp. 12:30 - 2:00. (Sunday)

6:00 P.M. Dad gave me some geographics and photographer maps. — I'll now search them for more photos to add to my ___ (514) "child" "Porno Collection"

Mon 9-4-89 9:35 A.M. Awoke 3-4 times last night. Seem to have maintained a stiff erection all night. Only a boy can make it soft again now. Now ready for my 2nd day of the hunt. Will start about 10:00 A.M. and take a lunch so I don't have to return home. Got to thinking last night I'm better off taking them somewhere else to do them, if I have M'd ones there, I'll lose hunting ground for up to 2 or 3 months; But if they just disappear, it won't be as bad. At this time I know of no other hunting grounds — which is even better than the river in Richland.

5:40 P.M. — got home — at park for all but ½ trips totalling ½ hr. Only 2 incidents. 1) 1:15 P.M. 2 boys on bikes — I passed them, watched for 2-3 minutes; passed again they were 9-10 yrs old. I started walking away; they followed a ways behind I finally decided to turn; confront & separate (they were a bit big), but they took another trail & left. 2) 4:30 P.M. A guy on bike passed me. I turned to run him down but his face was a little behind the boy and came into view as I saw the boy's great looking butt on the bike seat. If I was well rounded he would have been a great fuck.

(9-4-89)

5:45 P.M. I was going to call it quits, but believe I'd go try once more before weekend is over.

6:10 P.M. Arrived park

6:15 P.M. Began walking from end of trail.

6:18 P.M. Found 2 boys — no one else around - about proper age & figures.

6:19 P.M. I approached & said "I want you 2 to come w/ me." Older said "why?" so "Because I told you to — & you can bring your bikes if you want" — said that because younger was going to leave his behind. Didn't want someone to find it and start looking for him. ~~realize they were not American, but was committed~~ ~~and never saw sign of anyone to front.~~
They both followed me for about 5 minutes to most isolated part of park. As passed 2 teen-agers; I warned the boys not to talk to them.

aprox 6:25 P.M. ~~I~~ Had learned older was 11 yr. old Cole & younger was 10 yr. old Billie. ~~and~~ ~~having~~ with no one else ~~between them~~ near, we went a few yards into to trees & bushes.   Billie kept quiet, Cole always said "why" once to each command by me. I had ~~them~~ them stand back to back, ~~and~~ and tied their wrists together tightly — binding the boys together by a 10" piece of cord.
They then both faced me & I knelt in front of them.

aprox 6:30 P.M. I said one of them had to let me pull down their pants & Billy quickly said "yes." ~~the other two caught not to react his dick~~ Cole asked if it would hurt — I said no so he said OK. ; prettier, but I didn't want him to ~~see~~ scream, not to cry loudly when the ~~so~~ both knives he just ~~started~~. Cole ~~of~~ agreed. Billy was wearing jeans. Cole wearing shorts.

I pushed Cole's button down colored shirt up and slid fingers into waist of his shorts & undies, and pulled down to his knees.

one more thing", as I again took knife from sheath (hidden in sock under pant leg).

They were both facing me, about a foot apart, me centered in front of them. I reached out & shoved the knife into Billy's gut. I thought he'd drop, but & as I quickly turned to Cole before he could react, Billy grabbed his stomach & started running.

Cole had just started to turn & rise — ~~stand~~ so I aimed his gut, and caught him in the side. He may have then been dead then, but kept moving. I then got him in the chest, and the 3rd stab struck him, but I'm not sure where, as I was rising to chase Billy. I didn't want him to reach a nearby busy road.

I caught him by the right arm. We were both running — I stopped and stabbed him, I believe in the lower side, as he spun. He said "I'm sorry! I'm sorry!" as he spun around. I stabbed again in the left shoulder I think as he went down. I didn't stay to make sure he was dead this time.

I ran to where their bikes were on the trail and started walking. I put the knife back under my pant leg. I went about 30 yards & decided to run back to make sure I hadn't left any evidence behind. I found Cole on flat on his back, head tilted to the left, eyes (the one I could see) still open, arms at his side. He was covered with blood and not moving. At first I thought something was poking out of his belly, then realized his pants were still 1/2 way to his knees and I was looking at his dick & balls.

He was definitely dead. That only took a second to take it all in, and I started looking around and found no evidence. I thought about running back to be sure Billy was dead, and decided not to risk the extra time.

[4]

I then noticed blood on my left hand. Keeping it in my pocket I calmly climbed to the main park, greeting an old man, and throwing a stray baseball to a couple guys on the way back to my car.

I circled around and on other side of park found a guy running down the hill. I figured he'd found Billy, since I'd left him out on the trail, ~ I didn't want to leave fingerprints on his bloody clothes, or get his blood on me trying to get him into hidden bushes as Cole was. I had expected Billy to die right with Cole - still hidden. It turns out luckily I didn't go back to check Billy, or the guy would have seen me too. It was about 6:45 P.M. when I got out to the main park.

My total time with the boys had been 18-20 minutes. Billy was reported found at 6:50 P.M. by phone and 9-1-1, and taken by helicopter to a Portland hospital at 7:37 P.M. I didn't know for sure he was dead until the 6:00 A.M. news on radio the next morning. (Tuesday Morning) I already knew for sure Cole was dead.

After the incident Monday I was pretty shook up. I thought about it all day - couldn't get picture of Cole's body, or Billy's in way out of my mind. By time I got home from work on Tuesday 9-5-89, about 4:10 P.M., I was able to masturbate to fantasy & mind pictures of Cole, both alive & dead and bloody. I climaxed in about 3 minutes. ~~~~ I dumped knife, wrapped in old used man's envelope, in garbage dumpster at work at lunch time Tuesday 9-5-89.

Wednesday
9-6-89

Now trying to figure out a location for next hunt. Must spend more time with boy (or girl?) before killing, and restore body is hidden better.

The newspaper articles on this incident are attached to the following pages.

9-6-89   While most of my future victims will ~~die~~ die (in various ways) I also hope to have some long relationships with children as well. (Lies with Robert & Jeremy (and even Chad - though unwilling he kept quiet)). I'd like to make some child porno ~~movies~~ movies. I also hope to get "before & after" photos of my "sex-murder" victims as well.

When each fucking she was to die, I'll always tie kid well before killing, and ~~the~~ deposit my sperm in something to remove it as "forensic evidence". When butt-fucking, I'll use a well greased rubber. (May fuck either way before or after they die, depending on whether they're bloody or not.) Some of them will also be forced to perform certain acts on me.

I think I got more of high out of killing, than molesting. I had fantasized previously of my stomach against a boy's back, my arms around him, and ~~over~~ his arms. He's blindfolded so as not to see the knife I'm holding to a point just below ~~the~~ breast-bone. My cock in his crotch or maybe his butt, I squeeze my arms, pinning him and holding him so he can't move as I slowly push the blade into him, then back out, holding him or fucking him as he dies.

I also dream of sucking him erect, do a long oral on him, then cutting off his erect cock. Then I butt fuck him as his cock bleeds into the ground under him. If he's still alive after ~~that~~ that I finish him off. - Of course taking pictures each stage of the way.

Just read - you'll see what actually does occur. Just writing ~~this~~ this and previous story about my 1st murder makes

9-8-89

‖ 9-8-89   Yesterdays "Columbian" news article had me worried. It said
8:45 A.M.   that by talking to kids that were at the park Monday (day of killings),
            police had a artists sketch of a man seen at the park by several children.
                Then last night 3 sheriffs deputies pulled up in front of the
            house where I'm renting a room. I hoped they were here because
            the landlady called them after a verbal fight in which she evicted
            other guy living here. I also hoped they didn't realize I was one in
            their sight. They weren't interested in no other than what I'd
            heard of argument.
                Landlady said later that person they're looking for is "6 miles
            and darker" than the guy evicted. Well - I'm 6 miles - but not
            darker.

9-10-89 (Tuesday) (8 days after the fact)
        11:30 P.M.   just watched news. Two sketches of "Persons
            of interest" were released by Police & shown. Neither sketch
            resembles me at all. There was nothing for me to worry about. I'll
            just have to stay away from the park for awhile. A lot may не'
            remember me there or on Sunday, Monday. I've not looked at
            a paper since Sunday, but haven't heard on T.V. or radio of anything
            was found on the boys clothes, but I really doubt it. In case I can't
            get a news artist, the F.B.I. profile says the killer is a man
            comfortable and/or trained with knives.

for #3

~~Thursday~~ 11-4-89   11:10 P.M.

Now know how next one will die.
He'll be tied for a photo as #2 was, then,
when finished, he'll be tied - "just one
more time for another picture, but with
a bag on your head this time." O
plastic bag will be put over him and
secured about the neck. I'd suck
him as he dies - hopefully masting &
keeping him erect until death, then
learning if it stays erect after death.

WHY DID YOU DO IT?

In April of 1990 Dodd was in jail, and he got a letter from a female inmate named Mardi Harmon, who had volunteered to represent other inmates. She asked him why he abducted and killed children. He responded:

4-10-90.

Hi. I just got your letter. You said you "just have to know what kind of person" I am, and that "there is good in everyone." Well, I don't know what kind of person I am any more, to tell you the truth, and there was once some good in me.

I used to stop and help whenever I saw someone broken down on the highway. I stood by some friends and was there, for both when they divorced before I started molesting children, I was a real friend to many. I've rented a room from a single mother once. The kid's dad was never around. I sat up late at night more than once with her 9-year-old son. He often cried himself to sleep because his own dad wouldn't visit him. I would have done anything for that boy, and he knew it—he wanted to call me dad.

Other kids that knew me looked up to me and trusted me. They all seemed to like me. Then I started to change. Instead of being their friend, I started molesting them.

You asked "why did you do this?" I don't know why—I wish I did. Five years ago I would have put my own life on the line for any child, for any reason. Just last year I had an alcoholic roommate. I saved his 4-year-old son from many beatings while he was drunk.

I never wanted to hurt anyone in any way. Now 3 boys are dead. I don't know why.

You asked if I found God. Yes—about 3 months ago I was having trouble believing I could be forgiven for what I'd done. Several people reassured me I was already forgiven. I also feel I don't deserve to be forgiven—I don't deserve what God offers to all who ask in the name of Jesus. I guess I have these doubts because I know I can't forgive myself. I just don't understand how I could care about kids so much, and yet, do all I've done to some of them. Something made me change. I wish I knew what.

Material from Gary C. King, *Driven to Kill* (New York: Pinnacle Books, 1993); Diary of Death (July 1989–September 1989) material compliments of Gary C. King. Photo courtesy of Washington State Police.

5.

ALBERT FISH

BACKGROUND

As a defense witness for Albert Fish at his trial for murdering and cannibalizing ten-year-old Grace Budd, Dr. Frederic Wertham of Bellevue Hospital said that Fish had committed literally every human perversion that Wertham had ever heard of, including coprophagy (eating feces,) piquerism (sticking needles into his body), undinism (being urinated on or urinating on someone else), and a wide variety of sadomasochistic activities. Probably his favorite perverse activity was being whipped or imagining someone else being whipped.

Fish had a hellacious childhood, as the great majority of serial murderers do. Fish was the child of a thirty-two-year-old woman and a seventy-five-year-old man, who promptly died, leaving his young wife to care for the boy. Overwhelmed, she placed him in an orphanage, and Fish spent his early years learning all the perversions from other castaway kids that he was to practice as he grew into adulthood.

Fish often wrote to women trying to set up house with them, letters that were so crazy that at one point he was prosecuted by the Post Office and sent to Bellevue Hospital, the premier New York psychiatric hospital. His intense interest in sadomasochism and coprophagy was plainly evident in many of the letters he wrote. These letters became part of the record in

his trial for the murder of ten-year-old Grace Budd. When writing to various females, he did not use his real name but rather, either James W. Pell or Robert Hayden, and he posed as an important person. Following is a typical missive he wrote to a woman named Grace using the name Robert Hayden. The mentioned James W. Pell was Fish, who visited the woman and her daughter. The *x*'s shown are his kiss marks.

xx
xx
xx
xx

My Dearest Darling Sweetest Grace xx

Your dear loving little note at hand. We missed a train on acct of James W. Pell. When I told him we were going to Va. He said he wanted to go to you and be spanked and whipped with the rope on his bare ass by you and your daughter. He said you were the prettiest, sweetest loving little woman, he ever saw and your girl was just lovely. He said she made him a cup of coffee and he wanted to kiss her when she gave it to him. He was all set for a good whipping and expected you to strip him naked and both of you give it to him.

Now he thinks you were ashamed or else afraid of your husband. He spoke of what a cozy home you had. Said he would love it. I knew both of you would love him for he is a dear soul, with a heart of gold. He cried so I had to take down his pants and spank him good. Had you done so yesterday, the first letter would not now been written. You know my darling Grace, I was under the impression that you and the Mr were on the outs and that, you and your girl lived alone. Had I known what I know now with a Jealous hubby on guard I would not have told you of my love for you and the hopes of some day—making you my dear wife. But I do L O V E You Grace my darling with all my heart. If you were my own dear sweet wife, you would not be afraid of me. Oh girlie of my heart would I love you and How. Hug-Kiss-Squeeze you spank you then K I S S X Just where I spanked! Your nice xxxx pretty-fat-sweet ass. I am a very passionate xxxx xxx man. . . . Every night at bed time I would strip you naked kiss you all over—xxxxx—front and back—toes to heart, then turn you over to your back, get in bed and then you know just what I would do don't you dear. Yes you would have a baby 1—2—3. Out in Hollywood xxx at the clubs I often heard men say when they saw a pretty woman, if she was mine I would kiss her sweet ass, drink her #1 xx Eat Her #2. I thought at the time it was all hot air. Wallace Read was the first one I ever saw do it, to a boy. They say he did it to his own wife and sev-

eral girls to show how much he loved them. I can name 40 who do it now. In fact it is quite common among movie folks. The girls make 'the boys do it to show LOVE. If you ever are mine I shall xxxxx show how I LOVE—Grace Hayden I shall xxxx drink quarts of your sweet #1 xx Eat Pounds xxxx xx of your sweet #2—or Robert dont love—as he xxxx xx should. You know dearest I have asked you so many times to say—Yes Robert Dear I shall strip you naked and spank and switch your bare fat ass good. You never said you would. Now James tells me you would not do some of the things I asked you to do for Bobby and him. He said you were ashamed to milk their dickeys. You should not be, it is done now in hospitals to all boys over 17. Some boys have Cream at 14 and are able to become a—Daddy. Did you know that when I stood Naked in front of Mrs H. P. Whitney and she saw the size of my Prick She looked and acted as tho she wanted xxxx a taste. But that belongs to my dear sweet Grace.

xx xx xxx xxx xxxx

When you strip me naked you will see what Mrs H. P. W. called a most perfect form. Yours the sweet honey of my heart. I can taste your sweet— Piss Your sweet—shit. You must Pee xxxx xxx xx xxx Pee in a glass and I shall drink every drop of it as you watch me. Tell me when you want to do #2. I will take you over my knees, pull up your clothes, take down your drawers and hold my mouth to your sweet honey fat—Ass Holes and xxxx xxx x xx xxx Eat your sweet Peanut Butter & as it comes out fresh and hot. That is How they all do in—in Hollywood. You wont need toilet paper to wipe your sweet pretty fat Ass as I shall eat all xxx xxx xx xxx of it then Lick your sweet ass clean with my tongue

Oh my darling Sweetest Grace

How I do LOVE YOU Words are cheap, this will show you. You can write to James Monday so can Grace Jr. When you have him in his room—Naked. Not with a Pin, but a Paddle on his Ass. Now dearest you do this for me.

Soak the rope James brought you in a pail of water and have it all ready for my sweet bare ass Monday night. I want the first Dose of it, from You. Don't—be—stingy.

Ever and for ever Your boy Robert xxx xxx

A CHAT WITH ALBERT

Though Fish never testified at his own trial, he was questioned by the New York Police Department, and the transcript was read at his trial. Following are transcripts of what he told Captain Stein of the NYPD, chiefly concerning the abduction and murder of Grace Budd.

Q. Before you went to live with your daughter where were you living?
A. With another daughter in Astoria, Mrs. Gertrude De Marco.
Q. Did you ever live at 409 East 100th Street, Manhattan?
A. Yes.
Q. When?
A. In 1928.
Q. In 1928?
A. Yes.
Q. What time of the year was that?
A. I lived there from about April up until about the middle of June.
Q. Sometime in the month of May, 1928, in answer to an advertisement that appeared in the *World* did you go to a residence 406 West 15th Street, Manhattan? [the address of the Budds]
A. Yes sir.
Q. Just what was that advertisement that brought you to that address?
A. A young boy advertised for a job on a farm, any kind of work I went to the home of . . .
Q. When was that?
A. On a Sunday, June 3, 1928, and I had spoken in reference to taking the boy, because it was the boy she thought was going to go. When I got there a little girl came over and sat in my lap and I sort of had a feeling come across me to take the little girl.

Fish had left a package containing a cleaver, saw, and knife down by an unoccupied newsstand before walking to and entering the home of the Budds.

Q. Why did you have that cleaver, saw, and knife, why did you buy them?
A. I didn't have any intention at all of killing the girl, but I sort of had— I could not describe it—a sort of blood thirst, the notion got into my head and I intended to use those things on her—brother.
Q. What made you use them on her, then?
A. I never could account for it. I would have given my life within a half hour after I done it to restore it to her.
Q. This little girl you mention here, have you since learned her name was Grace Budd?
A. I knew that it was then. They told me at the house her name was Grace.

Q. The mother told you her name was Grace?

A. Yes.

Q. To the best of your recollection, what time of the day was this?

A. Between one and two. We [the family and Fish] had lunch together.

Q. And what time did you take this Grace Budd from her home?

A. Three PM.

Fish had been able to do this on the pretext that he was taking Grace to a birthday party at his sister's house. Mrs. Budd was reluctant to let her go, but Mr. Budd wasn't and he convinced her to let Grace go to the party.

Q. How did you travel?

A. We left the house and I took the elevated train on 9th Avenue and 14th Street. We went to Sedgwick Avenue and I forget just how we did it, but we transferred from there to Van Cortlandt Park. There we took the New York and Putnam Branch, 4368 New York Central Railroad, to Worthington, New York, Westchester County.

Q. And that makes it that you arrived in Worthington about what time?

A. We arrived there, I guess, about a little after three. Walked all the way in from Worthington to Elmsford, there was a trolley car at that time running into White Plains.

Q. When you got off the train at Worthington, you had forgotten the package [containing the cleaver, knife, and saw], is that right?

A. Yes, it was wrapped up and stood up in striped canvas and stood on its end, leaning up against the window side of the car, we were both almost out of the train and the girl happened to look back; she said "You forgot your package" and she ran back and got it.

Q. Did you tell her what was in it?

A. No.

Q. Then what?

A. We walked up the road to a two-family house.

Q. Was it occupied?

A. No; empty; it still is empty. Outside was a field of wildflowers, and I said, "You play out here in the yard while I go in." So I went in and I opened this package and spread it out on the floor. I expected to be spattered up with blood, so took off my clothing, put them in a closet.

Q. How was she dressed?

A. When we left her house she had on a blue coat, light pale blue hat, underneath that was a white dress, underwear, shoes, and stockings.

Q. What kind of shoes did she have on?

A. White shoes and stockings pure white. . . . On the way up to the house, it was kind of warm, so I said, "Take off your hat and coat."

She did. I rolled the hat under the coat and put it under a rock, the
water had formed an aperture running down the hill to put a package
there.

Q. That was on the way up.

A. Then I went to the window and called the little girl, Grace, to come
up. When she got to the top of the steps, one flight up, she appeared
to be kind of frightened [Fish was nude] and started to run back. I
grabbed her and she said she will tell her Mama, so I took her into
the room and choked her to death, and I cut the body up into three
pieces. I tried to drink the warm blood but it made me sick.

Q. What made you kill her, choke her and kill her?

A. I had been reading a lot of cases of children being kidnapped, that
Bobby White case, I recalled that and several other cases; then I had
a brother who served five years in the navy, United States Navy, was
honorably discharged, and he used to relate to me when I was quite
small—he was the oldest of my mother's seven children, Walter H.
Fish was his name is, he had been to China when there was a famine,
when they were using human flesh for food. He used to tell us a lot
of these things, and that got into my head.

Q. Did you commit any rape on her?

A. Never entered my head.

Q. What tools did you use to kill?

A. The knife to cut her throat, yes, and chopped her with the cleaver.

Q. Did you use the saw?

A. No.

A TERRIBLE LETTER

Six years after he had abducted and murdered Grace Budd, the Budds got
a letter from Fish, whom they knew as Frank Howard. It is fair to say that
it is one of the vilest letters ever penned and it proved to be Fish's undoing
because a brilliant, determined NYPD cop named William King used it to
help track Fish down. Following is the part of the letter that was most relevant to King.

*On Sunday June 3 1928 I called on you at 406 W. 15th St. . . . Grace sat
in my lap and kissed me. I made up my mind to eat her: On the pretense
of taking her to a party. You said Yes she could go. I took her to an empty
house in Westchester I had already picked out. When we got there, I told
her to remain outside. She picked wild flowers. I went upstairs and
stripped all my clothes off. I knew if I did not I would get blood on them.
When all was ready I went to the window and called her. Then I hid in*

the closet until she was in the room. When she saw me all naked she began to cry and tried to run downstairs. I grabbed her and she said she would tell her mamma. First I stripped her naked. How she did kick, bite and scratch. I choked her to death, then cut her in small pieces so I could take my meat to my rooms, Cook and eat it. How sweet and tender her little ass was roasted in the oven. It took me nine days to eat her entire body. I did not fuck her tho I could of had I wished. She died a virgin.

RANDOM UTTERANCES

I always had the desire to inflict pain on others and to have others inflict pain on me.

I always seemed to enjoy everything that hurt. The desire to inflict pain, that is all that is uppermost.

I am not insane, I'm just queer.

I saw so many boys whipped, it took root in my head.

None of us are saints.

Fish's trial, held in White Plains, New York, started on March 11, 1935, and concluded on March 22, 1935. Fish was declared guilty and electrocuted at Sing Sing Prison on March 26, 1936.

All material is from the transcript of Fish's trial for the murder of Grace Budd. Photo courtesy of author.

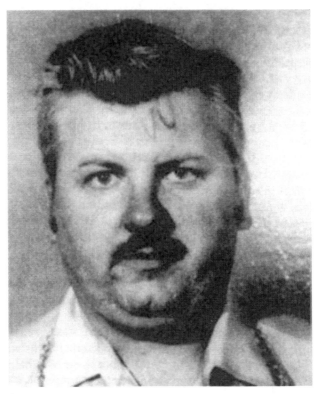

John Wayne Gacy

6.

JOHN WAYNE GACY

John Wayne Gacy lived in a suburb of Chicago and murdered thirty-three young men, mostly by suffocation, first torturing them by sticking an eighteen-inch wooden dildo up their behinds. (One dildo was recovered, half its length coated with dried blood and feces.) He buried most of his victims in a mucky crawl space under his house. He was executed by lethal injection, but while he was waiting in the death house in the Menard Correctional Center in Chester, Illinois, he was given a questionnaire, featuring very ordinary questions, and his answers were astonishing, granted who he was, demonstrating again that people—including serial killers—are able to separate their secret and public lives. Again, misspellings and grammatical errors have been left as is.

> Full name: John Wayne Michael Gacy
> Date of birth: March 17, 1942
> Age, Ht., Wt: 50, 5'9", 208
> Home: Menard Deathrow, Chester, Ill.
> Marital status: Twice Divorced
> Family: 2 sisters, 5 children
> My biggest fear: Dying before I have a chance to clear my name with truth
> Pet peeves: People who say things they have no intention of doing.
> Superstitions: none its for negative people
> Friends like me because: I am outspoken and honest, fun loving, dependable

Behind my back they say: The bastard got it made and he's grandiose
People in history I'd like to have met: Michelangelo, Leonardo DaVinci
If I were an animal I'd be: a Bear or Eagle
Personal goals in life: To see to it that my children are provided for.
Personal interests: Reading, Writing meeting people, classic movies and
   music
Favorite color: Red
Favorite number: nine
I view myself as a: positive thinker, self starter, open minded, non
   judgmental.
What I think of this country: Great, if people would work for it instead
   of against it, pointing fingers at others, the problem takes all races to
   [illegible]
Political views: semi-liberal Democrat, that one party doesn't have all
   winners.
Thoughts on crime: Too much political corruption, and allowed drugs by
   governed has set off the balance of the judicial reform and punishment.
Thoughts on drugs: Make some legal to avoid crime [illegible] I consider
   myself to be Conservative Moderate Liberal with values: Liberal with
   values
What I expect from friendships: lighthearted, fun loving, dependable
   [illegible]
Most treasured honor: 3 times son of the year Jaycees 3 different cities
Perfect woman or man: independent thinker, self starter, mind of her own.
Man: Bright, bold, honest dependable says what he is thinking
Childhood hero: J.F. Kennedy, R.J. Daley.
Current Hero: M. Cuomo, Donald Trump
Favorite TV shows: Unsolved Mysteries, National geographic Specials
Favorite movies: Once Upon A Time in America, Goodfellas, Ten
   Commandments
Favorite song: Send in the clowns, amazing grace
Favorite singers: Judy Collins. Bob Dylan, Neil Diamond, Roy Orbison,
   Shan na Na
Favorite Musicians: REO Speedwagon, Elton John, Zamfir
Hobbies: Correspondence, oil painting, study of human interests
Favorite meals: Fried Chicken, deboned lake perch drawn in butter, salad.
   Tea
Recommended reading: Texas Connection, Question of Doubt
Last book read: naked Lunch and wild boys William S Burroughs
Ideal evening: Dinner and concert or live show, drinks and a quiet walk
   by lake
Every Jan 1st: resolve: Correct things that I go year before
Nobody knows: I'm a character who loves to tease and joke around
My biggest regret: being so trusting and gullible. Taken advantage of.

If I were president I'd: make sure the people of this country had jobs and a place to live before worrying about other countries

My advice to children: Be yourself, think positive respect parents

What I don't like about people: Phonies, people who don't keep their word.

Religious thinking: My faith is in Churches need to work on the family unit.

What you're thinking now: why the hell did I fill this out and who cares what I have to say.

Your artistic interests: To please myself first and hope that expression is enjoyable to others. Art as in life is a journey not a destination. If you don't like it move on. Just like music to the ear, food to the smell and taste.

Gacy was executed by lethal injection on May 10, 1994.

Questionnaire reprinted from Frances Farmer's Revenge, http://www.francesfarmersrevenge.com/stuff/serialkillers/gacyquestion.htm (accessed July 15, 2010). Photo courtesy of Iowa State Men's Reformatory, Anamosa, Iowa, 1968.

7.

ROBERT HANSEN

BACKGROUND

Robert Hansen was born in Pocahontas, Iowa, and was a troubled child, given to wetting his pants, setting fires, and shoplifting. He moved to Anchorage, Alaska, following in the footsteps of his father, and there he opened a bakery. During times when his wife and kids were away, he started trolling areas where prostitutes plied their trade, and eventually he started to murder them. Sometimes he would pick them up in his truck and go to his house. He was a licensed pilot, so other times he would fly them into the Alaskan wild, release them, and then hunt them down with a rifle or bow and arrow. Hansen admitted to seventeen murders, but Alaska state investigator Glenn Flothe felt that Hansen had killed four or five women a year from the early 1970s to 1983, the year he was tracked down.

Hansen was finally caught when one of the women, Kitty Larson, he took to his house escaped, running from his house dressed only in the handcuffs he had put on her. Larson went to the police. In February of 1984, he admitted to some of the killings during questioning, though at times for investigators it was like pulling teeth. Following is a part of the interrogation. Hansen was questioned by Glenn Flothe, assistant district attorney Frank Rothschild, and Anchorage district attorney Victor Krumm.

In his confession, Hansen went to great pains to rationalize his behavior. He explained that he had had problems with women since he was a teenager and that women wouldn't go out with him because of his acne and his

stutter. He said he always "loved" women, but he made a distinction—a sharp distinction—between good and bad girls. Bad girls could die.

In the following portion of his confession he is being questioned by district attorney Victor Krumm. It provides insight into the mind of Robert Hansen. The final questioning is by Glenn Flothe, state investigator, and the simple answer at the end by Hansen is quite chilling when one realizes its homicidal implications.

KRUMM: Why did you drive out to the road instead of just going to a motel in town?

HANSEN: You know if you go to a motel or something with it, it's more or less like a prostitute deal. I'm going and, or I'd—I guess I'm trying to even convince myself maybe I really wasn't buying sex, it was being given to me, in the aspect that I was good enough that it was being given to me. Uh, if I can explain that a little bit better, gentlemen. Going back in my life, way back to my high school days and so forth, I was I guess what you might call very frustrated, upset all the time. I would see my friends and so forth going out on dates and so forth and had a tremendous desire to do the same thing.

From the scars and so forth on my face you can probably see, I could see why girls wouldn't want to get close to me and when I'm nervous and upset like this here; if I, I'll try to demonstrate if I can think about exactly what I'm going to say and if I talk slow I can keep myself from stuttering. But at the time during my junior high or high school days I could not control my speech at all. I was always so embarrassed and upset with it from people making fun of me that I hated the word school, I guess this is why I burned down the bus barn way back in Iowa . . .

I can remember going up and talking to someone, man or woman, classmate or whatever and start to say something and start to stutter so badly that especially in the younger years I would run away crying, run off someplace and hide for a day or so. The worst there was that I was the rebuttal of all the girls around the school and so forth. The jokes. If I could have faced it, I know now I could have laughed along with them it would have stopped but I couldn't at the time and it just, it got so it controlled me, I didn't control it. I didn't start to hate all women, as a matter of fact I would venture to say I started to fall in love with every one of them. Every one of them became so precious to me 'cause I wanted their—I wanted their friendship. I wanted them to like me so much. On top of things that have happened, I don't want to, I'm not saying that I hate all women. I don't. Quite to the contrary, if, I guess in

my own mind what I'm classifying is a good woman, not a prostitute. I'd do everything in my power, any way, shape, or form to do anything for her and to see that no harm ever came to her, but I guess prostitutes are women I'm putting down as lower than myself. I don't know if I'm making sense or not. And you know, when this started to happen I wanted—you know—it happened the first time there you know and I went home and I was literally sick to my stomach . . .

Over the years I've gone in many, many topless and bottomless bars in town and I never, never touched one of the girls in there in any way, shape, or form until they asked. It's like, it's like it was a game, they had to pitch the ball before I could bat. They had to approach me first saying about I get off at a certain time, we could go out and have a good time, or something like this here. If they don't say that we weren't playing the game right. They had to approach me. I've talked to, I suppose I made it a point to try to talk to every girl in there. Sometimes if I thought there was a possibility that she didn't say it the first time but she might come back and say it again, now I've invited two or three table dances with her and comment to her how nice she looked and everything else and I try to keep it in a joking tone, "Gosh you know, you sure would be something, you know, for later on," but that's as far as it would go, until she, then she had to make, I guess play out my fantasy. She had to come out and say, ah, we could do it but it's going to cost you some money. Then she was no longer—I guess what you might call a decent girl. I didn't look down at the girls dancing, what the hell they're just trying to make a buck.

FLOTHE: But when they propositioned you, then it made things different?
HANSEN: Then, yes.

Material from the confession of Robert Hansen, elicited in February 1984 by Assistant District Attorney Frank Rothschild, Anchorage District Attorney Victor Krumm, and Alaska State Investigator Glenn Flothe. Photo courtesy of Alaska Police Department.

H. H. Holmes, aka Herman Mudgett

8.

H. H. HOLMES

BACKGROUND

He's often been called it, but H. H. Holmes was certainly not, in a strict sense, America's first serial killer. There were many people before him who would qualify as serial killers under the FBI's definition of what constitutes a serial killer, which is a person who murders three or more people and has a cooling-off period between his kills. But H. H. Holmes, born Herman W. Mudgett in Gilmanton, New Hampshire, was the first American serial killer who achieved any measure of fame.

Certainly he was one of the most notorious. At the core of his murderous forays was a three-story, block-long "Castle"—so named by neighbors. It debuted as a hotel for the World's Columbian Exposition in 1893. Part of the building was rented out for commerce. The ground floor of the Castle contained a drugstore, which he had gained ownership of by murdering the owner, a variety of stores, the top two offices, and a maze of over one hundred rooms, none with windows. The labyrinth featured stairs that led to nowhere, brick walls behind doorways, door locks that could only be turned to open from the outside, and strangely angled hallways. Only Holmes understood the entire layout.

If you were a female employee of H. H. Holmes, you had problems. He would obligate them to take out life insurance policies with him as the beneficiary (he would pay the premiums), and then he would torture and kill them, as well as lovers and hotel guests. His techniques were horrific.

Some victims were locked in soundproof bedrooms and gas was pumped in, asphyxiating them, some were stuffed into trunks, some suffocated in a vault near his office while he listened to the screaming and the death. The bodies were then put down a chute that led to a room, where they were eventually sold to medical schools. Some were cremated—while alive— and some were destroyed in lime and acid pits, also within the Castle. Holmes also performed over one hundred abortions in a secret room. If the women died there during the procedure, their bodies would be sold.

At one point police got on to Holmes and he was arrested in a fake life insurance scheme involving a man named Benjamin Pitezel who was going to fake his own death, but Holmes made sure the genuine article died. He was arrested in 1894. Police investigated the Castle and eventually the whole story came out. The authorities pinned twenty-seven murders on Holmes, though like most serial killers, the figure is likely much higher.

Shortly before he died he penned his account of these murders, which was published in the *Philadelphia Inquirer* on April 12, 1896, for which he was paid $7,500. He was executed by hanging on May 7, 1896, his body—at his request—buried in concrete so it couldn't be unearthed and dissected. He was thirty-five years old. Following is the complete text of his confession.

THE CONFESSION OF H. H. HOLMES

During the past few months the desire has been repeatedly expressed that I make a detailed confession of all the graver crimes that have with such marvelous skill been traced out and brought home to me. I have been tried for murder, convicted, sentenced, and the first step of my execution upon May seventh, namely, the reading of my death warrant, has been carried out, and it now seems a fitting time, if ever to make known the details of the twenty-seven murders, of which it would be useless to longer say I am not guilty, in the face of the overwhelming amount of proof that has been brought together, not only in one but in each and every case; and because in this concession I speak only of cases that have been thus investigated and of no others, I trust it will not give rise to a supposition that I am still guilty of other murders which I am withholding.

To those inclined to think thus, I will say that the detectives have gone over my entire life, hardly a day or an act has escaped their closest scrutiny, and to judge that I am guilty of more than these cases which they have traced out is to cast discredit upon their work. So marvelous has been the

success of these men into whose hands the proving of my guilt was given, that as I look back upon their year's work it seems almost impossible that men gifted with only human intelligence could have been so skillful, and I feel that I can here call attention to what the prosecution at the close of my trial was denied the pleasure of stating, concerning their ability, though no words of mine can fittingly express what the world at large owes to these impartial and untiring representatives, and more especially to Assistant District Attorney Barlow and Detective Frank Geyer and La Forrest Perry, of the Fidelity Mutual Life Association of Philadelphia; for it is principally owing to their unerring judgment, skill and perseverance that in a few days I am to be forever placed beyond the power of committing other, and, perhaps, if possible, more horrid wrongs. Surely justice, if attended by such servants as these could no longer, in the sense of making mistakes, be appropriately portrayed as being blind. I am moved to make this confession for a variety of reasons, but among them are not those of bravado or a desire to parade my wrongdoings before the public gaze, and he who reads the following lines will, I beg, make a distinction between such motives and a determination upon my part to enter plainly and minutely into the details of each case without favor towards myself. And having done so I have chosen to make it public by publishing it in the *Philadelphia Inquirer.*

A word as to the motives or causes that have led to the commission of these many crimes and I will proceed to the most difficult confessional task of my life, the setting forth in all its horrid nakedness the recital of the premeditated killing of twenty-seven human beings and the unsuccessful attempts to take the lives of six others, thus branding myself as the most detestable criminal of modern times—a task so hard and distasteful that beside it the certainty that in a few days I am to be hanged by the neck until I am dead seems but a pastime.

I am convinced that since my imprisonment I have changed woefully and gruesomely from what I was formerly in feature and figure. My features are assuming a pronounced satanical cast. I have become afflicted with that dread disease, rare but terrible, with which physicians are acquainted, but over which they have no control whatsoever. That disease is a malformation or distortion of the osseous parts. . . . My head and face are gradually assuming an elongated shape. I believe fully that I am growing to resemble the devil—that the similitude is almost completed. Acquired homicidal mania, all other causes, save time occasional opportunity for pecuniary gain having by others been excluded for me, is the only constant cause, and in advancing it at this time I do not do so with the expectation of a mitigation of public condemnation, or that it will in any way react in my favor. Had this been my intention I should have considered it at the time of my trial, and had it used as my defense.

All criminologists who have examined me here seem to be unanimous in the opinions they have formed, although one inexplicable condition presents itself, viz.: that while committing the crimes these symptoms were not present, but commenced to develop after my arrest.

Ten years ago I was thoroughly examined by four men of marked ability and by them pronounced as being both mentally and physically a normal and healthy man. Today I have every attribute of a degenerate—a moral idiot. Is it possible that the crimes, instead of being the result of these abnormal conditions, are in themselves the occasion of the degeneracy?

Even at the time of my arrest in 1894 no defects were noticeable under the searching Bertillon system of measurements to which I was subjected, but later, and more noticeably within the past few months, these defects have increased with startling rapidity, as is made known to me by each succeeding examination until I have become thankful that I am no longer aghast with which to note my rapidly deteriorating condition, though nature, ever kind, provides in this, as in the ordinary forms of insanity where the sufferer believes himself always sane, so that, unless called to my attention, I do not notice my infirmity nor suffer there from. The principal defects that have thus far developed and which are all established signs of degeneracy, are a decided prominence upon one side of my head and a corresponding diminution upon the other side; a marked deficiency of one side of my nose and of one ear, together with an abnormal increase of each upon the opposite side; a difference of one and one-half inches in the length of my arms and an equal shortening of one leg from knee to heel; also a most malevolent distortion of one side of my face and of one eye, although I wore a beard at the time to conceal it as best I could, described

that side of my face as marked by a deep line of crime and being that of a devil—so apparent that an expert criminologist in the employ of the United States Government who had never previously seen me said within thirty seconds after entering my cell: "I know you are guilty."

Would it not, then, be the height of folly for me to die without speaking if only for the purpose of justifying these scientific deductions and accrediting what is due to those who society owes so much for bringing me to justice?

DR. ROBERT LEACOCK

The first taking of human life that is attributed to me is the case of Dr. Robert Leacock of New Baltimore, Mich., a friend and former schoolmate. I knew that his life was insured for a large sum and after enticing him to Chicago I killed him by giving him an overwhelming dose of laudanum. My subsequently taking his dead body from place to place in and about Grand Rapids, Michigan, as has been an often-printed heretofore, and the risk and excitement attendant upon the collection of the forty-thousand dollars of Insurance were very insignificant matters compared with the torturing thought that I had taken human life. This will be understood that before my constant wrongdoing, I had become wholly deaf to the promptings of conscience. For prior to this death, which occurred in 1886, I begged to be believed in stating that I had never sinned so heavily either by thought or deed. Later, like the man-eating tiger of the tropical jungle, whose appetite for blood has once been aroused, I roamed about the world seeking whom I could destroy. Think of the awful list that follows. Twenty-seven lives, men and women, young girls and innocent children, plotted out by one monster's hand, and you, my reader of a tender and delicate nature, will do well to read further, for I will in no way spare myself, and he who reads to the end, if he be charitable, will, in the words of the District Attorney at my trial, when the evidence of all these many crimes had been collected and placed before him by his trusty assistants, exclaim: "God help such a man!" If uncharitable only just will he not rather say: "May he be utterly damned," and that it is almost sufficient to cause one to doubt the wisdom of Providence that such a man should have so long been allowed to live. If so I earnestly pray that this condemnation and censure may not extend to those whose only crime has been that they knew and trusted, aye in some instances, loved me, and who today are more deserving of the world's compassion than censure.

DR. RUSSELL

My second victim was Dr. Russell, a tenant in the Chicago building recently renamed the "The Castle." During a controversy concerning the nonpayment of rent due me, I struck him to the floor with a heavy chair, when he with one cry for help, ending in a groan of anguish, ceased to breathe. This quarrel and death occurred in a small outer office, and as soon as I realized that my blow had been a fatal one and I had recovered somewhat from the horror of having still another victim's blood upon my hands, I was forced to look about for some safe means of concealing the crime. I locked the doors of the office, and my first intention was to dispose of the body to a Chicago medical college, from one of whose officers I had previously obtained dissecting material, as they believed, but in reality to be used in insurance work. I found it difficult, if not impossible, to thus dispose of it, and was directed to call upon a party to whom I sold the bodies and whose name I withhold, but I have confessed his name to parties in whom I have confidence. To him I sold this man's body, as well as others at later dates. In short, in this writing, in each instance when the manner of the disposal of their remains is not otherwise specified, it will be understood that they were turned over to him, he paying me from $25 to $45 for each body, and right easily could he, during the recent investigations, go from room to room in the building when each was more or less gruesomely familiar to him. It is not necessary for me to add that my efforts to shield him when it became evident that he had talked too freely for his own safety should not have saved him from being compelled to turn over the remains of these persons for decent burial or to point out the various museums where they were sold.

JULIA L. CONNOR AND DAUGHTER PEARL

The third death was to a certain extent due to a criminal operation. A man and woman are cognizant of and partially responsible for both the operation and death. The victim was Mrs. Julia L. Connor. A reference to almost any newspaper of August, 1895, will give the minute details of the horrors of this case, as they were worked out by the detectives, therefore, making it unnecessary to repeat it here, save to add that the death of the child Pearl, her little daughter, who is the fourth victim, was caused by poison, and that the man and woman above referred to for its administration, although it was at my instigation that it was done, as I believed the child

was old enough to remember of her mother's sickness and death. They wished, at first, to place the child in the care of the city, but were overruled by my opposition. Owing to the suddenness of the third death, a certain note of considerable value, well secured by property south of the Castle, was uncollectible, and at the time of my death it will be sent to such of her relatives as it may appear have the greater right to receive it.

RODGERS

The fifth murder, that of Rodgers, of West Morgantown, Va., occurred in 1888, at which time I was boarding there for a few weeks. Learning that the man had some money I induced him to go upon a fishing trip with me, and being successful in allaying his suspicions, I finally ended his life by a sudden blow upon the head with an oar. The body was found about a month thereafter, but I was not suspected until after my trial here, and even then by a fortunate circumstance succeeded in having the report publicly denied, but did not succeed in changing the opinion of fifty or more persons living in the town who had recognized my picture in the daily papers.

CHARLES COLE

The sixth case is that of Charles Cole, a Southern speculator. After considerable correspondence this man came to Chicago, and I enticed him into the Castle, where, while I was engaging him in conversation, a confederate struck him a most vicious blow upon the head with a piece of gas pipe. So heavy was the blow it not only caused his death without a groan and hardly a movement, but it crushed his skull to such an extent that his body was almost useless to the party who bought the body. This is the first instance in which I knew this confederate had committed murder, though in several other instances he was fully as guilty as myself, and, if possible, more heartless and bloodthirsty, and I have no doubt is still engaged in the same nefarious work, and if so is probably aided by a Chicago business man.

LIZZIE

A domestic, named Lizzie, was the seventh victim. She, for a time, worked in the Castle restaurant and I soon learned that Quinlan was paying her

too close attention and fearing lest it should progress so far that it would necessitate his leaving my employ I thought it wise to end the life of the girl. This I did by calling her to my office and suffocating her in the vault of which so much has since been printed, she being the first victim that died therein. Before her death I compelled her to write letters to her relations and to Quinlan, stating that she had left Chicago for a Western State and should not return. A few months ago the prosecution, believing from certain letters purporting to have been written by her that she was alive, at once showed me their willingness to give me a fair trial by having this publicly known, she being a witness that I could have used to great advantage in the Pitezel case, here.

MRS. SARAH COOK, HER UNBORN CHILD, AND MS. MARY HARACAMP

The eight, ninth and tenth cases are Mrs. Sarah Cook, her unborn child, and Miss Mary Haracamp, of Hamilton, Canada. In 1888 Mr. Frank Cook became a tenant in the Castle. He was engaged to be married to a young lady living at some distance from Chicago who later came there and was married to him in my presence, by the Rev. Dr. Taylor, of Englewood, Ill. They kept house in the Castle, and for a time I boarded with them. Shortly Miss Mary Haracamp, of Hamilton, a niece of Mrs. Sarah Cook, came to Chicago and entered my employ as a stenographer. But Mrs. Cook and her niece had access to all the rooms by means of a master key and one evening while I was busily engaged preparing my last victim for shipment, the door suddenly opened and they stood before me. It was a time for quick action, rather than for words of explanation upon my part, and before they had recovered from the horror of the sight, they were within the fatal vault, so lately tenanted by the dead body, and then, after writing a letter at my dictation to Mr. Cook that they had tired of their life with him and had gone away not expecting to return, their lives were sacrificed instead of giving them their liberty in exchange for their promise to at once and forever leave Chicago, which had been promised them in return for writing the letter. These were particularly sad deaths, both on account of the victims being exceptionally upright and virtuous women and because Mrs. Sarah Cook, had she lived, would have soon become a mother.

EMMELINE CIGRAND

Soon after this Miss Emmeline Cigrand, of Dwight, Ill., was sent to me by a Chicago typewriter firm to fill the vacancy of stenographer. She had formerly been employed at Dwight where she had become acquainted with a man who visited her from time to time while she was in my employ. She was finally engaged to him and the day set for their wedding. This attachment was particularly obnoxious to me, both because Miss Cigrand had become almost indispensable in my office work, and because she had become my mistress as well as stenographer. I endeavored on several occasions to take the life of the young man and failing in this I finally resolved that I would kill her instead, and upon the day of their wedding, even after cards had been sent out announcing that it had occurred, she came to my office to bid me goodbye. While there I asked her to step inside the vault for some papers for me. There I detained her, telling her that if she would write her husband that at the last moment she had found that it would be impossible to live happily with him and consequently had left Chicago in such a way that search for her would be useless, I would take her to a distant city and live openly with her as my wife. She was very willing to do this and prepared to leave the vault upon completing the letter only to learn that the vault would never be again opened until she had ceased to suffer the tortures of a slow and lingering death.

MURDER TOTAL COULD HAVE BEEN 33

Then follows an unsuccessful attempt to commit a triple murder for the $90 that my agent for disposing of "stiffs" would have given me for the bodies of the intended victims, who were three young women working in my restaurant upon Milwaukee Avenue, Chicago. That these women lived to tell their experience to the police last summer is due to my foolishly trying to chloroform all of them at once and the same time. By their combined strength they overpowered me, and ran screaming into the street, clad only in their night robes. I was arrested next day, but was not prosecuted. To this attempt to kill could very justly be added my attempt to take the lives of Mrs. Pitezel and two of her children at a later date, thus making the total number of my victims 33, instead of 27, as it was through no fault of mine that they escaped.

ROSINE VAN JASSAND

My next attempt was carried out with more caution. The victim was a very beautiful young woman named Rosine Van Jassand, whom I induced to come into my fruit and confection store, and, once within my power, I compelled her to live with me there for a time, threatening her with death if she appeared before any of my customers. A little later I killed her by administering ferro-cyanide of potassium. The location of this store was such that it would have been hazardous to have sent out a large box containing a body, and I therefore buried her remains in the store basement, and from day to day during the recent investigation at the Castle I expected to hear that excavations had been made there as well.

ROBERT LATIMER

Robert Latimer, a man who had for some years been in my employ as janitor, was my next victim. Several years previous, before I had ever taken human life, he had known of certain insurance work I had engaged in, and when, after years, he sought to extort money from me, his own death and the sale of his body was the recompense meted out in him. I confined him within the secret room and slowly starved him to death. Of this room and its secret gas supply and muffled windows and doors, sufficient has already been printed. Finally, needing its use for another purpose and because his pleadings had become almost unbearable, I ended his life. The partial excavation in the walls of this room found by the police was caused by Latimer's endeavoring to escape by tearing away the solid brick and mortar with his unaided fingers.

ANNA BETTS

The fourteenth case is that of Miss Anna Betts, and was caused by purposely substituting a poisonous drug in a prescription that had been sent to my drug store to be compounded, believing that it was known that I was a physician, I should be called in to witness her death, as she lived near the store. This was not the case, however, as the regular physician was in attendance at the time. The prescription, still on file at the Castle, drug she took should be considered by the authorities if they still are inclined to attribute this death to causes that reflect upon Miss Betts' moral character.

GERTRUDE CONNER

The death of Miss Gertrude Conner, of Muscatine, Iowa, though not next in order of occurrence, is so similar to the last that a description of suffices for both, save in this case Miss Conner left Chicago immediately and did not die until she had reached her home in Muscatine. Perhaps these cases show more plainly than others the light regard I had for the lives of fellow beings.

MISS KATE

The sixteenth murder is that of Miss Kate ——, of Omaha, a young woman owning much valuable real estate in Chicago, where I acted as her agent. This was at the time so graphically described by a local writer—as when to hold property under one name, act as notary public under another and carry on a general business under still another title. I caused Miss K to believe that a favorable opportunity had come for her to convert holdings into cash, and having accomplished this for her, she came to Chicago and I paid her the money, taking a receipt in full for the same, and thus protected myself in the event of an inquiry at a later date. I asked her to look about my offices and finally to look within the vault, and, having once passed that fatal door, she never came forth alive. She did not die at once, however, and showed her anger when first she realized that she was deprived of her liberty then her offer of the entire forty thousand dollars in exchange for same and finally her prayers are something terrible to remember. It was stated I had also killed a sister of Miss Kate ——but I think this report has been contradicted.

WADE WARNER

The next death was that of a man named Warner, the originator of Warner Glass Bending Company, and here again a very large sum of it was realized, which prior to his death had been deposited in two Chicago banks, nearly all of which I secured by means of two checks, made out to me. To these I later added the word thousand and the necessary numbers, and by passing them through a bank where I had a regular open account I secured by means of two checks made out and properly signed by him for such a small amount I promptly realized the money save a small amount not covered by the checks in the Park National Bank, northwest corner Dearborn and Washington

streets, in that city. It will now be remembered that the remains of a large kiln made of fire brick was found in the Castle basement. It had been built under Mr. Warner's supervision for the purpose of exhibiting his patents. It was so arranged that in less than a minute after turning on a jet of crude oil atomized with steam the entire kiln would be filled with a colorless flame, so intensely hot iron would be melted therein. It was into this kiln that I induced Mr. Warner to go with me, under pretense of wishing certain minute explanations of the process, and then stepping outside, as he believed to get some tools, I closed the door and turned on the oil and steam to their full extent. In a short time not even the bones of my victim remained. The coat found outside the kiln was the one he took off before going therein.

In 1891 I associated myself in business with a young Englishman, whose name I am more than willing to publish to the world, but I am advised it could not be published on my unsupported statement, who by his own admission, had been guilty of all other forms of wrongdoing, save murder, and presumably of that as well. To manipulate certain real estate securities we held so as to have them secure us a good commercial rating was an easy matter for him and he was equally able to interest certain English capitalists in patents so that for a time it seemed that in the near future, our greatest concern would be how to dispose of the money that seemed about to be showered upon us. By an unforeseen occurrence our rating was destroyed and it became necessary to at once raise a large sum and this was done by my partner enticing to Chicago a wealthy banker named Rodgers from a North Wisconsin town in such a manner that he could have left no intelligence with whom his business was to be. To cause him to go in the Castle and within the secret room under the pretense that our patents were there was easily brought about, more so than to force him to sign checks and drafts for seventy thousand dollars, which we had prepared. At first he refused to do so, stating that his liberty that we offered him in exchange would be useless to him without his money, that he was too old to again hope to make another fortune: finally by alternately starving him and nauseating him with the gas he was made to sign the securities, all of which were converted into money and by my partner's skill as a forger in such a manner as to leave no trace of their having passed through our hands. I waited with much curiosity to see what propositions my partner would advance for the disposal of our prisoner, as I well knew he, no more than I, contemplated giving him his liberty. My partner evidently waited with equal expectancy for me to suggest what should be done, and I finally made preparation to allow him to leave the building, thus forcing him to

suggest that he be killed. I would only consent this upon the condition that he should administer the chloroform, and leave me to dispose of the body as my part of the work. In this way I was enabled to keep him in ignorance of my dealings with the medical college agent. That evening this large sum of money was equally divided between us, and my partner went to the Palmer house, where he was well known, and passed the night at cards with three other men, and at 10 o'clock the next morning came to the office to borrow $100 with which to redeem his overcoat, watch, and rings that he had left to secure a final stroke.

So much has already been written of my own extravagancies and wrong methods of living that I can add little to what the detectives have already pointed out, save to say that during these years, reckoning only the amount of money which they have discovered that I defrauded others of, and as it is known to them that when I was arrested I had very little money, it is evident that my disbursements were over ten thousand dollars per month.

UNKNOWN VICTIM

The nineteenth case is that of a woman, whose name has passed from my memory, who came to the Castle restaurant to board. A tenant of mine at the time immediately became very much infatuated with the woman, who he learned was a widow and wealthy. This tenant was married, and his wife occasionally came to the restaurant when this boarder was there, which did not tend to decrease a family quarrel that for quite a time had threatened this tenant's family with disruption. Finally he came to me for advice, and I was very willing to have him in my power in order that I could later use him in my work if need be. I suggested that he live with the woman in the Castle for a time, and later if his life became unpleasant to him, we would kill her and divide her wealth. Soon, he suggested it was time to take his companion's life. This was done by my administering chloroform while he controlled her violent struggles. It was the body of this woman within the long coffin-shaped box that was taken from the Castle late in 1893, of which the police were notified.

THE WILLIAMS SISTERS

The Williams sisters come next. In order that these deaths may be more fully understood it is necessary for me to state that what has been said by

Miss Minnie R. Williams' Southern relatives regarding her pure and Christian life should be believed; alas, that prior to her meeting me in 1893 she was a virtuous woman, thus rendering truthful the statements of Mr. Charles Goldthwaite, of Boston, that he had never known her other than as an intimate friend of his wife, and that in June 1893, he did not wire her a considerable sum of money to Chicago in response to a demand for some from her; that she was not temporarily insane at a hotel opposite the Pullman Building. Chicago, May 20–23, 1893; was not a little later secluded within the Baptist Hospital at Chicago under the name of Mrs. Williams, and still later at a retreat in Milwaukee, and that she did not kill her sister and threaten to kill a nurse having her in charge at 1230 Wrightwood Avenue, Chicago. All these statements it gives me a certain amount of satisfaction to retract, thereby undoing so far as I can these additional wrongs I have heaped upon her name.

I first met Miss Minnie R. Williams in New York in 1888, where she later [returned] under the same name in Denver, as has been testified by certain young women who recognized my photograph. Early in 1893 I was again introduced to her as H. H. Holmes in the office of Campbell & Dowd, of Chicago, to whom she had applied for them to secure her a position as a stenographer. Soon after entering my employ, I induced her to give me $2500 in money and to transfer to me by deed $50,000 worth of Southern real estate and a little later to live with me as my wife, all this being easily accomplished owing to her innocent and child-like nature, she hardly knowing right from wrong in such matters. Thereafter I succeeded in securing two checks from her for $2500 and $1000 each, and I also learned that she had a sister Nannie in Texas who was an heir to some property and induced Miss Minnie Williams to have her come to Chicago upon a visit. Upon her arrival I met her at the depot and took her to the Castle, telling her Miss Minnie Williams was there. It was an easy matter to force her to assign to me all she possessed. After that she was immediately killed in order that no one in or about the Castle should know of her having been there save the man who burned her clothing. It was the footprint of Nannie Williams, as later demonstrated by that most astute lawyer and detective, Mr. Copps, of Fort Worth, that was found upon the painted surface of the vault door made during her violent struggles before her death. It was also easy to give to Miss Minnie Williams a delayed letter, stating that her sister's proposed visit had been given up and also by intercepting later letters and substituting others to keep her from learning that the sister had left the South. Having secured all the money and property Miss Williams had, it was time that she were killed. Owing to a fire that

had occurred in the Castle I was unable to resort to the usual methods in taking her life, and after some delay, took her to Momence, Ill., about November 15, 1893, registering at a hotel near the post-office under an assumed name, but as man and wife. My intention was to quietly kill her in some sure manner but a freight wreck that occurred upon the outskirts of the town the day following my arrival there, which, out of curiosity, I visited, brought me in contact with a passenger conductor named J. Peck, who knew me, and I therefore abandoned it, but later returned and took her eight miles East of Momence upon a freight line that is little used, and I ended her life with poison and buried her body in the basement of the house spoken of at about the time of the Irvington discovery in 1895. It was a great wonder that the body was not found at the time if the detectives in reality went to that location. Nothing would at the present time give me so much satisfaction as to know that her body had been properly buried, and I would be willing to give up the few remaining days I have to live if by so doing this could be accomplished, for, because of her spotless life before she knew me, because of the large amount of money I defrauded her of, because I killed her sister and brother, because not being satisfied with all this, I endeavored after my arrest to blacken her good name by charging her with the death of her sister, and later with the instigation of the murder of the three Pitezel children, endeavoring to have it believed that her motive for so doing was to afford an avenue of escape for herself if ever apprehended for her sister's death, by pointing to her as a wholesale murderess, and, therefore, presumably guilty of the sister's death as well; for all these reasons this is without exception the saddest and most heinous of any of my crimes.

FORGOTTEN CHICAGO MAN

A man who came to Chicago to attend the Chicago Exposition, but whose name I cannot recall, was my next victim. The Chicago authorities can, if they choose, learn the name by inquiries made of the Hartford Insurance Company, Mr. Lasher, of the Stock Exchange Building; D. F. Duncombe, Metropolitan Building, all of Chicago; a sash and door manufacturing company opposite the Deering, Illinois Station or F. L. Jones, a notary public at Indianapolis, at some one of which places I hope either his name or handwriting may have been preserved, thus affording a clue for identification by his friends. I determined to use this man in my various business dealings, and did so for a time, until I found he had not the ability I had first thought

he possessed, and I therefore decided to kill him. This was done, but as I had not had any dealings with the "stiff" dealer for some time previous to this murder, I decided to bury the body in the basement of the house that I formerly owned near the corner of Seventy-fourth and Honore streets, in Chicago, where, by digging [deeply] in the sandy soil, the body will be found. After Miss Williams' death I found among her papers an insurance policy made in her favor by her brother, Baldwin Williams, of Leadville, Col. I therefore went to that city early in 1894, and, having found him, took his life by shooting him, it being believed I had done so in self-defense. A little later, when the assignment of the policy to which I had forged Miss Williams' name was presented to John M. Maxwell, of Leadville, the administrator of the Williams estate, it was honored and the money paid. Both in this instance and that of a $1000 check given to Dr. Tolman and checks aggregating $2500 by I. R. Hitt & Co., both of Chicago, inasmuch as the endorsements are forgeries, the Williams heirs can now recover these amounts, although it will be an undeserved hardship upon those who have once advanced the money upon them.

BENJAMIN F. PITEZEL

Benjamin F. Pitezel comes next. So much has already been printed (even in South Africa, where the case was recently given considerable prominence in a local issue there) regarding this case that there will be little for me to tell, save the actual manner in which his death was brought about. It will be understood that from the first hour of our acquaintance, even before I knew he had a family who would later afford me additional victims for the grati-fication of my bloodthirstiness, I intended to kill him, and all my subsequent care of him and his, as well as my apparent trust in him by placing in his name large amounts of property, were steps taken to gain his confidence and that of his family so when the time was ripe they would the more readily fall into my hands. It seems almost incredible now as I look back that I could have expected to have experienced sufficient satisfaction in witnessing their deaths to repay me for even the physical exertion that I had put forth in their behalf during those seven long years, to say nothing of the amount of money I had expended for their welfare, over and above what I could have expected to receive from his comparatively small life insurance. Yet, so it is, and it fur-nishes a very striking illustration of the vagaries in which the human mind will, under certain circumstances, indulge; in comparison with which the seeking of buried treasure at the rainbow's end, the delusions of the expo-

nents of perpetual motion. Pitezel left his home for the last time late in July, 1894, a happy, light-hearted man, to whom trouble or discouragements of any kind were almost unknown. We then journeyed together to New York and later to Philadelphia, where the fatal house upon Callowhill Street in which he met his death September 2, 1894, was hired. Then came my writing to him the discouraging letters, purporting to be from his wife, causing him to again resort to drink. Then the waiting from day to day until I should be sure of finding him in a drunken stupor at midday. This was an easy matter, as I was acquainted with his habits and so sure was I of finding him thus incapacitated that when the day came upon which it was convenient for me to kill him, even before I went to his house I packed my trunk and made all arrangements to leave Philadelphia in a hurried flight immediately after death. After thus preparing I went to the house, quietly unlocked the door, stole noiselessly within and to the second story room, where I found him insensibly drunk, as I had expected. But even in this condition the question may be asked had I no fear that he might be only naturally asleep or partly insensible and therefore liable to at any moment come to his senses and defend himself? I answer no, and that even had he done so my great strength would have enabled me to have still overpowered him.

Only one difficulty presented itself. It was necessary for me to kill him in such a manner that no struggle or movement of his body should occur or otherwise his clothing being in any way displaced it would have been impossible to again put them in a normal condition. I overcame this detail by first binding him hand and foot and having done [that,] I proceeded to burn him alive by saturating his clothing and his face with benzene, igniting it with a match. So horrible was this torture that in writing of having been tempted to attribute his death to some humane means—not with wish to spare myself, but because I fear that it will not be believed that I could be so heartless and depraved, but such a course would be useless, by excursion, the authorities have determined for me that his death could only have occurred in this manner, no blows or bruises upon his body and drug administered, save chloroform, which was not placed in his stomach until at least 30 minutes after his death, and to now make a misstatement of the facts would only serve to draw out additional criticism from them. The least I can do is to spare my reader a recital of the victim's cries for me, his prayers and finally, his plea for a more speedy termination of sufferings, all of which upon me had no effect. Finally, he was removed from the straps and ropes that had bound him and I extinguished flames, and a little later, poured into his stomach one and one half ounces chloroform. It has been asked why I did this after I knew that he was dead, what

possible use it could have served? My answer to this is that I placed it there so that at the time of the post mortem examination, which I knew was to be held, the Coroner's physician would be warranted in reporting that death was accidental, and due to an explosion of a cleaning fluid, composed of benzene and chloroform, and that the chloroform had at the time of explosion separated from the benzene and passed into his stomach and receipt of such intelligence I believed the insurance company would at once pay the full amount of the claim. The chloroform did worse than this however, and developed a condition of this body that in my limited medical experience I have never seen or read of, and I mention it here as a fact of scientific interest, that I believe is not generally known. It drove from entire body tissue, brains and viscera, all evidence of recent intoxication to such an extent that the physicians who examined the body after death warranted in stating under oath that there was no evidence of, and they did not believe the man was drunk at the time of his death, or within twelve hours thereof. That they were wrong in making such deductions is proven by well-known fact that all other testimony and circumstances at my trial tend to show that he must have been insensible from liquor, and that only in that condition could I have killed him; a fact so strongly brought out that a learned trial judge in his arguments commented upon it at some length. At his death I gathered together various assignments of patents and deeds property he had held for me that I had been careful to have him sign some days before, so I should not suffer pecuniary loss. I also wrote the cipher message found by the insurance company among my papers after my arrest, imitating his handwriting, and after placing the body in such a position that by an arrangement of a window shutter upon the South side of the building the sun would be reflected upon his face the entire day, I left the house without the slightest feeling of remorse for my terrible acts.

For one month and six days thereafter I took no human life, although about three weeks after Pitezel's death I was afforded an opportunity to gratify my feverish lust for blood by going to the graveyard where he had been buried and under pretense of securing certain portions of his body for microscopical examination removed the same with a knife, and the heartless manner in which I did this and the evident gratification it afforded me has been most forcibly told by Mr. Smith upon the witness stand. As an instance of the infallibility of justice, as a triumph of right over wrong, and of the general safety of condemnation to death upon circumstantial evidence alone this case is destined to long remain prominent as a warning to those viciously inclined that their only safe course is to avoid even the [appearance] of evil.

Two questions that have been often asked I would answer—why did I make no defense at my trial when by so doing I could lose nothing, and possibly could have gained? I answer that after which we could not at that time in any way refute, and in the face of Dr. Leffmann's learned statements to the effect that no one could or had ever been known to lose consciousness by chloroform self-administered, provided they had not first confined their movements. It would have been but a waste of my counsel's energies, and of my own, to have had to convince the most impartial juries that it was a case of suicide and not a murder. Is it to be wondered at that I hesitated before placing the defense of suicide before a jury composed of men who had, with three exceptions, stated under oath, before being passed upon by the court as competent, that they had already formed opinions prejudiced to my interests? The second question is, did Pitezel during his eight years' acquaintance and almost constant association with me, know that I was a multi-murderer, and if he did know was he a party to such crime? I answer that he neither knew of nor was a party to the taking of any human life, and I believed, both in justice to his memory and on account of the surviving members of his family. The worst acts he ever participated in were dishonesties regarding properties and unlawful acts of trade, in which he aided me freely. In support of my statement that he was not cognizant of any of the graver crimes, which I have so freely confessed herein, I will mention one of many instances already known to the authorities; that for six months previous to his death he had planned openly with his wife that their daughter Alice should spend a year at a school he believed Miss Williams intended to open near Boston, and these plans were of such a nature that Mrs. Pitezel knows he was not deceiving her. He would not have made these arrangements, and there would have been no occasion for him to have deceived his own family, if he believed Miss Williams was not alive.

HOWARD PITEZEL

The Irvington, Indiana, tragedy is next. Upon the 1st day of October, 1894, I took the three Pitezel children to the Circle House in Indianapolis, where I engaged permanent board for them until such a time as I could kill one or more of them. Upon the evening of that day I went to St. Louis, where I remained until October 4, busily engaged in settling up the insurance matter with McDonalds and Howe, the attorneys. During this time I also called upon the agent or owner of the Irvington House. This was my first incau-

tious step, and was destined to fasten the crime upon me, for later when the detectives learned that I made this call upon the date that they knew the insurance settlement took place, they no longer hesitated in stating that I, and I alone, could have murdered the boy. Upon October 4, I returned to Indianapolis and later in that same day went to Franklin, Indiana, which is situated South of Indianapolis, while Irvington is East thereof, Franklin to Irvington representing the hypotenuse of a triangle—Franklin to Indianapolis and Indianapolis to Irvington the two shorter sides—so that one could go from Franklin to Irvington direct without making the longer journey via Indianapolis. On October 5th the rent of the house was paid and at about 9 A.M. October 6th I called upon Dr. Thompson at Irvington for the keys, he having been a former occupant. At 5 o'clock upon the same I called upon Mr. Brown at Irvington to engage him to make some repairs upon the house, and upon his appearing indifferent I became very angry with him and my only wonder is that I did not entice him to the house and kill him also. This small circumstance aided in bringing the crime home to me when it was made known to the detectives and considered by them in connection with many other complaints of my violent and ungovernable temper that had come to their knowledge. On October 7th I called at the Irvington drug store and purchased the drugs I needed to kill the boy and the following evening I again went to the same store and bought an additional supply, as I feared I had not obtained a sufficient quantity upon my first visit. My next step was to secure the furniture for the house. This was done upon October 8, late in the afternoon, at such an hour that made it impossible for the store owner to deliver them, and as I wished to stay at Irvington that night I hired a conveyance and carted the goods to the house myself, keeping the horse there until the next day. It was also upon the 8th, early in the forenoon, that I went to the repair shop for the long knives I had previously left there to be sharpened. Early in the afternoon of October 10th, I had the boy's trunk and a stove I had bought taken to the depot, and they arrived at the Irvington house at about 6 P.M. at which time Mr. Moreman was the last person who saw the boy alive, for almost immediately I called him into the house and insisted that he go to bed at once, first giving him the fatal dose of medicine. As soon as he had ceased to breathe I cut his body into pieces that would pass through the door of the stove and by the combined use of gas and corncobs proceeded to burn it with as little feeling as 'tho it had been some inanimate object. If I could now recall one circumstance, a dollar of money to be gained, a disagreeable act or word upon his part, in justification of this horrid crime, it would be a satisfaction to me; but to think that I committed this and other crimes for the pleasure

of killing my fellow beings, to hear their cries for mercy and pleas to be allowed even sufficient time to pray and prepare for death—all this is now too horrible for even me, hardened criminal that I am, to again live over without a shudder. Is it to be wondered at that since my arrest my days have been those of self-reproaching torture, and my nights of sleepless fear? Or that even before my death, I have commenced to assume the form and features of the Evil One himself?

After I had finished the cremation of my victim I made the excavation in which the few remaining portions were found at the time the horror was brought to light, which together with the stove and other evidences of my wrongdoings, were brought here to Philadelphia at the time of my trial to mock me in my efforts to save my life. Then after I had removed the blood and other evidences of the crime, and had burned the contents of the trunk, I went to the office of Powell & Harter, at Indianapolis, for my mail; from there to the hotel for the other two children, whom I took at once to Chicago. I immediately returned to the Irvington House, and was seen there by Mr. Armstrong, a teamster, or such, in time as to have made it a foolish act for me to have persisted in saying that it was some other person whom he saw. My identification in Chicago by a woman with whom the children boarded and by the station agent at Milwaukee, and later at Adrian, Mich., all show the uselessness of trying to escape from one's self or from the responsibility of one's wrong acts.

In Detroit I hired a house and made an excavation in the basement, where I left a note in my own handwriting, all of which I hastened to tell the detectives as soon as I was arrested, so that by their going to the house and finding both the excavation and the note they would not be inclined to prosecute a similar search in Toronto or other places.

ALICE AND NELLIE PITEZEL

I now, with much reluctance, come to the discussion of the twenty-sixth and twenty-seventh murders. The victims were Alice and Nellie Pitezel, whose deaths will seem to many to be the saddest of all, both on account of the terribly heartless manner in which it was accomplished, and because in one instance, that of Alice, the oldest of these children, her death was the least of the wrongs suffered at my hands. Here again I am tempted to either pass the matter by without speaking of it, or to altogether deny it, but to what purpose? It is publicly known and was freely commented upon at my trial, and to deny it now would only serve the double purpose of

breaking my resolution to hold nothing in reserve, and of causing many who are somewhat familiar with the details of the different cases to disbelieve me in other matters; moreover, the testimony already given by Mrs. Actlia Allcorn, and the opinion of Coroner Ashbridge and a Mr. Perry, who knew the mental condition of the child upon the following day, would, if called for, be sufficient to decide the matter. These children, after boarding in Detroit for about one week, reached Toronto, October 19, and were taken to the Albion Hotel, where they boarded until they were killed. Upon October 20 I hired the Vincent Street house, having the lease made in the name of H. M. Howard, in order to avert suspicion as much as possible in case an investigation followed. Between 5 and 6 P.M. the same day I took a large empty trunk to the house and then passed the following day at Niagara Falls. On the 22d I bought and had taken to the house the furniture, stove and bedding, and on the 23d, the children went to the house for a few hours. The 24th was passed in other parts of the city, but upon the 25th, the fatal day of these deaths, they were seen at the house at 1 P.M., and a little later they accompanied me to several clothing stores in a restaurant near-by. I entered a large store in which I believed I should meet Mrs. Pitezel, holding in my hands some heavy winter underwear I had bought for the little boy already dead. Of this meeting Mrs. Pitezel has said: "I believe my children were at that time in that store with me."

I immediately took them to the Vincent Street house and compelled them to get within the large trunk, through the cover of which I made a small opening. Here I left them until I could return and at my leisure kill them. At 5 P.M. I borrowed a spade of a neighbor and at the same time called on Mrs. Pitezel at her hotel. I then returned to my hotel and ate my dinner, and at 7:00 P.M. went again to Mrs. Pitezel's hotel, and aided her in leaving Toronto for Ogdensburg, N.Y. Later than 8:00 P.M. I again returned to the house where the children were imprisoned, and ended their lives by connecting the gas into the trunk, then came the opening of the trunk and the viewing of their two blackened and distorted faces, then the digging of their shallow graves in the basement of the house, the ruthless stripping off of their clothing and burial without a particle of covering save the cold earth, which I heaped on them with fiendish delight. Consider what an awful act this was! These little innocent and helpless children, the oldest only being 13 years of age, a puny and sickly child, who to look at one would believe much younger; consider that for eight years before their death I had been almost as much a father as though they had been my own children, thus giving them a right to me for care and protection, and in your righteous judgment let your curses fall upon me, but again I pray

upon me alone! There is little else to tell. The next day was passed in burning the children's clothing, and resting from my terrible night's work, and upon the 27th I called a pressman and had the trunk removed from the house, and after giving the keys to a neighbor went away never to return. From Toronto I went to Ogdensburg, from there to Burlington, Vermont, where I hired a furnished house for Mrs. Pitezel's use, and a few days prior to my arrest in Boston I wrote her a letter in which I directed her to carry a bottle of dynamite that I had previously left in the basement so arranged that in taking it to the third story of the house it would fall from her hands, and not only destroy her life, but that of her two remaining children, who I knew would be with her at the time. This was my last act, and happily did not have a fatal termination. The eighteen intervening months I have passed in solitary confinement and in a few days am to be led forth to my death. It would now seem a very fitting time for me to express regret or remorse in this, which I intend to be my last public utterance for these irreparable shortcomings. To do so with the expectation of even one person who has read this confession to the end, believing that in my depraved nature there is room for such feelings, is I fear, to expect more than would be granted. I can at least, and do refrain, from calling forth such a criticism by openly inviting it.

Signed,
H. H. Holmes

Material and photos from "The Confession of H. H. Holmes," *Philadelphia Inquirer*, April 12, 1896.

A Ripper victim

9.

JACK THE RIPPER

BACKGROUND

For some reason—even though there are seemingly far more blood-thirsty serial killers, Jack the Ripper's shadow looms large ever since he started his five-person killing spree on August 3, 1888 (the same year the Brooklyn Bridge went into service), eviscerating a prostitute named Mary Nichols and, subsequently, four others. Perhaps part of the reason why The Ripper was so shocking was because he flaunted his homicidal achievements, writing letters to the police and having them published in the newspapers.

The first of these alleged letters penned (in red ink) by the killer was written on September 25 and mailed three days later, addressed to London's Central News Agency. It read:

Dear Boss,

I keep on hearing the police have caught me but they won't fix me just yet. I have laughed when they look so clever and talk about being on the right track. That joke about Leather Apron gave me real fits. I am down on whores and shan't quit ripping them till I do get buckled. Grand work the last job was. I gave the lady no time to squeal. How can they catch me now. I love my work and want to start again. You will soon hear of me and my funny little games. I saved some of the proper red stuff in a

ginger beer bottle over the last job to write with but it went thick like glue and I can't use it. Red ink is fit enough I hope ha ha. The next job I do I shall clip the lady's ears off and send to the police officers just for jolly wouldn't you. Keep this letter back till I do a bit more work, then give it out straight. My knife is nice and sharp I want to get to work right away if I get the chance. Good luck.

Yours truly,

Jack the Ripper

Don't mind me giving the trade name. Wasn't good enough to post this before I got all the red ink off my hands curse it. They say I am a doctor now ha ha.

The Ripper claimed two more victims in September. A third communication was mailed on October 16 to George Lusk, head of the newly organized Whitechapel Vigilance Committee. It read:

From hell
Mr. Lusk
Sir

I send you half the Kidne I took from one woman prasarved it for you tother piece I fried and ate it was very nise I may send you the bloody knif that took it out if you only wate a whil longer

[signed]
Catch me when you can Mishter Lusk

Examining the partial kidney that accompanied the letter, Dr. Openshaw, the pathological curator of the London Hospital Museum, pronounced it "ginny," typical of an alcoholic. It showed symptoms of Bright's disease, as (allegedly) did the kidney left from a victim named Catherine Eddowes.

Material from Michael Newton, *Encyclopedia of Serial Killers* (New York: Checkmark Books, 2000).

10.

EDMUND KEMPER

BACKGROUND

Edmund Kemper is another serial killer for whom we have documented information about his childhood. Perhaps one incident says it all: He was seven or eight at the time, and did something that deserved punishment. But the punishment meted out was, quite simply, horrific. He owned a pet chicken, a creature he loved as much as another boy might love a dog. Because of his bad behavior his parents ordered him to kill the chicken, which he did, and then his mother cooked it and the Kempers ate his pet for dinner. And all during the killing and the eating, tears ran down young Edmund's face.

His father, who was giant size—six foot ten or so—deserted his mother (who was six foot tall and big overall). Kemper withstood a steady stream of abuse from his towering mother. We know Edmund was

Edmund Kemper

119

very bright, and we also know he started acting out in response to the abuse.

With two psychopaths as parents, it was hardly a mystery why Kemper turned out the way he did. It was determined he was deeply disturbed as a young boy, and he provided persuasive proof. Sent to live with his paternal grandparents at the age of fifteen, he first shot his grandmother to death with a rifle and then his grandfather when he came home. Kemper's reason for the double murder was that he wanted to "feel what it was like."

He was then confined to Atascadero Hospital and started getting treatment, and five years later, at twenty-one, now a six-foot-nine-inch giant weighing three hundred pounds, he was released. A few of the doctors bitterly objected.

Kemper, of course, was as crazy as a bedbug, but he didn't start to kill anyone for a while. According to Michael Newton, writing in *The Encyclopedia of Serial Killers*, he spent 1970 and 1971 cruising the roads around Santa Cruz, a college town, where there were frequent Fresno State College coed hitchhikers. They might be chary of most cars driven by males, but Kemper's car had a Fresno State sticker on the bumper. Kemper's mother worked at the college. Kemper also developed a smooth style of talking, which would reassure them.

But eventually he did kill six coeds in all, plus his mother and her friend, and he finally turned himself in and was very cooperative with police in providing details of his crimes. Indeed, Kemper seemed to relish laying out all the gory details of his killings, and they were gory. Please note that his accounts of his killings are extremely detailed and not for the fainthearted.

Following are stories he told in his own words to police officers, Lieutenant Scherer and Sergeant Aluffi, on tape.

MARY ANN AND ANITA

"Last May seventh (1972) at approximately 4 P.M.," Kemper said, "I picked up two girls on Ashby Avenue, which is also Highway 13, in Berkeley, who were carrying a sign which said they wanted to go to Stanford. Their names were Anita Luchessa and Mary Ann Pesce. Each was eighteen and enrolled at Fresno State College.

"I asked them a few questions and determined to my satisfaction that they were not familiar with the area. Without pressing too hard, and doing a few loopy-loops around freeways and bypasses, I managed to think up

some method for following through with this act with the least amount of jeopardy.

"What I did was, I stopped for gas in Alameda, where I was living." At the station he went into the restroom, taking a map, and checked to make sure that Stanford University was to the south.

"So I took them the other way, out on 680, which would come in on the rural highway. I told them a story about how I was working for the Division of Highways. They were impressed with my radio transmitter, and they thought I was a secret agent or something. I kept telling them that I wasn't a policeman . . . and they'd give each other little looks. But I didn't really make much of an effort to deceive them because they were terribly naive. Anything I said just went over fine."

Kemper drove them south, in the opposite way they wanted to go, and eventually found what he wanted, a rural cul-de-sac. He pulled in and parked.

Under the seat he had a 9-mm Browning automatic. He pulled it out.

"I was scared, and kept telling myself I didn't really want to do it. But I was determined. I was very frustrated, because it was like a game to me. Up to that point, it always had been a big adventure, a big thrill. But I never permitted myself . . . to follow through and take a chance on getting in serious trouble. I mean avoid the possibility . . . of rape; but I had decided from my past stay at Atascadero and listening to a lot of stories, that what I thought was my past experience—it seemed to me a lot more efficient not to have someone, unless you're absolutely sure that they weren't going to go to anybody, and in this case, thinking back on it, I really honestly think I could have gotten away with doing exactly what I told them I was going to do, which was rape. I didn't say that word. But one of them asked me, 'What do you want?' and I pointed the gun. I just lifted it up between the two of them, and I told her, 'You know what I want.'

"The one girl, Mary Ann, assumed command over the two and over conversation, and immediately when I turned the gun up, I turned to her and spoke and ascertained from our conversations that she was not the talkative one, but the one who was more in a leadership position. The other girl was Anita, who was overpowered, despite the presentation of that weapon, without any threats."

Mary Ann did most of the talking. That impressed him.

"I was really quite struck by her personality and her looks," he said. Anita was silent but Mary Ann kept up her "very good efforts of communicating and discussing the thing, rather than just jumping hastily into action, before anything serious happened."

He said he told them "that if either one of them had gotten any funny ideas about communicating with anybody, or pulling the lights out in the back so I wouldn't have any signal for brakes, or something—I told them that that was going to be the end of both of them.

"At this time, I had full intentions of killing both of them. I would have loved to have raped them. But not having any experience at all in this area, I'd had very limited exposure to the opposite sex and I guess the learning point—fifteen to twenty-one—I was locked up with all men, and there wasn't any opportunity to be with women or girls, and this is one of the big problems I had, and one of the biggest things that caused me to be so uptight.

"So even trying to communicate [with girls] before this happened, just casually, I felt like a big bumble butt, and I think it's just like an over-aged teenager trying to fit in. They were both eighteen at the time, I think, and I was twenty-three, which isn't that much of a gap, but it was just like a million years.

"Anyway, I decided that Anita was more gullible and would be easier to control, so I told her that she was gonna go into the trunk. And she stepped right out of the car, and I had a pair of handcuffs I had purchased. I took the cuffs out and I reached for one of Mary Ann's arms and she grabbed it back. I picked the gun up like I was gonna hit her with it and told her not to do that again. I said, you know, 'I'm running the show here,' or some such cliché. So she allowed me to put my handcuffs on her arm, and I put the other one around the seat belt, behind the lock so it wouldn't come up, and left her back there.

"I took the other girl to the trunk. Just before she got in Mary Ann said: 'Please don't do this' or something like that.

"I said, 'What, are you gonna start in too?'"

Back in the car, he found that Mary Ann was not quickly following through on his instructions. "I almost stuck the gun up her nose to impress her that that was a real gun and that she kept getting me more uptight than I was. And then my lips started quivering, rather than her friend's, and I started losing control, and I told her that if she kept that up, that they were all gonna be in a whole lot of trouble. At this point, she cooperated. I handcuffed her behind her back and turned her over, and I tried to put a plastic bag over her head. I had this nifty idea about suffocating her. I was going to be really smart, and the windows were rolled up, and just normal conversation wouldn't carry—it was a fairly populated area. It was up on the hill. You couldn't hear voices or anything way off in the distance. So I didn't want anything carrying that would be conspicuous. . . . She was complaining that she couldn't breathe. I said I'd tear a hole in the bag, not

intending to really, and I had a terrycloth bathrobe with a long rope tie. I put a loop in it and started pulling it down over what I thought was her neck. I pulled it tight. That's about where I blew it."

Kemper said he became overly tense and snapped the rope in two. It had caught her around the mouth anyway, and she complained. She also bit a hole in the plastic bag. Enraged, he reached into his pocket, pulled out his knife, and flipped the blade open. Blinded by the bag over her eyes and with her back to Kemper, she asked him what he was doing.

"I poised the blade over her back, trying to decide where her heart was, and struck and hit her in the middle of the back, and it stuck a little bit; and she said something like Ow! or Oh! and I pulled it back out.

"And I did it again and did the same damn thing, and I was getting mad now and I told her to shut up after the second time, and she said 'I can't,' and was moaning. She was struggling . . . but she couldn't move too much. . . . Then I started thrusting hard and I was hitting, but apparently I wasn't hitting or the blade wasn't long enough, which wasn't conceivable to me because she wasn't that large a girl, rather small in fact, about five feet two inches and maybe 105 pounds. I struck in several places in both sides of the back and noticed as I went further down the back, that she was a little louder and more painful in her cries, but none got really loud. That always bothered me. I couldn't figure out why. It was almost like she didn't want to blow up and start screaming or something. She was maintaining control. But when I started doing this, then it got to be too much for her, she twisted around, and I hit her once in the side with the knife.

"She turned completely over to see what the hell I was doing, I guess, or to get her back away from me, and I stabbed her once in the stomach in the lower intestine. It didn't have any effect. There wasn't any blood or anything. There was absolutely no contact with improper areas. In fact, I think once I accidentally—this bothers me, too, personally—I brushed, I think with the back of my hand when I was handcuffing her, against one of her breasts, and it embarrassed me, I even said, 'Whoops, I'm sorry,' or something like that. She was pretty cognizant of what was going on, and it was getting pretty messy there in the back seat. She turned back over on her stomach, and I continued stabbing. I don't know how many times I stabbed her. I'm trying to think. I usually checked something like that—you might say, almost comparing notes—and in this case I didn't. I did with Anita, 'cause that really amazed me. With Mary Ann, I was really quite struck by her personality and her looks, and there was just almost a reverence there. I didn't even touch her, really too much, after that. That is, other than to get rid of physical evidence, such as clothing, and later the body.

"Anyway, she was across the back of the seat with her head down towards the door, towards the space between the front seat and back seat, and I don't think the bag was on. She had shaken it off. She was crying out a little louder, and I kept trying to shut her up, covering her mouth up, and she kept pulling away, and one time, she didn't, and like it was a cry, and I could have sworn it came out of her back. There were several holes in the lung area and bubbles and things coming out, and the sounds shook me up, and I backed off; at that point, she turned her head to the back of the seat and she called her friend's name, her first name. It was slow and it was not loud. That was the last thing that she said. She wasn't passing out at that point. I don't think at that point that the full impact of what had happened had really hit her. I think she was pretty well in shock or something.

"I felt I was getting nowhere, not that I wasn't getting any kicks out of stabbing her, but hoped that one more would do it. When it got quite messy like that, I reached around and grabbed her by the chin and pulled her head back and slashed her throat. I made a very definite effort at it, and it was extremely deep on both sides. She lost consciousness immediately, and there were no more vocal sounds anyway."

At that point, Kemper got up in a daze or shock, he said, and headed to the back of the car. "I knew I had to do it to the other girl right then, because she had heard all the struggle and she must have known something very serious was going on."

He concealed his hands as he raised the trunk lid because of the blood on them. Anita said, "What's happening with Mary Ann?" Kemper said, 'Well, she was getting smart with me.'

"And I pulled my hands down kind of unconsciously, and she noticed how bloody they were and she panicked. Her lip was really quivering, and she was really scared. I was scared."

He told her that he thought he had broken Mary Ann's nose and that she should help her. Anita, in her new, heavy coveralls, started to get out. While Kemper was talking to her, he picked up another knife from the trunk, with a very large blade. "It was called the Original Buffalo Skinner or something," and it had been "very expensive, about eight or nine dollars."

Then he used the Original Buffalo Skinner and stabbed Anita as she got out of the trunk, but the knife didn't penetrate. Anita saw what was happening. As Kemper stabbed at her again and again, she threw herself back into the trunk, saying "Oh, God, God." She began fighting back. He tried to slash her throat but in the process stabbed his own hand, a fact he did not realize for all of an hour.

As Anita covered her throat with her hands he stabbed through her fin-

gers. Kemper said she was "putting up a hell of a fight." He tied to drive the knife though her heart. "I was thrusting and the knife was going very deep, and it amazed me that she was stabbed three times and then was still going at it. I tried stabbing her in the front again, or towards the throat area, and she was making quite a bit of noise and was trying to fight me off, and I stabbed her in the forearms. One was so bad you could see both bones, and she saw it. When I hit, I didn't think it really hurt so much, as it was the shock of everything happening so fast. She looked at it, and I could see the expression on her face of shock.

"I hate to get into such detail on that," Kemper said, "but my memory tends to be rather meticulous."

Finally, Anita began screaming, very loudly and piercingly. Her murderer was scared, he said, and unsure of what to do. He had heard voices in the distance. Therefore he renewed his attack with greater fury. The stab with which he hoped to penetrate her eye socket failed, but he knocked her glasses off.

"She reacted to each one of these things with a completely different thing," Kemper noted. "Where the other girl was just one continuous motion, this girl was actually fighting me, almost succeeding. But she really didn't have a chance."

Gradually she slowed down and became both semiconscious and delirious. She was dying.

Kemper looked in the back seat. Mary Ann was there, dead. He pushed her body down and covered it with an old jacket.

He thought he had lost the keys, but he found them.

"I said, 'Oh, Jesus, that's just what I need, and a bunch of people are gonna be charging up here any second.' And I ran around the car looking for anything that might have fallen out." Mary Ann's wallet was by the passenger seat. He picked it up and threw it into the car.

"I jumped in the car," he said, "and was sweating very heavily and there was blood splattered here and there and on my hands, which I had to keep concealed. But I drove out of the area. Very close by, right down on the main road, were two couples looking at property. They looked rather disgruntled as I went by. I tried to look nonchalant."

At home, Kemper opened the trunk of his car and looked at the body of Anita.

"What surprised me was how many blows she took. They were all heavy blows. I didn't think I could have taken one of them. For them being such small females, both of them about the same size and build, the knife had to go well over halfway through her chest from side to side, and they

were direct. It was shocking to me. But anyway, she was in a rather peaceful position, with one arm across her."

The blood was highly noticeable. "My intention all along," he said, "was to get rid of any physical evidence that might make someone suspicious, and like I said to the officers today, when I discussed this, the whole series of things was very sick, I realize that better than anybody. The thing that hits me is that when I'm lucid and thinking normally and rationally, it's very painful at that point. But I had set up certain rules. What these were, were fantasies come to life. I decided I was tired of hiding in my little fantasy world while the rest of the world was trampling upon my head with their just living their normal lives. So I decided on this rebellion . . . like conquests or something like this, physical sights, my fantasies were usually around women. Rather than like having an orgasm with a dead woman or something; that was my fantasy, but it would be more along the lines of a not so forceful rape, or I would be in command and she would not be that unwilling, but I imagine everybody likes to have dreams like that. Mine did get a little bit more lurid than that."

AIKO

Aiko Koo was not yet sixteen years old, a small but well-built Eurasian female with dark hair. Though she had had a rough background—for starters, she was illegitimate and her father had deserted her mother—she had turned out quite well, this mainly due to her mother, who was a woman who didn't let life defeat her. Aiko had been active and involved, particularly in dancing, and everyone who knew her felt she was on track to becoming a successful classical dancer.

On the evening of September 14, 1972, however, she was invited to attend a class in advanced dance in San Francisco, and she decided to go via bus. While waiting for the bus she started to talk to a girl named Ann. As noted in *The Coed Killer* by Margaret Cheney, Ann remembered, "She told me she was going to San Francisco to a dance class and that she was waiting for a bus. We talked for about five minutes—about her family, school, things like that." She added that she had been surprised to learn that Aiko was only fifteen, saying she had looked "much, much older."

Horribly, Ann didn't learn Aiko's name until she saw her photo on a telephone pole on University Avenue. Underneath the picture was a question: "Have you seen this girl?" Ann called the Berkeley Police Department immediately and recalled, "She got tired of waiting and decided to hitchhike."

Ann saw Aiko catch a ride. She described the car as "a cream or tan-colored sedan, late sixty model." (Kemper's car was usually caked with mud and dust from his travels.) Driving the car had been "a fairly tall male Caucasian with light brown, medium brown hair. That is the best description I can give."

"When Aiko failed to return home by eleven o'clock that night, her mother began to worry. She telephoned first to the dance studio and learned that her daughter had never arrived. Between midnight and 1 o'clock she communicated with the Berkeley police and reported Aiko missing," writes Margaret Cheney in *The Coed Killer*.

Then her mother and her friends started putting up posters and the like, and the cops intensified their search efforts.

But Aiko was already dead.

She had gotten into Edmund Kemper's car.

Kemper was driving along University Avenue in Berkeley around seven in the evening when he saw a "small Oriental girl" holding up a sign that said SF, for San Francisco. He went past her but circled the block and picked her up. "There was absolutely no problem," he said. "Apparently she was not an accomplished hitchhiker."

Right away he was determined to drive her to a place where he could kill her.

"After blowing [past] her off-ramp and making it sound like an accident," he said, "I said, 'Whoops,' and she said, 'Whoops.' I think it was slightly cutting."

He took a series of other wrong moves until they were far down the coast when Aiko realized what was happening. She told him she'd be late for class, and she knew she was in danger. He told her to "knock it off." At one point Aiko said, "Please don't kill me."

"... You know, that type of thing, and was shrieking sort of. I pulled out this great .357 magnum six-inch Trooper that I borrowed from [a friend] who works where I worked at the Division of Highways ... him not knowing what I was using it for."

He poked the big gun in her ribs. "Do you know what this is?"

But then he convinced her that he was depressed and just wanted to talk. Aiko suggested she get in the back seat. "Now behave," Kemper said, "I don't want to hurt you or anyone else. But if you try to signal a policeman or anyone else, I'll have to kill him and you. You wouldn't want to be responsible for the death of a man who probably has a family and kids, would you?"

In the Santa Cruz area he drove into a private spot blocked from view from the road by trees. Then he lowered his body on hers and she went berserk, fighting for her life, grabbing his testicles. She fought like a tiger but gradually he was smothering her, pinching her nostrils closed. Then she seemed to be unconscious, but "For a moment she opened her eyes and just looked at me, and I guess she became conscious enough, to where she remembered what was happening, and went back into the extreme panic she had been in, and the whole process started over again, for just about the same amount of time, identical to the other forty-five seconds. Every move—I mean, still grabbing at my testicles and still grabbing at my body."

But she continued to suffocate, and then she was almost dead. He pulled her out of the car and onto the ground, and then raped her "violently, and I achieved orgasm—I guess it was only fifteen to twenty seconds. It was very quick. At that time I noticed her hair falling over her face and nose. She was still breathing, starting to breathe again. I took the muffler that she had around her neck still and just wrapped it very tight and tied a knot in it and . . . I even choked her around the throat for a moment, but by that time I was convinced that she was dead. I picked her up by the shoulders, and she wasn't a heavy girl. I think she told me she weighed 104 pounds."

He wrapped a blanket around her, and tied it with a cord he had used in killing Mary Ann and Anita.

He felt the skin and it was cool.

He then stopped at a bar for a few beers, "to check up to see how apparent my—whatever it was, grief, excitement, exultation, anxiety—whatever, was showing.

"I wanted to test on these people in the bar and correct it before I went any further. Besides, I was hot, tired, and thirsty."

Outside, he opened the trunk again to make sure she was dead.

He said, "I suppose as I was standing there looking, I was doing one of those triumphant things, too, admiring my work and admiring her beauty, and I might say, admiring my catch like a fisherman. I closed the lid, got back into the car, drove to Santa Cruz, out to Aptos, where I stopped at my mother's home . . . and went inside the house.

"I talked to my mother for approximately half an hour about nonessential things, just passing the time, telling her why I was down from the Bay Area, which was a lie, a fabrication, testing on her whether or not anything would show on my face or my mannerism or speech as to what I was doing and why, and it didn't. She absolutely took no alarm or asked any undue questions.

"I left her home and by then it was probably nine-thirty at night."

This time Kemper's travels took him back to his apartment in Alameda. He put Aiko's corpse on the bed, then looked at her possessions. One thing was a little handbag "that was very crudely made by crocheting, and she had crochet materials and tools in her bag. I gathered it was an article she had made herself."

He also looked closely at one of her pencils. "She had scraped the enamel away, down to the bare wood, for about half an inch or three-quarters of an inch, and had written her name in blue with a ballpoint pen, and had etched it, actually, into the wood, her full name. . . . In fact she had a little flower pattern in it. It was a little stem with four little dots around it."

Later, he would tell the police: "This was something I usually tried—to talk to the girls about, and gently probe about different things; to find out their lifestyle, their living conditions, whatever. She was very free and prolific in her speech, and I believed from her speech that she came from a home of meager means, that her parents had either divorced or her father had left her at an early age, and she and her mother apparently were living alone, and possibly with someone else. That wasn't quite cleared up.

"And there was no family car. The only transportation that she had was a bus to and from where she would go. I got no indication at all that she was from a family of any means. Her clothing was rather plain and she apparently had taken pains to dress herself—well, I don't know how to say it exactly, but as clean-cut as possible. Rather than just wear her hair long, she apparently had gone to some effort to look a little better dressed than she actually was." In the beginning he thought she was pure Asian. "I only saw bits of her hair from under the hat, and it appeared to be black. But when she took her cap off and her hair fell out, and also on the back seat when I was choking her, I noticed that it was a dark brown and almost had some auburn highlights to it, but it was not black. It was definitely brown and not black, and that surprised me."

He buried her in the Santa Cruz Mountains. "I just wanted the exultation over the party. In other words, winning over death. They were dead and I was alive. That was the victory in my case." But in taking her head off, "I remember . . . there was actually a sexual thrill. . . . It was kind of an exalted, triumphant-type thing, like taking the head of a deer or an elk or something would be to a hunter. I was the hunter and they were the victim." Death brought living creatures closer. "Alive, they were distant, not sharing with me. I was trying to establish a relationship, and there was no relationship. . . . When they were being killed, there wasn't anything

going on in my mind except that they were going to be mine. . . . That was the only way they could be mine."

CINDY

About four months after he had murdered Aiko, Edmund Kemper said, "I was cruising around, close on five o'clock or so. I had been cruising around the campus [UCSC] and I'd picked up three different girls, two of them together, that were possibilities, but I cancelled those out because there were too many people standing around that possibly knew them when they got in. But all the other conditions were perfect.

"It had been drizzling, it had been raining real hard, and people were getting any ride they could get, and windows were fogging up. Nobody was paying any attention, and it was during that real heavy rain. But I had given up on those other two and I was kind of uptight about it; and driving down the street, I spotted her standing out there with her thumb out. She was large, I think, five foot four inches, maybe 160 pounds, straight, medium-long blond hair, and very large chested—uh, breasted, I should say."

He had driven her to the little town of Freedom near Watsonville and then into the hills and up a side road. They talked. "I was playing a little game of not blowing it, you know. Somebody's going to talk with me or, you know, that's it, by God. So I said, you know, I convinced her that I don't like guns and all that, it was just bull, and that I wasn't going to use it, and I just nonchalantly tucked it away under my leg there and didn't refer to it again until later. And now and then I picked it up and played around with it, but did everything but hand it to her. To calm her down. Several times she asked me not to kill her and it got to the point later on it was very nonchalant. . . . Lying through my teeth."

Then, he asked her to climb into the trunk—which she resisted. He lied and said to her that he would take her to his mother's house, where they could talk. Kemper talked her into the trunk finally and arranged the blanket as a pillow.

He squeezed the trigger.

"There was no jerk," Kemper said, referring to the motion of the girl's body. "Every other case there has always been at least you know, a jerk, a little reflex. There was absolutely nothing. . . . She followed through with the motion."

The bullet had bored into her skull. "It amazed me so much because the one second she's animated and the next second she's not, and there was

absolutely nothing between. Just a noise and absolute, absolute stillness."

He covered her body in the trunk with the blanket and began to drive to his mother's house. The fresh cast on his arm, he noticed, was now spattered with new blood. At home he would have to put white shoe polish on it. When he arrived home, he noticed with pleasure that the neighbors were not at home. And the weather was drizzly. Perfect. The weight in the trunk caused the car to sag a little.

Then, his mother—whom he was living with at the time—came home, and the next morning when she left for work he sprang into action. He brought the body into his bedroom, then dissected it in the shower with an ax, putting sections in plastic bags that he later discarded along the Pacific Coast Highway. He also told investigators he used a knife. "I used the same knife in all of them. It's a buck knife; it's called the General; and it's the largest. It's something like a Bowie knife, but it has more of a straight blade, rather than real fancy or curved."

Then he got an unpleasant surprise. Cindy's body had been discovered, this less than twenty-four hours after he had disposed of it! "It quite noticeably shocked me when I heard on the radio, the very next day."

The cops wanted to know, in one point of his interrogation, why he trolled college campuses.

"Well, I didn't actually," Kemper said. "At first that was one of my rules, don't ever hit around town, but then, sometime after that (I don't remember whether it was after the first two, or the third one, Aiko or someone named Mary was abducted and disappeared, apparently, from what I read in the paper. . . . And I couldn't see someone—like the paper said—of her apparent background disappearing like that when they're going to college. So I assumed that someone else was doing the same thing I was doing, and they had hit in town [indeed, it turned out to be a serial killer named Herbert Mullin] and that kind of made me mad because that could throw everything in my lap if an investigation started around Santa Cruz. Because up until that point, I had assumed that the authorities were looking for someone in the Bay Area that was depositing the heads in the Santa Cruz area.

"When I was disabled and staying with my mother, when I first started to live with her, when I . . . realized that no investigation was coming my way at all, I realized that I was being a little too careful. And there was a much better opportunity around the Santa Cruz area to attack these coeds. I had been hitting primarily the Berkeley area . . . the University of California, and I saw no reason to ease my—completely leave out Santa Cruz as long as I was careful.

"So this is why I started out with the Cabrillo school; it was quite by

accident. I had been looking for university coeds when I picked up Cindy. I kind of picked her up as an afterthought. I was pretty pleased."

Surprisingly, just before he picked up Cindy, he had picked up two university girls on the UCSC campus and planned to kill them, but he couldn't follow through.

"I guess I just emotionally wasn't quite prepared to jump anybody," he said, "and they were quite beautiful girls, and the opportunity was so great and everything; it just caught me off guard. Before I knew it, I was dropping them off, and apparently they lived on Locust Street where Alice, a later victim, also lived."

He had then circled back through the campus but had found no one else "readily available" for a "hit."

On the rainy evening of February 5, 1973, Kemper was in the mood to kill. "My mother and I," he said, "had had a real tiff. . . . I told her I was going to a movie, and I jumped up and went straight to the [UCSC] campus because it was still early.

"I said, the first girl that's halfway decent that I pick up, I'm gonna blow her brains out."

Rosalind was a big, usually happy girl who had entered the university right after graduating from high school in 1968. She emerged into the rain from her evening class just as Kemper drove past. He noticed she had "light brown (hair) with blondish tints" and was wearing "black felt bell-bottom sailor pants, pink-and-purple zip-up boots.

"I said, Well, she's not too bad looking. So I stopped and she hesitated—she was probably twenty yards behind the car—and looked to the rear, and she saw the wrecked-up car there and hesitated for a moment. Then," he continued, "I'm sure that she saw the A tag, and ran right along and hopped in.

"She asked me where I was going. And that had always been a problem with me, because when they ask me where I'm going and I say the wrong thing, they won't get in. If I say I'm going down Mission and they say they're going up the other end of Mission or something like this, sometimes it's an excuse not to get in. Sometimes they're going the other way, and I'll blow an awful good opportunity 'cause I don't think quick enough."

At one point while the tapes were being recorded the machine broke down. Kemper had gone into a long-winded dissertation on how this reminded him of how brutal this could be to loved ones who had to listen. "I asked the sergeant this morning especially about that," he said, "because that's an awful touchy thing where the family's involved, and I'm

being very frank here, and it's going to be hard enough as it is there, and I'm sure that parents should be talked to. I wouldn't even attempt to approach any of them. I doubt that any of them would be anywhere near me as far as wanting to ask me anything. Having been through that type of situation with my uncle, with my grandparents there the first time I was in court." At fifteen, Edmund had been deeply hurt because a favorite uncle disapproved of his first murders. "It's an awfully touchy subject, you know, what happened and what didn't happen, and some of these things that did happen which you know weren't all that bad; still it's going to be awfully terrible for the family to have to listen to this. I've heard of things like where certain tapes are played just in front of the judge, or just in front of the jury, as evidence rather than play it in front of the whole court because I—that, that starts to look like an arena, you know, and everything is in there . . . all the gory details. That would get me very upset, and I'd probably ask to leave the court and the judge would say, no, you're going to sit there and listen, and then I'd start throwing chairs and having a fit, scream on the floor and all that stuff.

ROSALIND AND ALICE

"All right," one of Kemper's questioners said. "Let's go into Rosalind here. You had her in the car. What was your next move?"

"Basically, she carried the conversation. She was very outgoing and I was just trying to be amicable, and I was trying to think of what I was gonna do. I had decided, after we rode a little ways, that that was it, I was gonna get her, definitely, and I had my little zappel! through my body there that always confirmed it. I never had one of those where it didn't actually happen. It's just where everything would click just right; circumstances were perfect. Nobody else was around, the guard didn't notice me coming in, nothing would look unusual going out, and she was not the least bit suspecting. And, also, it was somebody I didn't know in any way, shape, or form, or knew anybody that I knew about. Those were certain things I held as absolutes. One I had held as an absolute for a long time was, don't ever do anything like that around the Santa Cruz area because that's too close to home, and having been in the past I was in, I would naturally come under suspicion. But then I started getting sicker and sicker later on and a little more and more careless in my approach, in taking care of things, and afterwards—which I'm sure got obvious, because more and more evidence started popping up, in different forms.

"Okay, what happened next is, we were talking and she's more or less popping little questions here and there, talking along. I noticed Alice standing on the side. She saw us coming. She threw out a great big beautiful smile, and stuck her thumb out very helpfully, and you know, not a cheesecake-type thing, but you know, throwing her best foot forward there. I figure later on what happened was, that she looked to me from different little details, that she was probably a careful hitchhiker. Very good looking, built nicely and everything, and intelligent and moderate in her dress and everything, nothing outlandish.

"From some of her ID, college friends, stable background, and all that, I imagine she was a cautious hitchhiker, and she always made sure of her ride before she got in, and we appeared to be a couple, and with that A tag on there. . . . So she didn't hesitate at all about getting in."

He had been relieved to note that the girls did not know each other. As the car approached the kiosk on the way out, "I was very careful in eyeballing the guard as I went by, and he glanced, and I'm sure he didn't see Alice in the back seat because of the lighting and the fact that her clothes were dark, except for the top, light-colored tweed peacoat.

"It surprised me, [Alice] being an Oriental, that she was built like she was. Nothing fantastic, I mean, but you know, very nice build. Anyway, she had long, black hair, rather coarse, and very square sort of a face, very wide, high cheekbones.

"What struck me about Rosalind was that she didn't have any money at all, not even change in her purse. She had just gotten a letter from home with a check in it."

"Where's the check?" asked one of the interrogators, Lieutenant Scherer.

"At the bottom of the ocean."

"What happened," asked Lieutenant Scherer, "when you had both girls in the car, now?"

"Well, they had gotten past the campus guard . . ." Kemper and Rosalind were chatting. Alice sat quietly in the back seat. As they went down around the first curve of the broad new road from the campus to where it straightened out and where the city lights became visible, Kemper commented on the beautiful view. He slowed down, asking Rosalind if she minded. She said, "Not at all." Alice in back also said she did not mind, but Kemper got the feeling she was just saying it to be polite, and that she was beginning to feel disgusted.

"I had never done something like that before," he said, "where I just come out and shot somebody, just right out in the blue. But I was mad that night."

But a night that had started out badly had developed well.

"As it was, I improved. It was two in a perfect situation. Anyway, we slowed down there, almost to a stop. We were just barely moving and I had been moving my pistol from down below my leg in my lap, a solid black pistol, and the interior of the car was black, so she couldn't see it and I picked it up and had it in my lap, talking with them; and I moved it up to the side like this, 'cause I knew the minute I picked it up like that, the girl in the back was gonna see it and I didn't want any problems. So as soon as I picked it up, I hesitated maybe a second at the very most and then pulled the trigger."

The car was moving very slowly.

"Like, I didn't want the brake lights on in case somebody was around the corner, 'cause that would be something to stick in their memory."

As he lifted the gun up, Rosalind started to turn her head. Alice gasped. He pulled the trigger. The bullet had entered Rosalind's head just above her left ear.

"She had a rather large forehead and I was imagining what her brain looked like inside, and I just wanted to put it right in the middle of that."

Alice cowered in a corner of the car and covered her face with her hands and Kemper shot through them, missing twice. A third shot "hit her just right around the temple area." He shot her several more times. She was unconscious, "But she was making a very strange sound. I almost threw up as we were going down the hill. It was a sigh. A constant, over and over, sigh."

Lieutenant Scherer asked Kemper to describe the killing again.

"With her, I fired the first time and it went through her hand. She was moving around quite rapidly, trying to get away from the gun because I had to fire right-handed because of the cast. Otherwise, in both cases I would have fired left-handed. It was awkward in both cases. I had to turn around like this, so I was at a bad angle with her and I missed. They were bad shots the first two times. But the third shot, I moved it almost out of my hand and around at a direct angle. The first shot through her hand missed her completely, and the second one grazed her head and also went through her hand, and embedded itself in the car, and ricocheted back out the front. Then the third shot, I was positive that she was unconscious, I don't really think I needed to do that.

"She was very slumped over in the seat and she was scrunched way down. . . . So her head was not visible above the cushion like it normally would be. So I just put the coat over her, grabbed the blanket, and unfolded it enough—and I tried to push Rosalind over into the floorboard

area, and she wouldn't budge. She was just sitting there, slumped over completely. And so finally I just pulled her over sideways on the seat and put the blue velveteen sort of blanket over her and made sure it stayed below the level of the windows there and that it wasn't an obvious shape or anything. I kept it double thickness, and just opened it enough so it looked like a flat blue surface."

He continued down the hill.

"Right after I put the blanket over her, a car came down. I smoothly accelerated so there wouldn't be a blast of gas and a jerk or anything. So I am sure that to them it appeared as if I just came along. They came down behind us, and I came right down in front of the guard station at the bottom where the cars were parked and everything. And there were two guards standing right by the road out there, having a little conversation. They were, maybe, twenty feet from the car, on their side of the car."

Scherer asked if Alice was still making sounds.

"Yeah, it was a sigh, a very strange sigh. It would start out very sharp, almost like a sniffle, and then it would taper off and become a little bit more like a masculine sigh than [from] a fine girl, a petite-type girl like she was. It wasn't low or anything, but it was very disconcerting and it was constant. After we stopped, and went on down Bay Street, obviously there was quite a bit of blood because of the wounds, and there was blood from that last hole in the forehead."

Kemper proceeded straight down to Mission, turned right, and headed out of town.

"I was making sure that I broke absolutely no rules and was doing my damnedest to look cool while I was freaking out about Alice in the back seat there, which I am sure she was unconscious. At first I didn't think so and I made a couple of loud statements, and it just continued right on through, so I knew she was unconscious. But the blood started running and she started gurgling, and the sighing was still there. So as soon as I got out to the edge of town, I stepped on the gas and got the hell away from there, and a little further down the road, where no cars were coming, I slowed down very slow, turned her head around to the side, and fired point-blank at the side of her head.

"The reason she didn't go instantly like the other girl was that the automatic had a kind of quirky ramp, and it would not—you couldn't load all the points into the clip, or I would have always used those. I could only put one in the barrel and nine regular solid-head long rifles in the clip, and everything I fired at her was solids. So one solid slug she got in there—and she was doing the moaning. I got out of town and turned her head to the

side and fired point-blank, and the flash was so great that I could see some of the tissue coming out. She stopped immediately. There was silence, and then I turned back around about two seconds later and it started up again, and it was really getting to me.

"There's a place down the road, you know, that popular beach area where the sign is, like where it says Davenport, Bonny Doon, and all that? A lot of people park there. Well, the next one back from there is the loop. Some people get on that and think they're going to Bonny Doon, and it loops right back out. Laguna. I circled back down through that and went up on that little cul-de-sac up in there and parked. I had the parking lights on. I jumped out and put both of them in the trunk."

Kemper then drove to Santa Cruz.

"There was a Chinese girl pumping gas. I went into the rest room and cleaned off as much of the blood on the cast as I could, and I cleaned a little off my pants. To myself I called them my murder clothes because it was those dark pants; they were a dark blue denim Western-style pants with very light, not quite white, markings. But they were very dark. That was in case I got them splattered. I used them on the first two girls. I think I used them when Aiko and Cindy were killed. I am not sure, but in the vast majority of the cases I used those pants and shirt."

At home, he told his mother he fell asleep at the movie. He said, "'How do you like that? You go and pay all that money and then fall asleep.' Then I said I would go back and see it tomorrow night, and that gives me an alibi."

Then, Kemper went outside.

"The way the house is laid out, there's a big picture window that's enclosed with curtains, and the TV is right over here against the wall, and my mother sits right where that picture window is. All she would have to do is get up and take a couple of steps and open the curtain in order to see if I am still out there; and she hadn't heard the car leave. But what I didn't realize was that she wouldn't hear that over the TV. So I just went out there, pulled the car around and opened up the trunk, and this is the way the entire series happened. I took out that big knife and I cut both of their heads right off out there on the street.

"It was maybe ten o'clock at night, or possibly eleven. But that's where I did that because of the blood problem. Because they both had bled very badly in the trunk during the time of riding around and sitting at the gas station. It was getting all over everything. Then I went down and got my cigarettes at this little bar down by Seacliff, walked back out, got in the car, and drove home and went back into the house and watched TV and

went to bed. The next day my mother was at work, and it was drizzling, and I just backed the car into the garage." He carried Alice into his mother's house, right in through the back door. "Because I knew the old biddy in the back there never was out in the rain, so I just wandered on in there and committed this act, which was actually rather difficult. And actually I think that being the last time I did anything like that. It was rather distasteful. I guess maybe the first time I did something like that, there was a little bit of a charge, you know. But that time—"

On the following day he brought the girls' heads into the house, "I cleaned the blood off both of them in the bathroom, so I wouldn't get all bloody." Then he put Alice's body on the floor and had sex with it.

During the taping Kemper looked at and told Lieutenant Scherer, "This is kind of bad tonight 'cause you remind me a lot of my father. I've never met you personally, or seen you personally. My first impression was—my father's taller, but you have a lot of his features. So that makes it rather, uh, macabre here. A John Wayne image of my father . . . so anybody that looks like him, I immediately cast him as a father hero."

Lieutenant Scherer remained mute.

Kemper continued. "This is a bummer. Which is why I get depressed in that damn cell 'cause I realized earlier today after talking to you guys that I do not—I make a very strong attempt not to think about any of this stuff, anything related to it, and especially my mother while I'm in that cell, because I just get super depressed. I'm just sitting there. I still haven't slept in four days. I tried two more times back there to sleep, and I'd lay down—and the first thing, I'd start thinking about this last weekend. And I get super torqued-up and I'm wide awake; just absolutely not drowsy. And this is including fifteen hundred miles of driving almost constantly, and the last nine hundred miles of it was nothing but gas—a bottle of pop once in a while, and a lot of NoDoz."

Then Kemper started talking about when he was young.

"Before I got into that trouble when I was fifteen, I . . . and ever after that I got in trouble . . . was one very hard point of consternation. It had a lot to do with my getting upset with society and deciding to attack. It was that I was frustrated in my dreams and desires totally. It was sad, really. I didn't blame society for me not being able to be a policeman, but—"

"All right," Lieutenant Scherer said. "Now we've got Alice in your room. Now, what happened after the sexual act?"

"I just wandered right out there with her and put her in the trunk right under the window. That's one thing that amazes me about society. That is, that you can do damn near anything and nobody's gonna say anything or notice."

He had decided against doing any more dissecting.

"At that point, I was just not caring if somebody finds those portions of their bodies, but hoping that it would be at least a few days.

"I went up [to Alameda] and visited that friend—a good friend of mine, up there, that lived in the same neighborhood as I did when I worked with the state, and I dropped by and I was fairly agitated that night, and she noticed it. I was kidding around a lot and was very nervous. My stomach was killing me. I think I'm developing ulcers because of all this. Not so much now, but I was in a great tension whenever something like that was happening, especially people in the trunk and having to dispose . . . I'd get close to the point of panic until it was done. Then I would just completely relax. But this tension would just build and build to the point of removal of the bodies; and I'll tell you, on that road, Eden Road there—"

To dispose of the bodies, he drove up Highway 17.

"I wanted to distract the heat from Santa Cruz. So I figured I knew both areas, and the authorities wouldn't necessarily know that I knew the Bay Area well, because the job that I do entails intensive travel through those areas. Especially like with the disposal of Alice's head and hands, I knew that this was an ideal place because the authorities would figure it was somebody that knew that particular area really well, and I knew that people at two o'clock in the morning would not be traveling the road at all. So they would think it would be at least somebody within five or ten miles of that area, and that's what I wanted people to think."

"I arrived on the scene up in Eden Canyon Road about two A.M." He drove to an area known as Devil's Slide. He drove into Pacifica to see if cops were around—they were at a local diner—so he drove back to the cliff and threw the body parts off.

MRS. KEMPER

At one point, Kemper started to think about killing his mother. "I laid there in the bed thinking about it. And it's something hard to just up and do. It was the most insane of reasons for going and killing your mother. But I was pretty fixed on that issue because there were a lot of things involved. Someone just standing off to the side, watching, isn't really going to see any kind of sense, or rhyme or reason.

"I had done some things, and I felt that I'd had to carry the full weight of everything that happened. I certainly wanted for my mother a nice, quiet, easy death, like I guess everyone wants."

He thought about the best way to do it. At 5:15 in the morning, "I went into the kitchen and got a hammer. We have a regular claw hammer at home. I picked up the pocket knife, the same one I had used to kill Mary Ann with, opened it up, and I carried that in my right hand and the hammer in my left, and I walked into her bedroom very quietly. She had been sound asleep. She moved around a little bit, and I thought maybe she was waking up. I just waited and waited and she was just laying there.

"So I approached her right side . . . I stood there a couple of minutes, I suppose, and I hit her just above the temple on her right side of the head. I struck with a very hard blow, and I believe I dropped the hammer, or I laid it down, or something.

"Immediately after striking that blow I looked for a reaction, and there really wasn't one. Blood started running down her face from the wound, and she was still breathing. I could hear the breathing. And I heard blood running into her; I guess it was her windpipe. It was obvious I had done severe damage to her, because in other cases where I had shot people in the head I heard the same—or it had the same effect—blood running into the breathing passages. And this all happened in a few seconds."

Then he held her head up and slashed her throat. This was when he decided, "What's good for my victims was good for my mother," so he cut her head off and dragged her headless corpse into the closet.

After going out with a male friend, he returned to his house and contemplated what to do.

SARA HALLETT

"I decided that someone else had to die too, a friend of hers, as a cover-up, an excuse; something that would be believable by other people and friends and possible family that might get in touch. So I started thinking about who would be a victim; who would be most available; who would be the easiest to kill; and who would be likely to be gone with my mother for the weekend. I fell upon a friend of hers, Sara or Sally Hallett, who had frequently gone places with my mother and done things on weekends.

"There was another friend, Mrs. Victoria Sims, who would have been just as easy if not for the fact that she was married and was with her husband for the weekend, and possibly with her daughter and her daughter's boyfriend. So that completely ruled that person out because it was too involved."

He lured his mother's friend over to the house, saying that they were

having a little party to celebrate Kemper's going back to work, and that he would love if she could come over for dinner and a movie, which was to be a surprise for his mother.

"The reason I did this," he said, "was I knew she'd accept. I had surmised from past acquaintance with her at home and out that she would leap at something like that, so that's what I thought to say. Of course she jumped at the idea. I told her that my mother was not home but would be a little later." He urged Sara come around seven-thirty and she said, "Fine."

He got ready for her visit by closing all windows and pulling shades and blinds. No one could see in, and hearing anything would be difficult as well.

He got some rope, a drill shank as a bludgeon, and a carbine in case things went awry and he needed to shoot the friend. He also had clear plastic bags and handcuffs.

Sara came in at eight o'clock. Edmund met her at the door, greeting her warmly.

"So anyway she came and we talked, and we were crossing the living room towards the couch. I was balking at what I had to do or what I felt I had to do, and that was the last thing I wanted to do. I didn't want to seem obvious at anything being wrong. I was stalling around as we moved across the room. My first intention was to strike her in the midsection, around the solar plexus, and knock the wind from her so that she couldn't cry out, and then strangle her. It was this first move that I was kind of dreading. I guess what worked me into it really quick was that she said, 'Let's sit down. I'm dead.'

"And I kind of took her at her word there. I guess I saw that as a cue, and I struck her in the stomach. She fell back or jumped back mostly, I guess. I was quite surprised at her reaction. I hit her hard, and she jumped back and said, 'Guy, stop that.' I struck her again immediately after the first blow, and her last words were, 'Oh!' and she stumbled back. I pulled her around toward me, facing away from me, threw my left arm around her neck. It was hurting at that point but I didn't realize it then because I was so wrapped up in what I was doing.

"It's almost like a blacking out. You know what you're doing but you don't notice anything else around. But in striking her, I had held my thumb wrong when I made a fist, and had jammed my thumb and hurt my wrist. It's weak anyway, being in a cast so long. But I grabbed her around the neck with the left wrist at her throat, put her into a choke hold, and pulled her up off the floor. In fact, she was dangling across my chest with

absolutely no sounds coming from her. She was holding my arm with both of her hands, trying to pull away apparently. There was no real tugging, just holding on to my arm. Her legs weren't really kicking at all. She was moving around a little, very little. But no sound at all came from her, and at that time I thought that she was so embarrassed or so shocked at what had just happened that she really couldn't say anything and that she was waiting for me to make a move. I didn't really think that I had cut her wind off so completely that not even a little squeak or any gasp or anything had come out.

"So I pulled her back farther and looked down into her face, and her eyes were bulging badly. Her face was turning black at that point, and this was moments after I had grabbed her. Her face was turning from a bright red to a black, and I realized that I was actually cutting her wind off completely. Later on I realized I had crushed her larynx or at least dislocated it to where she couldn't breathe. . . . When she went limp completely, I dropped her to the floor and tied the bags around her head with a cord after I had put the tape over her mouth, which really didn't work; so I just pulled that off.

"When she completely quit struggling, there were some automatic reflexes in the lung area. Her chest was heaving once in a while. When that all stopped, I took her into the bedroom, and her belongings—removed all her clothes, put her on my bed in my bedroom, covered her up with a blanket, went into the other room with her belongings, removed the money from her wallet.

"I had been keeping track of things like that with the other victims, but in this case I was blowing wide open. I just took any money that anybody had. It might have been ten dollars or fifteen, maybe twenty. I don't know. The credit cards—I had already taken some from my mother. I had several gas credit cards and took a couple I didn't have from my mother's pocketbook, which I had placed under the bed, out of the way."

He went out for a beer at the Jury Room, driving Mrs. Hallett's car there, then drove back. He decided to cut her head off, as he had with his mother. He spent the night sleeping in his mother's bed.

Sergeant Aluffi asked: Had he sexually attacked his mother or Mrs. Hallett? Kemper replied only that he had attempted to have intercourse with the latter, the night before fleeing.

"Do you feel," asked Sergeant Aluffi, "that you've got urges to kill people, or is it just something kind of spontaneous?"

"Well, it's kind of hard to go around killing somebody just for the hell of it," Kemper said. "It's not a kicks thing, or I would have ceased doing

it a long time ago. It was an urge. I wouldn't say it was on the full of the moon or anything, but I noticed that no matter how horrendous the crime had been or how vicious the treatment of the bodies after death. . . . But when I'm actually beginning to get myself involved in a crime, it was a big thrill. It was a very strong, sensual, sexual excitement, and in some ways it replaced the sexual drive, let's say; but there was always a disappointment in not achieving a sexual rapport, let's say, with the victim. That's why the sex after death sometimes, because it's through frustration."

Aluffi asked if killing was a "sexual achievement."

"Yes," Kemper said, "I'm sure it's happened before, but the only time I actually noticed an ejaculation was as I was killing Mrs. Hallett on Saturday night. As she was dying, it was a great physical effort on my part, very restraining, very difficult. I went into a full complete physical spasm. . . . I just completely put myself out on it, and as she died, I felt myself reaching orgasm. In the other cases, the physical effort was less."

Aluffi questioned him about why he dissected the bodies and beheaded them. "Originally," Kemper said, "the decapitations, I think part of it was kind of a weird thing I had in my head. It was a fantasy I had had in childhood. I don't know where it came from, but it was always something I had wanted to do. And it did facilitate part of my plan later; that is, if someone was found they would be harder to identify.

"But there was satisfaction gained in the removal of the head. In fact, the first head I ever removed was that of Anita in the trunk of the car with the knife that killed Mary Ann, and I remember it was very exciting, removing Anita's head. There was actually a sexual thrill. And, in fact, there was almost a climax to it. It was kind of an exalted, triumphant-type thing, like taking the head of a deer or an elk or something would be to a hunter."

Aluffi expressed curiosity about the different time intervals that separated Kemper's killings.

"Part of it was fear," Kemper said. "Some of it was regret. Other parts of it were the opportunities. I didn't just rush out and look for the opportunities. If you will notice, there was a greater time span between the first and second, and the second and third, than there was anywhere else. But I had started to really get into gear towards the end there. I was getting what I think is sicker, and it was much more of a feel for more of the blood—and the blood got in my way. It wasn't something I desired to see. Blood was an actual pain in the ass. What I wanted to see was the death, and I wanted to see the triumph, the exultation over the death. It was like eating, or a narcotic, something that drove me more and more and more."

He said that when he had the pistol it made everything go faster. It stepped everything up, "made it much simpler, much easier, much quicker, less of a threat to me personally. I was less afraid to attack. I didn't like attacking people. My whole thing was that if I had been obsessed by attacking people, I would have been in bar fights and street fights, and would have been physically and verbally assaulted. There I wasn't.

"It was a matter of—I didn't care how I got there. I just wanted the exultation over the other party. In other words, winning over death. They were dead and I was alive. That was a victory in my case.

"I suppose I could have been doing this with men, but that always posed more of a threat. They weren't nearly as vulnerable. And that would have been quite odd and probably noticeable, picking up other men and having killed them. Plus, like in the case where sex is involved, or the thrill of having a woman around, alive and dead, wasn't there with a man. So, like I said, there was a threat of the possible retaliation or the possible defense that would throw me off, and after I had broken my arm this was absolutely unthinkable.

"So it wasn't just deaths I wanted. It was, like I said, somewhat of a social statement in there too, and I was jumping upon—I could have gotten children, I suppose. Children are vulnerable. But there are two things against that. One is the most important—that is that children are innocent.

"Children are unknowing. And I have always been very protective of children for that reason."

Material from Margaret Cheney, *Why: The Serial Killer in America* (Lincoln, NE: I.Universe.com, 2000); originally titled *The Coed Killer*. Used by permission. Photo courtesy California Prison System.

ii.

PETER KÜRTEN

BACKGROUND

Peter Kürten

Like most other serial murderers, Peter Kürten didn't have much of a chance for normalcy from the beginning of his life. Born in Cologne-Mulheim, Germany, in 1883, economic circumstances forced him to live with ten other family members in a single room. His father was a sadistic drunk who forced his wife to strip nude in front of the other family members and have sex with him. His father also tried to rape his thirteen-year-old daughter and was sent to prison. The psychotic, as it were, doesn't fall far from the tree; Peter also had sex with a number of his sisters. But incest was hardly abnormal enough for Kürten. As he grew up, he also came to enjoy homicidal bestiality, and he tortured all kinds of animals. He took particular pleasure in stabbing sheep to death and watching the blood spurt from them as he had intercourse with them. Such an activity would frequently bring him to orgasm.

Kürten committed his first murder—actually two murders—at the ripe old age of nine. He was with another boy on a raft in the Rhine River, and Kürten pushed the boy into the water. A mutual friend jumped into the river to save him, and Kürten was able to keep both boys from getting on the raft, instead forcing them to go under it—and drown.

RANDOM UTTERANCES

In the case of Ohliger, I also sucked blood from the wound on her temple, and from Scheer from the stab in the neck. From the girl Schulte I only licked the blood from her hands. It was the same with the swan in the Hofgarten. I used to stroll at night through the Hofgarten very often, and in the spring of 1930 I noticed a swan sleeping at the edge of the lake. I cut its throat. The blood spurted up and I drank from the stump and ejaculated.

The whole family suffered though his drinking, for when he was drunk, my father was terrible. I, being the eldest, had to suffer most. As you may well imagine, we suffered terrible poverty, all because the wages went on drink. We all lived in one room and you will appreciate what effect that had on me sexually.

After my head has been chopped off, will I still be able to hear, at least for a moment, the sound of my own blood gushing from my neck? That would be the pleasure to end all pleasures.

Material from Tom Philbin, *The Killer Book of Serial Killers* (Naperville, IL: Sourcebooks, 2008). Photo courtesy of author.

12.

HENRY LEE LUCAS

BACKGROUND

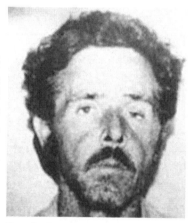
Henry Lee Lucas

As mentioned earlier, not all of the childhoods of serial killers are well known. But there is enough of the childhood story for Henry Lee Lucas known to indicate why he turned out the way he did.

He was born and raised—if that's the word—on a farm in Blacksburg, Virginia.

His mother, Viola, was a prostitute and his father was an alcoholic known by the townspeople as "No Legs," because he lost his legs from the hips down to a slow-moving freight train when he was drunk.

Lucas's mother was a prostitute and she used to service some of her customers on the farm. On at least one occasion, however, she made her husband watch her do it, and he reportedly was so upset that he got totally drunk and crawled out in the yard, away from her. Snow fell that night and he froze to death.

Viola also terribly mistreated Lucas. She never bathed him, she let his hair grow into a dirty mass of curls, and then she dressed him like a little

147

girl and sent him off to school to be laughed at by the other students. It is said that even in dirt-poor Blacksburg, Lucas stood out.

Perhaps his mother's ultimate act of cruelty toward her son was when one day she asked him what animal he liked best on the farm.

"I like the mule," he said.

Viola went and got a shotgun and shot the animal dead.

Lucas followed classic lines in developing into a serial killer, including skinning small animals alive, starting when he was about ten years old.

Just how many people Lucas killed is debatable, ranging in estimates from hundreds to perhaps four or five. Evidence suggests he probably killed twenty or twenty-five people, because for a while he prowled I-35, which ran between Laredo, Texas, and Gainesville, Florida, and quite a few bodies were found on that stretch of road. Indeed, cops dubbed it the "Henry Lee Lucas Memorial Highway." And for a time, he also palled around with another serial killer, Ottis Toole.

"I was brought up like a dog," Lucas told Ron Rosenbaum of *Vanity Fair* magazine in a death row interview. "No human being should have to be put through what I was."

In prison, Lucas heard his mother's voice ordering him to kill himself. He pulled a razor across his abdomen and wrists to comply, but failed. It was to be one of many suicide attempts. And he heard other voices that told him to do bad things. Prison doctors had him diagnosed as schizophrenic, a sexual psychopath who only felt potent—and became potent—when he was having relations with dead bodies. (An FBI agent once asked Lucas why he only had sex with women after he killed them and his answer was, "I like peace and quiet.")

Precisely what Lucas and Toole as murdering partners did together is debatable, but by all odds their life together was a spine-tingling amalgam of strangling, stabbing, cutting, shooting, necrophilia, dismemberment, and cannibalism. They also had sex with each other. Rosenbaum of *Vanity Fan* reports a classic line uttered by Lucas. Lucas told Rosenbaum that Toole would often crucify his victims, after which Toole would often barbecue and eat them. He himself, Lucas said, never joined Ottis in these unholy feasts.

"Why not?" he was asked.

"I don't like barbecue sauce," Lucas said.

Another murder Lucas definitely committed and the one that put him on death row in Huntsville was the killing of "Orange Socks." She was an unidentified young woman, found facedown on the side of I-35, strangled and nude except for some long, pumpkin-colored stockings, which were

pulled down around her ankles and prompted one of the cops to dub her "Orange Socks."

She was an attractive young woman with reddish brown hair, perfect teeth, a nice body, and venereal disease. Lucas said he picked her up in Oklahoma City, and they drove to Texas. At one point they stopped and Lucas made her an exception. He had sex with her while she was still alive. Then they continued on, and Lucas wanted to make it an even rarer day. He wanted to have sex with her again. She told him "Not now."

Lucas did not readily take no for an answer. As he described what happened in *Serial Killers* by Joel Norris, "She tried to jump out of the car and I grabbed her and pulled her back. We drove for a little piece further than that, and I pulled off the road because she was fighting so hard that I almost lost control of the car. . . . After that I pulled her over to me and I choked her until she died."

Then he had sex with the corpse and dumped the body in a culvert.

RANDOM UTTERANCES

Sex is one of my downfalls. I get sex any way I can get it. If I have to force somebody to do it, I do . . . I rape them; I've done that. I've killed animals to have sex with them, and I've had sex while they're alive.

I took her bra and panties off and had sex with her. That's one of those things I guess that got to be a part of my life—having sexual intercourse with the dead.

I was brought up like a dog. No human being should have to be put through what I saw.

Material from Tom Philbin, *Murder USA* (New York: Warner Books, 1992). Photo courtesy of author.

Dennis Nilsen

13.

DENNIS NILSEN

BACKGROUND

When he was very young, Dennis Nilsen started to feel emotionally drawn to boys. At sixteen he joined the army, and then in 1972 he became a cop. This gave him access to the morgue, where he could act out deep-seated necrophiliac urges. Eventually, Nilsen started a relationship with a man named David Gallichan, and when Gallichan broke it off, Nilsen felt profound abandonment. He began a series of gay relationships, taking men to his apartment in the Cricklewood section of London. On December 29, 1978, he brought a young man home. When the young man wanted to leave, Nilsen strangled him.

He related to the corpse as if it were still alive, even trying to have sex with it, and spent the entire day marveling at the corpse. He then carefully pried up the floorboards, laid the body between the wooden frames, and replaced the floorboards.

Then he started his murder career in earnest, and over the next few years Nilsen killed thirteen men and stored their bodies in various places in his apartment—under floorboards, the cupboard, the closet, outside in a garden shed. Eventually, because of the stench inside his apartment, Nilsen cut up and tried to flush the bodies, but this led to a clogging of the plumbing drain lines, and to his arrest.

MURDERING A GUEST

Below Dennis Nilsen describes how he murdered a young man he had picked up and brought back to his apartment named Stephen Sinclair.

"I am sitting cross-legged on the carpet, drinking and listening to music. It finished with the theme from *Harry's Game*. I drain my glass and take the phones off. Behind me sits Stephen Sinclair on the lazy chair. He was crashed out with drink and drugs. I sit and look at him. I stand up and approach him. My heart is pounding. I kneel down in front of him. I touch his leg and say, 'Are you awake?' There is no response. 'Oh Stephen,' I think, 'here I go again.' I get up and go slowly and casually through to the kitchen. I take some thick string from the drawer and look at it on the stainless steel draining board. 'Not long enough. I think, I go to the cupboard in the front room and search inside. On the floor therein I find an old tie. I cut a bit off . . . I go back into the kitchen and make up the ligature. I look into the back room and Stephen has not stirred. Bleep [Nilsen's dog] comes in and I speak to her and scratch her head. 'Leave me just now, Bleep. Get your head down, everything's all right.' She wags her tail and slinks off into the front room. Her favourite place is on one of the armchairs in there, where she curls up. Looking back I think she knew what was to happen. Even she became resigned to it. If there was a violent struggle, she would always become excited and start barking. I was relaxed. I never contemplated morality. This was something which I had to do. . . . I draped the ligature over one of his knees and poured myself another drink. My heart was pounding very fast. I sat on the edge of the bed and looked at Stephen. I thought to myself, 'All that potential, all that beauty, and all that pain that is his life. I have to stop him. It will soon be over.' I did not feel bad. I did not feel evil. I walked over to him. I removed the scarf. I picked up one of his wrists and let go. His limp arm flopped back on to his lap. I opened one of his eyes and there was no reflex. He was deeply unconscious. I took the ligature and put it around his neck. I knelt by the side of the chair and faced the wall. I took each loose end of the ligature and pulled it tight. He stopped breathing. His hands slowly reached for his neck as I held my grip. His legs stretched out in front of him. There was a very feeble struggle, then his arms fell limp down in front of him. I held him there for a couple of minutes. He was limp and stayed that way. I released my hold and removed the string and tie. He had stopped breathing. I spoke to him. 'Stephen, that didn't hurt at all. Nothing can touch you now.'"

Material from Brian Masters, *Killing for Company: The Case of Dennis Nilsen* (New York: Stein and Day, 1985). Photo courtesy Full Sutton Prison.

14.

DENNIS RADER

BACKGROUND

Dennis Rader

No one has yet pieced together a fully fledged background of the BTK Killer, Dennis Rader, so while we can assume he was subject to the same kind of emotional forces as other serial killers during childhood and adolescence, we don't have the specifics pointing to his motivations.

Rader started to kill on January 15, 1974, when he invaded the home of the Otero family: a mother, father, and two young children were all strangled to death. For the next sixteen years, Radar terrorized Wichita and the area around it, killing six other people. He always identified himself—via communications with the police and news media—as the BTK (bind-torture-kill) Killer, which was the method he used to murder people.

Rader would usually stalk his intended victims—all female—and then strike, sometimes gaining entry into the home by knocking on the door but also by breaking into the home when the potential victim wasn't there and waiting for her to come home.

In 1991 Rader did something strange for a serial killer: he stopped killing. Why this occurred no one has yet determined, but one thing was for sure: the police hadn't forgotten about him. Indeed one cop suggested that one of his friends write a book about BTK, that it might possibly lure the killer into a dialogue with the police because BTK clearly liked the attention and notoriety. Sure enough, Robert Beattie's book was published and Rader started to communicate again with the cops, and at one point he asked them if they could determine, if he sent them a floppy disc, who the sender was. The police said they couldn't, and Rader sent the disc. Of course the police could tell, and they tracked the sender as one Dennis Rader of the Christ Lutheran Church in Wichita. One thing led to another, and police eventually collected enough evidence to arrest, try, and convict Rader.

The testimony below, given by Rader before a Kansas judge, describes what happened when Rader, on January 15, 1974, invaded the Wichita home of Joseph Otero and his family, and others.

THE MURDER OF THE OTERO FAMILY

The Defendant: On January 15, 1974, I maliciously, intentionally, and [with] premeditation killed Joseph Otero. Count Two—

The Court: All right. Mr. Rader, I need to find out more information. On that particular day, the fifteenth day of January 1974, can you tell me where you went to kill Mr. Joseph Otero?

The Defendant: Mmm, I think it's 1834 Edgemoor.

The Court: All right. Can you tell me approximately what time of day you went there?

The Defendant: Somewhere between 7:00 and 7:30.

The Court: This particular location, did you know these people?

The Defendant: No. That's no, that was part of my—I guess my, what you call, fantasy. These people were selected.

The Court: All right. So you—you were engaged in some kind of fantasy during this period of time?

The Defendant: Yes, sir.

The Court: All right. Now, where you use the term "fantasy," is this something you were doing for your personal pleasure?

The Defendant: Sexual fantasy, sir.

The Court: I see. So you went to this residence, and what occurred then?

The Defendant: Well, I had did some thinking on what I was going to do to either Mrs. Otero or Josephine, and basically broke into the house—or

didn't break into the house, but when they came out of the house I came in and confronted the family, and then we went from there.

The Court: All right. Had you planned this beforehand?

The Defendant: To some degree, yes. After I got in the house it—lost control of it, but it—it was—you know, in back of my mind I had some ideas what I was going to do.

The Court: Did you—

The Defendant: But I just—I basically panicked that first day, so—

The Court: Beforehand, did you know who was there in the house?

The Defendant: I thought Mrs. Otero and the two kids—the two younger kids were in the house. I didn't realize Mr. Otero was gonna be there.

The Court: All right. How did you get into the house, Mr. Rader?

The Defendant: I came through the back door, cut the phone lines, waited at the back door, had reservations about even going or just walking away, but pretty soon the door opened, and I was in.

The Court: All right. So the door opened. Was it opened for you, or did someone—

The Defendant: I think one of the kids—I think the Ju—Junior—or not Junior—yes, the—the young girl—Joseph opened the door. He probably let the dog out 'cause the dog was in the house at the time.

The Court: All right. When you went into the house what happened then?

The Defendant: Well, I confronted the family, pulled the pistol, confronted Mr. Otero and asked him to—you know, that I was there to—basically I wanted, wanted to get the car. I was hungry, food, I was wanted, and asked him to lie down in the living room. And at that time I realized that wouldn't be a really good idea, so I finally . . . the dog was the real problem, so I—I asked Mr. Otero if he could get the dog out. So he had one of the kids put it out, and then I took them back to the bedroom.

The Court: You took who back to the bedroom?

The Defendant: The family, the bedroom—the four members.

The Court: All right. What happened then?

The Defendant: At that time I tied 'em up.

The Court: While still holding them at gunpoint?

The Defendant: Well, in between tying, I guess, you know.

The Court: All right. After you tied them up what occurred?

The Defendant: Well, they started complaining about being tied up, and I reloosened the bonds a couple of times, tried to make Mr. Otero as comfortable as I could. Apparently he had a cracked rib from a car accident, so I had him put a pillow down on his—for his—for his head,

had him put a—I think a parka or a coat underneath him. They, you know, they talked to me about, you know, giving the car, whatever, money. I guess they didn't have very much money, and the—from there I realized that, you know, I was already—I didn't have a mask on or anything. They already could ID me, and I made—made a decision to go ahead and—and put 'em down, I guess, or strangle them.

The Court: All right. What did you do to Joseph Otero Sr.?

The Defendant: Joseph Otero?

The Court: Yeah, Joseph Otero Sr. Mr. Otero, the father.

The Defendant: Put a plastic bag over his head and then some cords and tightened it.

The Court: This was in the bedroom?

The Defendant: Yes, sir.

The Court: All right. Did he in fact suffocate and die as a result of this?

The Defendant: Not right away, no sir, he didn't.

The Court: What happened?

The Defendant: Well, after that I—I did Mrs. Otero. I had never strangled anyone before, so I really didn't know how much pressure you had to put on a person or how long it would take, but—

The Court: Was she also tied up there in the bedroom?

The Defendant: Yes, uh-huh. Yeah, both their hands and their feet were tied up. She was on the bed.

The Court: Where were the children?

The Defendant: Well, Josephine was on the bed, and Junior was on the floor—

The Court: All right.

The Defendant: —at this time.

The Court: So we're, we're talking, first of all, about Joseph Otero. So you had put the bag over his head and tied it.

The Defendant: I don't know. I have no idea. Just—

The Court: What happened then?

The Defendant: I got the keys to the car. In fact, I had the keys I think earlier before that, 'cause I wanted to make sure I had a way of getting out of the house, and cleaned the house up a little bit, made sure everything's packed up, and left through the front door, and then went there—went over to their car, and then drove to Dillons, left the car there. Then eventually walked back to my car.

The Court: All right. Now, sir, from what you have just said, I take it that the facts you have told me apply to both Counts One, all of Counts One, Two, Three, and Four. Is that correct?

The Defendant: Yes, sir.

The Court: Now, Mr. Rader—

Ms. Parker: Your Honor?

The Court: Yes.

Ms. Parker: There is one thing that needs to be corrected on that record and that is originally I believe he indicated 1834 Edgemoor. The address was actually 803 Edgemoor.

The Court: All right. But I'd asked him if it occurred in Sedgwick County. He's indicated what had happened. I don't believe the exact address is important.

The Defendant: Mm-hmm.

The Court: And he did not die right away. Can you tell me what happened in regards to Joseph Otero?

The Defendant: He moved over real quick like and I think tore a hole in the bag, and I could tell that he was having some problems there, but at that time the—the whole family just went—they went panicked on me, so I—I—I worked pretty quick. I got Mrs. O—

The Court: All right. What did you, you worked pretty quick. What did you do?

The Defendant: Well, I mean, I—I—I strangled Mrs. Otero, and then she was out, or passed out. I thought she was dead. She passed out. Then I strangled Josephine. She passed out, or I thought she was dead. And then I went over and put a—and then put a bag on Junior's head and—and then, if I remember right, Mrs. Otero came back. She came back and—

The Court: Sir, let me ask you about Joseph Otero Sr.

The Defendant: Senior.

The Court: You indicated he had torn a hole in the bag.

The Defendant: Mm-hmm.

The Court: What did you do with him then?

The Defendant: I put another bag over it—or either that or a—if I recollect, I think I put a—either a cloth or a T-shirt or something over it—over his head, and then a bag, another bag, then tied that down.

The Court: Did he sub—did he subsequently die?

The Defendant: Well, yes. I mean—I mean, I was—I didn't just stay there and watch him. I mean, I was moving around the room, but—

The Court: All right. So you indicated you strangled Mrs. Otero after you had done this. Is that correct?

The Defendant: Yeah, I went back and strangled her again.

The Court: All right.

The Defendant: And that—and that—that finally killed her at that time.

THE MURDER OF KATHRYN BRIGHT

The Court: All right, Mr. Rader. We will now turn to Count Five. In that count it is claimed that on or about the fourth day of April 1974, in Sedgwick County, Kansas, that you unlawfully killed Kathryn Bright, maliciously, willfully, deliberately, and with premeditation, by strangulation and stabbing, inflicting injuries from which she did die on April 4, 1974. Can you tell me what happened on that day?

The Defendant: Well, the—I don't know how to exactly say that. I had many, what I call them, projects. There were different people in town that I followed, watched. Kathryn Bright was one of the next targets, I guess, as I would indicate.

The Court: How did you select her?

The Defendant: Just driving by one day, and I saw her go in the house with somebody else, and I thought that's a possibility. There was many, many places in the area, College Hill even. They're all over Wichita. But anyway, that's—it just was basically a selection process, worked toward it. If it didn't work I'd just move on to something else, but in the—in the—my kind of person, stalking and strolling [sic]—you go through the trolling stage and then a stalking stage. She was in the stalking stage when this happened.

The Court: All right, sir. So you identified Kathryn Bright as a potential victim.

The Defendant: Yes, sir.

The Court: What did you do here in Sedgwick County then?

The Defendant: Pardon?

The Court: What did you do then here in Sedgwick County?

The Defendant: On this particular day?

The Court: Yes.

The Defendant: I broke into the house and waited for her to come home.

The Court: How did you break into the house?

The Defendant: Through the back door on the east side.

The Court: All right. And you waited for her to come home.

The Defendant: Yes, sir.

The Court: Where did you wait?

The Defendant: In the house there, probably close to the bedroom. I walked through the house and kind of figured out where I'd be if they came through.

The Court: All right. What happened then?

The Defendant: She and Kevin Bright came in. I wasn't expecting him to be there. And come to find out, I guess they were related. That time I

approached them and told them I was wanted in California, needed some car—basically the same thing I told the Oteros. Kind of eased them, make them feel better, and proceeded to—I think I had him tie— I think I had him tie her up first, and then I tied him up, or vice versa. I don't remember right now at that time.

The Court: Let—let me ask—

The Defendant: Mm-hmm.

The Court: You indicated that you had some items to tie these people with. Did you bring these items, both to the Oteros' and to this location?

The Defendant: The Oteros', I did. I'm not really sure on the Brights. There were some—I—when I had—in working with the police there was some controversy on that. Probably more likely I did, but if—if I had brought my stuff and used my stuff, Kevin would probably be dead today.

The Court: All right.

The Defendant: I'm not bragging on that. It's just a matter of fact. It's the bond had tau—row [sic]—tied him up with that he broke them, so that—

The Court: All right, sir.

The Defendant: It may be same way with—same with Kathryn. It was . . . they got outta . . . got outta hand.

The Court: All right. Now, you indicated you believe you had Kevin tie Kathryn up.

The Defendant: Mm-hmm.

The Court: Tell me what happened then.

The Defendant: Okay. I moved—well, after—I really can't remember, Judge, whether I had her tie him up or she tied him up; but anyway, I moved, basically I moved her to another bedroom, and he was already secure there by the bed. Tied his feet to the bedpost, one of the bedposts so that he couldn't run. Kind of tired her in the other bedroom, and then I came back to strangle him, and at that time we had a fight.

The Court: Were you armed with a handgun at that time also?

The Defendant: Yes, I had a handgun.

The Court: All right. What happened when you came back?

The Defendant: I actually had two handguns.

The Court: All right.

The Defendant: Well, when I started strangling, the—either the garrote broke or he broke his bonds, and he jumped up real quick like. I pulled my gun and quickly shot him. It hit him in the head. He fell over. I could see the blood. And as far as I was concerned, he—you know, I

thought he was down and was out, and then went and started to strangle Kath—or Kathryn. And then we started fighting, 'cause the bonds weren't very good, and so back and forth we fought.

The Court: You and Kathryn?

The Defendant: Yeah, we fought, uh-huh. And I got the best of her, and I thought she was going down, and then I could hear some movement in the other room. So I went back, and Kevin—no. No. I thought she was going down, and I went back to the other bedroom where Kevin was at, and I tried to restrangle him at that time, and he jumped up, and we fought, and—and he about—at that time about shot me, 'cause he got the other pistol that was in my shoulder here. I had my Magnum in my shoulder. So—and really—

The Court: A shoulder holster?

The Defendant: Hmm?

The Court: Did you have it in a shoulder holster?

The Defendant: Yes, mm-hmm. I had the Magnum in my shoulder holster. The other one was a .22.

The Court: All right.

The Defendant: And we fought at that point in time, and I thought it was gonna go off. I jammed the gun, stuck my finger in the—in there, jammed it; and I think he thought that was the only gun I had 'cause once I either bit his finger or hit him or something, got away, and I used the .22 and shot him one more time, and I thought he was down for good that time.

The Court: All right. So you shot him a second time.

The Defendant: Yes, sir.

The Court: Went back to finish the job on Kathryn, and she was fighting. And at that point in time I'd been fighting her. I just—and then I heard some—I don't know whether I was losing—basically losing control. The strangulation wasn't working on her, and I used a knife on her.

The Court: You say you used a knife on her.

The Defendant: Yes. Yes.

The Court: What did you do with the knife?

The Defendant: I stabbed her. She was stab—either stabbed two or three times, either here or here, maybe two back here and one here, or maybe just two times back here.

The Court: And you're—you're pointing to your lower back and your—your—

The Defendant: Yeah, underneath the ribs.

The Court: —and your lower abdomen.

The Defendant: Yeah, underneath the ribs, up—up under the ribs.

The Court: So after you stabbed her what happened?

The Defendant: Actually I think at that point in time . . . well, it's a total mess 'cause I didn't have control on it. She was bleeding. She went down. I think I just went back to check on Kevin, or at that basically same time I heard him escape. It could be one of the two. But all the sudden the front door of the house was open and he was gone, and— oh, I tell you what I thought. I thought the police were coming at that time. I heard the door open. I thought, you know, that's it; and I stepped out there, and he—I could see him running down the street. So I quickly cleaned up everything that I could and left.

The Court: All right. Now, Mr. Rader, you indicated that at the Oteros' you did not have a mask on. Did you have a mask on at the Brights'?

The Defendant: No. No, I didn't, huh-uh.

The Court: All right. So what happened then?

The Defendant: I tried—I had—already had the keys to the cars, and I thought I had the right key to the right car. I ran out to their car, what—I think it was a pickup out there. And I tried it, didn't work; and at that point in time I was—he was gone, running down the street. I thought well, I'm in trouble, so I tried it, didn't work. So I just took off, ran. I went down, went east and then worked back toward the WSU campus, where my car was parked.

The Court: All right. So you had parked your car at the Wichita State University—

The Defendant: Yes, sir.

The Court: —campus?

The Defendant: The campus, uh-huh.

The Court: How far away were—was the Brights' residence?

The Defendant: Oh, I parked, what is that, 13th? And there, I want to say there—I parked by that park, and then I walked to 13th to the Brights' residence. So I basically ran back.

The Court: All right. So you were able to get to your car and get away.

The Defendant: Yes, sir.

THE MURDER OF SHIRLEY VIAN

The Court: Now let's turn to Count Number Six. In that count they claim on March 17, 1977, in Sedgwick County, Kansas, that you unlawfully killed Shirley Vian, maliciously, willfully, deliberately, and with pre-

meditation, by strangulation, inflicting injuries from which she did die on March 17, 1977. Can you tell me what you did on that day?

The Defendant: As before, Vian was a, actually on that one she was completely random. There was actually someone that across from Dillons was a potential target. I had project numbers assigned to it. And that particular day I drove to Dillons, parked in the parking lot, watched this particular residence, and then got out of the car and walked over to it. It's probably in the police report, the address. I don't remember the address now.

Knocked. Nobody—nobody answered it. So I was all keyed up, so I just started going through the neighborhood. I had been through the neighborhood before. I know or knew a little—little of the layout of the neighborhood. I'd been through the back alleys, knew where some certain people lived. While I was walking down Hydraulic I met a young boy and asked him if he would ID some pictures, kind of as a russ, I guess, or ruse as you call it, and kind of feel it out, and saw where he went, and I went to another address, knocked on the door. Nobody opened the door, so I just noticed where he went and went to that house and we went from there.

The Court: Now, you call these "projects." Were these sexual fantasies also?

The Defendant: Potential hits. That, in my world, that's what I called them.

The Court: All right. So you—

The Defendant: They were called projects, hits.

The Court: All right. And why did you have these potential hits? Was this to gratify some sexual interest or—

The Defendant: Yes, sir. I had—there—I had a lot of them, so it's just—if one didn't work I'd just move to another one.

The Court: All right. So as I am to understand it then, on the seventeenth of March 1977, you saw this little boy go into a residence.

The Defendant: Mm-hmm.

The Court: And you tried another residence?

The Defendant: Sir?

The Court: No one was there? You tried another residence. No one was there, so you—

The Defendant: Right, right, right, right. Yeah.

The Court: —went to the residence with the little boy—

The Defendant: And I watched. I watched where he went.

The Court: What happened then?

The Defendant: After I tried this once, the residence, nobody came to the

door. I went to this house where he went in, knocked on the door and told 'em I was a private detective, showed 'em a picture that I had just showed the boy and asked 'em if they could ID the picture; and that time I—I had the gun here and I just kind of forced myself in. I just, you know, walked in—just opened the door and walked in and then pulled a pistol.

The Court: What happened then?

The Defendant: I told Mrs.—Ms. Vian that I had a problem with sexual fantasies, that I was going to tie her up, and that—and I might have to tie the kids up, and that she would cooperate with this—cooperate with me at that time. We went back. She was extremely nervous. Think she even smoked a cigarette. And we went back to the—one of the back—back areas of the porch, I explained to her that I had done this before, and, you know, I think she, at that point in time I think she was sick 'cause she had a night robe on, and I think, if I remember right, she was—she had been sick. I think she came out of the bedroom when I went in the house. So anyway, we went back to the—her bedroom, and I proceeded to tie the kids up, and they started crying and got real upset.

So I said oh, this is not gonna work, so we moved 'em to the bathroom. She helped me. And then I tied the door shut. We put some toys and blankets and odds and ends in there for the kids, make them as comfortable as we could. Tied the—we tied one of the bathroom doors shut so they couldn't open it, and we shoved—she went back and helped me shove the bed up against the other bathroom door, and then I proceeded to tie her up. She got sick, threw up. Got her a glass of water, comforted her a little bit, and then went ahead and tied her up and then put a bag over her head and strangled her.

The Court: All right. Was this a plastic bag also?

The Defendant: Yes, sir. I think it was.

The Court: All right.

The Defendant: But I could be wrong in that.

The Court: You put a bag or—

The Defendant: It was something—I'm sure it was a plastic bag, yeah.

The Court: Now, you say you put a bag over her head and strangled her. What did you strangle her with?

The Defendant: I actually—I think that I had tied—tied her legs to the bedposts and worked up with the rope all the way up, and then what I had left over I looped over her neck.

The Court: All right. So you used this rope to strangle her?

The Defendant: Yes, uh-huh. I think—I think it was the same one that I tied her body with, mm-hmm.

The Court: All right. What happened then?

The Defendant: Well, the kids were really banging on the door, hollering and screaming, and—and then the telephone rang, and they had talked earlier that the neighbor's gonna check on 'em, so I cleaned everything up real quick like, and got out of there, left and went back in—to my car.

The Court: Now, when you say you cleaned everything—

The Defendant: Well, I mean put my stuff—I had a briefcase. Whatever I have laying around, ropes, tape, cords, I threw that in there, my—you know, whatever, you know, that I had that I brought in the house.

The Court: Had you brought that to the Bright residence also or—

The Defendant: Yeah, there is some—there, I, I think there's some basic stuff, but I don't remember bringing total stuff like I did to some of the others.

The Court: Was this a kit that you had prepared—

The Defendant: Yeah. I—

The Court: —beforehand?

The Defendant: Yes. I call it my hit kit.

The Court: All right, sir. You left the Vian residence, and had you parked your vehicle near there?

The Defendant: Yeah, still in the same parking lot there at Dillons—

The Court: All right.

The Defendant: —at Hydraulic and . . . what is that? Harry? Lincoln. Lincoln, yeah. Lincoln and—Lincoln and Hydraulic.

THE MURDER OF NANCY FOX

The Court: All right. In Count Seven it is claimed that on the eighth day of December, 1977, in Sedgwick County, Kansas, that you unlawfully killed a human being, that being Nancy Fox, maliciously, willfully, deliberately, and with premeditation, by strangulation, inflicting injuries from which the said Nancy Fox did die on December 8, 1977. Can you tell me what you did on that day here in Sedgwick County?

The Defendant: Nancy Fox was another one of the projects. When I was trolling the area I noticed her go in the house one night. Sometimes I would, and anyway, I put her down as potential victim.

The Court: Let me ask you one thing, Mr. Rader. You've used that term when you were patrolling the area. What do you mean by that?

The Defendant: It's called stalking or trolling.

The Court: So you were not working in any form or fashion. You were just—

The Defendant: Well, I don't know, if, you know, if you read much about serial killers, they go through what they call the different phases. That's one of the phases they go through is a trolling stage. Basically you're looking for a victim at that time, and that can either be trolling for months or years. But once you lock in on a certain person, then you become stalking, and that might be several of them, but you really home in on that person. They—they basically come the—that's—that's the victim, or at least that's what you want 'em to be.

Ms. Foulston: Excuse me, Your Honor. I think he said "trolling," with a T, not "patrolling."

The Court: He did say "trolling" with a T. I thought he said "patrolling."

The Defendant: Oh, okay.

The Court: All right, sir.

The Defendant: No, no. I wasn't working, sir.

The Court: All right.

The Defendant: No, this was—no, this was off—off—off my hours.

The Court: All right. So you basically identified Nancy Fox as one of your projects. What happened then?

The Defendant: At first she was spotted, and then I did a little homework. I dropped by once to check the mailbox to see what her name was, found out where she worked, stopped by there once at Helzberg, kind of sized her up. I had—the more I know about a person the, the more I felt comfortable with it, so I did that a couple of times; and then I just selected a night, which was this particular night, to try it, and it worked out.

The Court: All right. Can you tell me what you did on the night of December 8, 1977?

The Defendant: About two or three blocks away I parked my car and walked to that residence. I knocked at the—knocked at the door first to make sure, see if anybody was in there 'cause I knew she arrived home at a particular time from where she worked. Nobody answered the door, so I went around to the back of the house, cut the phone lines. I could tell that there wasn't anybody in the north apartment. Broke in and waited for her to come home in the kitchen.

The Court: All right. Did she come home?

The Defendant: Yes, she did.

The Court: What happened?

The Defendant: I confronted her, told her there—I was a—I had a problem, sexual problem, that I would have to tie her up and have sex with her.

The Court: Mm-hmm.

The Defendant: She was a little upset. We talked for a while. She smoked a cigarette. While the—while we smoked a cigarette I went through her purse, identifying some stuff, and she finally said, Well, let's get this over with so I can go call the police. I said, Yes. She went to the bathroom and came—and I told her when she came out to make sure that she was undressed. And when she came out I handcuffed her, and don't really remember whether I—

The Court: You handcuffed her?

The Defendant: Sir?

The Court: You handcuffed her? You had a pair of handcuffs?

The Defendant: Yes, sir, uh-huh, mm-hmm.

The Court: What happened then?

The Defendant: Well, anyway, I had her—I handcuffed her, had her lay on the bed, and then I tied her feet, and then I—I—I was also undressed to a certain degree, and then I got on top of her, and then reached over, took either—either—either her feet were tied or not tied, but anyway, I took—I think I had a belt. I took the belt and then strangled her with the belt at that time.

The Court: All right. All right. After you had strangled her what happened then?

The Defendant: Okay. After I strangled her with the belt I took the belt off and retied that with pantyhose real tight, removed the handcuffs and tied those with—with pantyhose. Can't remember the colors right now. I think I maybe retied her feet, if they hadn't already—they were probably already tied, her feet were, and then at that time masturbated, sir.

The Court: All right. Had you had sexual relations with her—

The Defendant: No.

The Court: —before?

The Defendant: No, no. I told her I was, but I did not.

The Court: All right. So you masturbated. Then what did you do?

The Defendant: Dressed and then went through the house, took some personal items, and kind of cleaned the house up, went through and checked everything and then left.

The Court: All right.

Ms. Foulston: Your Honor, for the record, the address?

The Court: He's established it was in Sedgwick County. I don't need an exact address. For purpose of this, it's in Sedgwick County. Do you remember the address, Mr. Rader?

The Defendant: Oh, the Fox? 913 or 903? No, I—I sure don't. I know it was on Pershing, South Pershing. That's all.

The Court: Here in Wichita?

The Defendant: It was nine something, sir, but I don't remember the other numb—digits.

Ms. Foulston: It's 843.

The Court: The address, as I said, is really not important as long as you remember it happened here in Wichita, Sedgwick County, Kansas.

The Defendant: Yes, sir.

THE MURDER OF MARINE HEDGE

The Court: All right, sir. Let's turn to Count Eight. In Count Eight it is claimed that on or about the twenty-seventh day of April, 1985, to the twenty-eighth day of April, 1985, in Sedgwick County, Kansas, it is claimed that you unlawfully killed a human being, Marine Hedge, maliciously, willfully, deliberately, and with premeditation, by strangulation, inflicting injuries from which Marine Hedge did die on April 27, 1985. Can you tell me what occurred on that day?

The Defendant: Well, actually, kind of like the others. She was chosen. I went through the different phases, stalking phase, and since she lived down the street from me I could watch the coming and going quite easily. On that particular date I—I had a—a other [sic] commitment. I dressed into—I had some other clothes on. I changed clothes. I went to the bowling alley, went in there under the pretense of bowling, called a taxi. Had a taxi take me out to Park City. Had my kit with me. It was a bowling bag.

The Court: All right. Now, is Park City in Sedgwick County, Kansas?

The Defendant: Yes, sir, uh-huh, mm-hmm.

The Court: All right. You had the taxi take you to Park City. What happened then?

The Defendant: There I asked—I—I pretended that I was a little drunk. I just took—I just took some beer and washed it around my mouth, and the guy could probably smell alcohol on me. I asked, told him to let me out so I could get some fresh air, and I walked from where the taxi let me off over to her house.

The Court: All right. Where does she live?

The Defendant: 62—what is it? 427.

The Court: All right. What was the—

The Defendant: —North Independence.

The Court: All right. When you walked over there what happened next?

The Defendant: Well, as before, I was going to have sexual fantasies, so I brought my hit kit, and lo and behold, her car was there. I thought gee, she's not supposed to be home. So I very carefully snuck into the house, she wasn't there. So about that time the doors rattled, so I went—went back to one of the bedrooms and hid back there in one of the bedrooms. She came in with a male visitor. They were there for maybe an hour or so. Then he left. I waited till wee hours of the morning. I then proceeded to sneak into her bedroom and flip the lights on real quick like, or I think the bathroom lights. I just—I didn't want to flip her lights on, and she screamed, and I jumped on the bed and strangled her manually.

The Court: All right. Now, were you wearing any kind of disguise or mask at this time?

The Defendant: No. No.

The Court: You indicated this woman lived down the street from you. Did she know you?

The Defendant: Casually. We'd walk by and wave. She liked to work in her yard as well as I liked to work, and it's just a neighborly type thing. It wasn't anything personal, I mean, just a neighbor.

The Court: All right. So she was in her bed when you turned on the lights in the bathroom?

The Defendant: Yeah, the bathroom, yeah, just to—so I could get some light in there.

The Court: All right. What did you do then?

The Defendant: Oh, I manually strangled her when she started to scream.

The Court: So you used your hands?

The Defendant: Yes, sir.

The Court: And you strangled her? Did she die?

The Defendant: Yes.

The Court: All right. What did you do then?

The Defendant: After that, since I was in the sexual fantasy, I went ahead and stripped her and probably went ahead and, I'm not for sure if I tied her up at that point in time, but anyway, she was nude, and I put her on a blanket, went through her purse, some personal items in the house, figured out how I was gonna get her out of there.

Eventually moved her to the trunk of the car. Took the car over to Christ Lutheran Church—this is with the older church—and took some pictures of her.

The Court: All right. You took some photographs of her. What kind of camera did you use?

The Defendant: Polaroid.

The Court: All right. Did you keep those photographs?

The Defendant: Yes. The police probably have them.

The Court: All right. All right. What happened then?

The Defendant: That was it. I went—I took—she went through—I tied—she was already dead, so I took pictures of her in different forms of bondage, and that's probably what got me in trouble is the bondage thing. So anyway, that's probably the main thing. But anyway, after that I moved her back out to the car, and then we went east on 53rd.

The Court: All right. What occurred then?

The Defendant: Sir?

The Court: What happened then?

The Defendant: Oh, trying to find a place to hide her, hide the body.

The Court: Did you find a place?

The Defendant: Yes. Yes, I did.

The Court: Where?

The Defendant: Couldn't tell you without looking at a map, but it was on 53rd, between Greenwich maybe—maybe—what's . . . what's the other one between Greenwich and Rock?

Mr. Osburn: Webb.

The Defendant: Webb. Between—I think between wed [sic] and—Webb and Greenwich I found a ditch, a low place on the north side of the rode, and hid her there.

The Court: All right. You say you hid her there. Did you—

The Defendant: Well, there were some—there were some trees, some brush, and I laid that over the top of her body.

The Court: All right. So you removed the body from the car, put her in the ditch, then laid some brush over the body.

The Defendant: Yes, sir.

THE MURDER OF DOLORES E. DAVIS

The Court: Now, sir, let's turn to Count Ten. In that count it's claimed that on or about the eighteenth day of January, 1991, to the eight—nineteenth day of January, 1991, in the County of Sedgwick, State of Kansas, that you did then and there unlawfully kill a human being, that being Dolores E. Davis, maliciously, willfully, deliberately, and with premeditation, by strangulation, inflicting injuries from which the said Dolores E. Davis did die on January 19, 1991. Mr. Rader, please

tell me what you did here in Sedgwick County, Kansas, on that day that makes you believe you're guilty.

The Defendant: That particular day I had some commitments. I left those, went to one place, changed my clothes, went to another place, parked my car, finally made arrangements on my hit kit, my clothes, and then walked to that residence.

After spending some time at that residence—it was very cold that night—I had reservations about going in 'cause I, I had cased the place before, and I really couldn't figure out how to get in, and she was in the house, so I finally just selected a—a concrete block and threw it through the plate-glass window on the east and came on in.

The Court: All right. Where is this residence located?

The Defendant: It's on Hillside, but I couldn't give the address. I know it's probably 61—probably 62 something. I don't know. 62 something.

The Court: North or South?

The Defendant: North. North Hillside.

The Court: All right. So you used a concrete block to break a window?

The Defendant: Mm-hmm, plate-glass window, patio door, mm-hmm.

The Court: All right. What happened then?

The Defendant: Noise. I just went in. She came out of a bedroom and thought a car had hit her house, and I told her that I was—I used a—the ruse of being wanted. I was on the run; I needed food, car, warmth, warm up, and then I asked her, I handcuffed her and kind of talked to her, told her that I would like to get some food, get her keys to her car, and kind of rest assured, you know, walked—talked with her a little bit and calmed her down a little bit. And then eventually I checked—I think she was still handcuffed. I went back and checked out where the car was, simulated getting some food, odds and ends in the house, kind of like I was leaving, then went back and removed her handcuffs and, and then tied her up and then, and then eventually strangled her.

The Court: All right. You say "eventually strangled her."

The Defendant: Well, after I tied her up. I went through some things in the room there and then, and then strangled her.

The Court: All right. You say you went through. Were you looking for something?

The Defendant: Mm-hmm. Well, some personal items, yes. I took some personal items from there.

The Court: Did you take personal items in every one of these incidents?

The Defendant: I did on the Hedge. I don't remember anything in Vicki's place. The Oteros we got the watch and the radio. I don't think I did

any in Brights'. Vian's, no, I don't think so. Fox, yes. I took some things from Fox. It was hit and miss.

The Court: All right. But in regard—

The Defendant: Prob—probably if it was a controlled situation where I had more time I took something, but if it was a confusion and other things I didn't 'cause I was trying to get out of there.

The Court: All right. So in regard to the Davis matter, you went around the room, took a few personal things. What did you do then?

The Defendant: Strangled her.

The Court: What did you strangle her with?

The Defendant: Pantyhose.

The Court: All right. What happened then? Did she die?

The Defendant: Kind of like Mrs. Hedge. I already figured out my—I had a, you know, plan on leaving and put her in a blanket and drug her to the car, put her in the trunk of the car.

The Court: So you were able to strangle her to death with these pantyhose.

The Defendant: Yes, sir.

The Court: All right. You put her in your car.

The Defendant: In her car.

The Court: Or in a car.

The Defendant: Her car.

The Court: Her car or trunk.

The Defendant: Uh-huh, the trunk of her car, uh-huh.

The Court: What happened then?

The Defendant: I really had a commitment I needed to go to, so I moved her to one spot, took her out of her car. This gets complicated. Then the stuff I had, clothes, gun, whatever, I took that to another spot in her car, dumped that off. Okay. Then took her car back to her house. Left that. Let me think now. [The defendant made a repetitive popping sound with his lips.] Okay. In the interim—I took her car back to her house. In the interim I realized that I had lost one of my guns. I dropped it somewhere. So I was distraught trying to figure out where my gun was. So I went back in the house, realized I had dropped it when I went in the—when I broke the plate-glass window. It dropped. It fell on the floor right there, and I found it right there. So that solved that problem. Anyway, I went back out, threw the keys—checked the car real quick—quick like and threw the keys up on top of the roof of her house, walked from her car back to my car, took my car, drove it back, and I either dropped more stuff off or I picked her up and put 'em in my car, and then I drove northeast of Sedgwick County and dropped her off underneath a bridge.

The Court: All right. So all of these incidents, these ten counts, occurred because you wanted to satisfy a sexual fantasy. Is that correct?

The Defendant: Yes, mm-hmm.

The Court: Does any party desire any further matters to be put on the record at this time?

Mr. Osburn: No, Your Honor.

The Court: All right. You may be seated, Mr. Rader.

Material from the transcript of Dennis Rader pleading guilty on June 27, 2005, in Sedgwick County District Court, Wichita, Kansas. Photo courtesy of Sedgwick County, Kansas Sheriff's Office.

15.

DAVID PARKER RAY

Vernon Geberth, America's top homicide cop—he has been involved in over eight thousand wrongful death investigations—believes that David Parker Ray was the most vicious serial killer he has ever encountered. "Clinically, I would describe him as the ultimate psychopathic sadist. Investigatively, I would define him as a human predator. Spiritually, I would describe him as the Devil-on-Earth." Please note, the following material is especially disturbing.

Ray, his wife, Hendy, their daughter, Glenda Jesse, and a friend named Roy Yancy participated in the abduction of women, usually prostitutes or runaways, from the streets of New Mexico towns. They would then take them to Ray's compound and inside a windowless trailer called the "Toy Box," where Ray and the others would strip them nude, tie them in obscene positions in a gynecologist's chair, and then torture them by administering electric current, inserting an assortment of large and odd-shaped dildos into their bodies, slicing them with razors and knives, and sexually assaulting them with homemade torture devices. The pain the women endured and their cries and screams provided David Parker Ray sexual stimulation. When the women were all used up, as it were, Ray would kill them, often by strangulation, and dump their bodies (he likely killed thirty or more) in a twenty-five-mile lake he had access to. To make sure the bodies wouldn't surface, he would first gut them and pack stones inside.

Ray also suffered from logorrhoea, meaning he wrote about his experiences extensively. Following are different passages on different topics from tapes he made that the FBI found and transcribed.

THE WORDS OF DAVID PARKER RAY ON WHAT CAPTURED WOMEN WILL DO TO BE FREED

REMEMBER
WOMAN WILL DO OR SAY ANYTHING TO GET LOOSE
THEY WILL:
SCRATCH
OFFER MONEY
YELL
BEG
SCREAM
RUN
OFFER SEX

EXCUSES and SOB STORIES:
MENSTRUATING
PREGNANT
VD
SICK
KIDS WITH BABYSITTER
A SICK BABY
A SICK PARENT
CLAUSTROPHOBIA
MISSED BY HUSBAND OR FRIEND
BAD HEART
CAN'T MISS SCHOOL
DON'T LET HER GET TO YOU
IF SHE WAS WORTH TAKING—SHE IS
WORTH KEEPING
AND
SHE MUST BE SUBJECTED TO HYPNOSIS BEFORE
THE WOMAN CAN BE SAFELY RELEASED
NEVER TRUST A CHAINED CAPTIVE

DAVID PARKER RAY ON NIKKIE

Nikkie was a whore in Phoenix, Arizona. I had known her two or three years, but I didn't screw around with her then. She had long blond hair, pretty well built, not beautiful, but not bad-looking, either. What really fascinated me about her was that she had these big, humongous tits: I used to watch her working, walking back and forth in front of Canal Motors, watching those big ol' tits bounce, fantasizing about what I would like to do to them.

Seven or eight months after I left that job, I had to go back over to Arizona for a few days. I pulled my trailer and, needless to say, I went and looked Nikkie up. What I had in mind was to keep her chained and locked up in my trailer for about a week and use her for a sex toy, but it didn't work out that way. When I picked her up, her boyfriend knew where she was at. I asked her what she would charge to let me tie her up and spank her before I fucked her. She said a hundred dollars, but I didn't want to spend a hundred bucks, so I just got a blowjob and took her back to town.

The bitch gave me the clap.

I didn't think you'd catch the clap with a blowjob, but the doctors assured me that you could. Needless to say, I was pissed, but I wasn't in Arizona anymore and there wasn't a whole hell of a lot I could do about it, at least not at that moment.

About six months later, I was in New Mexico and I took some stuff over to Arizona for an auction. I had my trailer and I looked Nikkie up. It took two days to find her [snicker]. That bitch got around. During that two days, I talked to several guys that had been fucking her pretty regular. She had gotten rid of the VD. Her boyfriend wasn't anywhere around when I picked her up that time. I took her back to the trailer and I told her I wanted to do the hundred-dollar deal: tie her up, spank her, and fuck her. And she went for it—made it almost too easy for me.

The bondage table and related equipment were in concealed compartments, so she didn't have a clue as to what my real motives were. She didn't know exactly what I wanted to do, so I led her through it. She sat on a small cot, I used a rope to tie her ankles together, and then I used two separate ropes to tie her wrists down to her ankles—one rope on each wrist. I had a specific reason for tying her wrists that way, as I will explain later.

She cooperated completely until I brought out a tube-tied breathing gag and a roll of duct tape.

That cunt did not want to be gagged. But I got it in her mouth and put

several wraps of duct tape around her head to hold it in place. To be double sure, I wrapped duct tape under her chin and over the top of her head several times so she couldn't open her jaws. She still wasn't too upset, just pissed off because I gagged her. I moved across the trailer, pulled the latches, and let the bondage table down. That bitch took one look at the table and the rack that had been concealed behind it holding whips, harnesses, dildos, and other devices related to bondage [snicker].

She became unglued!

She really got upset. I sat down beside her and told her in no uncertain terms what I thought of a whore who gave me the clap. About the aggravation, the problems with the girlfriends, the doctor bills, trips to the hospital, and that there was going to be a hell of a lot more retribution than just spanking. Payback's a real motherfucker [snicker].

She just sat there trying to get loose and shaking her head back and forth—like No, no, no, but it was really Yes, yes, yes. I picked her up and sat her on the table, pushed her over on the middle of it, and positioned her on her back with her feet and arms pointed up. I held her that way and locked the chain around her neck that was attached to the table. That settled her down a little bit, but not much. A rope from the ceiling ring was tied to her ankles so she couldn't kick. The wrist bindings on the upper corner of the table consist of an adjustable chain that is attached to the corner of the table with a handcuff on the other end. Releasing one rope at a time, I secured her arms up to the upper corners of the table. Her legs were folded back, spread well apart, and also chained to the upper corners. That little whore was bouncing her ass all over the table while I finished strapping her down. I buckled table straps across her upper chest, her rib cage, and her belly. Two more table straps were buckled over each side and pulled tight, holding her ass firmly down on the table. Two more straps went across the back of each knee, holding her legs securely down. That position gets uncomfortable as hell for a woman after a while, but it works pretty neat for me.

She was absolutely and totally immobilized, couldn't move any part of her body at all except her head. Legs folded back and spread, and hips turned up with the asshole and pussy fully exposed. With her knees strapped down to the table on each side of her chest, the legs didn't interfere with access to her tits. They sagged off each side a little bit, but that was okay. God, they must have weighed five pounds apiece. The bitch was top heavy. She had large fluffy cunt lips on each side of the slightly open pussy.

She was a hooker because she had a hundred-dollar-a-day drug habit,

she had already told me that that was why she agreed to let me spank her for a hundred bucks. She'd go get her drugs so she didn't have to work the rest of the night. I didn't tell her then that she wasn't going to be working for quite a while. She also didn't get the hundred-dollar bill. I'd already taken it out of her sock. Anyway, I picked up the whip and gave her about a dozen good whacks. . . .

By that time, I was horny as hell. I climbed on the table and put just a little bit of Vaseline right around the head of my dick and stuck it in her asshole. Apparently, she didn't get into that too much; it was nice and tight. After that, I gave her a damn good ass-fucking.

RAY'S BACKGROUND, RECORDED WHILE IN JAIL

"My grandmother's name was Dolly Parker. One afternoon, the year before I was born, her two youngest sons were left at the ranch while my grandpa went to town to get groceries. They lived thirty miles from Mountainair. Alden and David was left there alone. Alden was fifteen and David was thirteen and they was playin' cowboys and Indians with real guns—there was always guns at the ranch, and Alden shot David in the heart and killed him. There was a bullet in the old Winchester and Alden didn't know it.

"Alden put David's body in the old pickup and tried to, tried to take him to town and it run out of gas—so Alden run down a horse and rode to the highway and—and flagged a car and—and tried to get help.

"Of course, David was already dead. When she found out what had happened, my grandmother flipped out. I wasn't born yet—that was 1938—but I was born a year later and she decided that I was a reincarnation of her son, of her dead son David, and consequently I'm named David Parker Ray. . . . And that's why she always wanted to raise me.

"There really wasn't much affection in my childhood. I was there physically, but nobody paid any attention to me, you know, it was like . . . like I wasn't really there at all."

"What about the sexual fantasies?" asked the FBI agent.

"This thing is literally tearing me apart," David Ray said. "For forty years my life has been a private hell."

"How did you get interested in sex?"

"When I was a little kid, my mother and father pawned me and my sister Peggy off on Dolly, my mother's mother, who lived on a farm up in the hills near Mountainair, New Mexico. There wasn't anything to do up there. My

dad was a drunk and a drifter and every six months he would drop by and bring me a big pile of *True Detective* magazines, and when I was about ten years old, I started to have these fantastic dreams about raping and killing young girls. In the dreams I always used a broken beer bottle.

"I hated any grandmother. She didn't care about us.

"I wanted to have a skill so I could make a living. I was going to air-craft mechanics school in Tulsa and we didn't have much money. One day, out of the clear blue sky, my wife decided she was going to bring home the bacon for us by becoming a whore. I didn't like it at all, but it sure paid the bills. I still thought about the fantasy sometimes and she let me tie her up a couple of times, but that was it. I had this dungeon downstairs in our house and most of the time she didn't have the slightest idea what I was up to. By the late 1970s, I was designing custom-made torture equipment and selling the stuff in *Screw* magazine.

"I left her when I found her in my bed with another man. It was her day off, so I knew it didn't have anything to do with money. I walked out the next day with Joannie Lee, her sister-in-law.

"We drove to California and for the next year we lived in Grass Valley, up in the Sierra Nevada Mountains. We grew marijuana up in the hills for a year and lived out of our trailer, and then one day we just decided to leave. We wanted to get regular jobs. We drove down to the turnoff at Death Valley—the spot where the road forks one way to Las Vegas and the other way to Phoenix. We flipped a coin and so we went to Phoenix.

"I got a job as a mechanic at Canal Motors, a used-car dealership in Phoenix. We got married in 1983 and I changed my name back to my mother's maiden name, Parker. We were David and Joannie Lee Parker. I still had the fantasy, and about every six or eight months, I would get the urge. I can't tell you what it felt like working around all that temptation—any time of day you could see them—hookers—four or five of them walking by, night and day. I started hiring girls to help relieve the pressure of my fantasy. I'd hire a hooker to do the dirty deed and pay her three hundred dollars an hour.

"I'd whip them, but I'd never break the skin—never.

"We had a code word we would use when it got too rough. When it got too painful for one of them, all they had to do was say the code word out loud."

"And what was that word?" asked the agent.

"Raspberry," answered Ray.

"That's all?" asked the agent.

"Yeah, raspberry, that's all. . . . There was no way Joannie Lee would

take part in the fantasies. She knew what I liked, but she wouldn't let me use her. She was jealous of the fantasy. We kind of drifted apart. Over the years she just got more and more crazy. She was having epilepsy attacks and she started drinking real heavy and one time she held a pistol up to my head. I couldn't take it anymore. Finally I had to send her home to her mother in Pennsylvania.

"That was 1994, and after she left, I changed my name back to David Ray.

"For the next three years, it was just me and the fantasy.

"I'm past the point where therapists can help me. One year I had six different shrinks. I tried to change, but it didn't do no good. Anyway, it didn't seem like some of 'em was too bright in the head. They didn't understand my problem, I guess you could say.

"By 1994 I was getting the urge every two or three months. After that, it really got worse, especially after I started taking Viagra. I even started taking other pills to suppress my sex drive. Nothing worked. I have this master sketch notebook of drawings—some of them are real frightening. The sketches kind of track the progress of the fantasy. If the FBI would like, I'll give you the drawings. Maybe you could help other people with the same problem. If I can help other people, I'd be glad to—it's a curse that destroys your life.

"I also read a lot of true crime books. They kinda fuel the fantasy. I've been collecting books on serial killers for the last fifteen years. I've read all twelve of the Ted Bundy books and, of course, I really like Stephen King. I also like Dean Koontz. I read a book by Christine McGuire called *Perfect Victim* in 1989, and after that, I changed the way I did things. The killer in the book used to put a woman's head inside a box so she couldn't see what was going on around her and that really turned me on. I've got a library of about seventy-five true crime books and the FBI can have those, too.

"I was real lonely before I met Cindy Hendy. She moved here in 1997 and I met her after she got into trouble for fighting with one of her boyfriends—I think his last name was Arrey. Judge Fitch sentenced her to do community service work at Elephant Butte State Park, where I work. The first time I met her, she told me in a real matter-of-fact voice, 'I don't like women, and I don't like men much, either.'

"It didn't take long until I fell madly in love with her—even right now, I love her dearly.

"I did not discuss this thing from my past with Cindy. . . . I'm a very private person and I'm very ashamed of this hang-up. Slowly I manipulated her to my fantasy. She allowed me to do anything to her body, even though she

didn't like it. I softened my fantasies for her because I didn't want to alienate her. Once I showed her my album of drawings and it scared her.

"I am potentially dangerous. I'm like a time bomb—and one way or the other, the problem stops here. I'm fantasizing about ten and eleven-year-old girls, so if it takes a sterilization, that's what I'll do, you know. I'm serious about that. I like to cause pain, but I don't like to physically, actually hurt a girl. I'm old and I'm tired and there's not going to be any more incidents.

"I get the urge every two or three months now," said Ray. "This thing is ruining my life. I've been having the fantasy since I was ten years old, and gradually it has gotten worse and worse. The fantasy is a curse for everyone around me, but somehow I'm going to beat it, one way or the other."

GREETINGS FROM HELL

At one point, Ray began reading his captives the riot act on what was going to happen to them. The speech was part of the torture he administered and was used to break them down emotionally so that they would obey his every wish and command.

"Hello there, bitch. You're chained, handcuffed, scared, and disoriented. Listen to this tape. It was created July 23, 1993, as an advisory tape for female captives based on my several years of experience.

"You are here against your will. You probably think you're going to be raped. You're right about that—you will be raped thoroughly and repeatedly. . . . My female companion and I are very selective. We'll snatch anything clean, young, and well built. We're basically like predators. We're always looking. I don't want to kill unless it's absolutely necessary. If I killed every victim I ever kidnapped, there'd be bodies all over the country."

Then Ray said, tongue in cheek, "This audiotape contains very graphic material for adults only. It was designed and created to be used for entertainment purposes.

"Hello there, bitch! Are you comfortable right now? I doubt it. Wrists and ankles chained, gagged, probably blindfolded. You are disoriented and scared, too, I would imagine. Perfectly normal under the circumstances. For a little while at least, you need to get your shit together and listen to this tape. It is very relevant to your situation. I'm going to tell you in detail why you have been kidnapped, what's going to happen to you, and how long you'll be here.

"I don't know the details of your capture, because this tape is being created July 23, 1993. The information I'm going to give you is based on

my experiences dealing with captives over a period of several years. If at a future date, there are any major changes in our procedures, the tape will be upgraded. Now, you are obviously here against your will. Totally helpless. Don't know where you're at. Don't know what's going to happen to you. You're scared or pissed off. I'm sure that you've already tried to get your wrists and ankles loose, and know you can't. Now you're waiting to see what's going to happen next. You probably think you're going to be raped, and you're fucking sure right about that.

"Our primary interest is in what you've got between your legs. You'll be raped thoroughly and repeatedly in every hole you've got, because basically, you've been snatched and brought here for us to train and use as a sex slave. Sound kind of far out? Well, I suppose it is to the uninitiated but we do it all the time. It's gonna take a lot of adjustment on your part, and you're not going to like it a fucking bit, but I don't give a rat's ass about that. It's not like you're gonna have any say about the matter. You've been taken by force, and you're going to be kept and used by force.

"What all this amounts to is that you're going to be kept naked and chained up like an animal to be used and abused anytime we want to, any way that we want to. And you might as well start getting used to it, because you're going to be kept here and used, until such time as we get tired of fucking around with you, and we will eventually in a month or two, or three.

"It's no big deal. My friend Hendy and I have been keeping sex slaves for years. We both have kinky hang-ups involving rape, dungeon games, et cetera. We found that it is extremely convenient to keep one or two female captives available constantly to satisfy our particular needs. We are very selective when we snatch a girl for use for these purposes. It goes without saying that you have a fine body, and you're probably young, maybe very young. Because for our purposes, we prefer to snatch girls in their early to midteens, sexually developed, but still small body, scared shitless, easy to handle and easy to train. And they usually have tight little pussies and assholes. They make perfect slaves.

"Anytime we go on a hunting trip, if we can't find a little teenager, we usually start hitting the gay bars, looking for a well-built, big-titted lesbian. I thoroughly enjoy raping and screwing around with lesbians, and there's not as much danger of them carrying a sexually transmitted disease, and I don't like using condoms. Also, even though they're a little older, unless they've been playing with dildos a lot, they still have tight holes between their legs, like the younger girls. If we can't find a lesbian that we want, we snatch anything that is young, clean, and well built. We seldom

come back empty-handed, because there's plenty of bitches out there to choose from. And with a little practice in deception, most of them is very easy to get with little risks.

"At this point it makes little difference what category you fall into. You're here, and we're going to make the most of it. You're going to be kept in a hidden slave room. It is relatively soundproof, escape proof, and is completely stocked with devices and equipment to satisfy our particular fetishes and deviations. There may or may not be another girl in the room. Occasionally, for variety we like to keep two slaves at the same time. In any case, as the new girl, you will definitely be getting the most attention for a while. Now, as I said earlier, you're going to be kept like an animal. I guess I've been doing this too long. I've been raping bitches ever since I was old enough to jerk off and tie a little girl's hands behind her back. As far as I'm concerned, you're a pretty piece of meat to be used and exploited.

"I don't give a flying fuck about your mind or how you feel about the situation.

"You may be married, have a kid or two, boyfriend, girlfriend, a job, car payments—fuck it! I don't give a big rat's ass about any of that, and I don't want to hear about it. It's something you're going to have to deal with after you're turned loose. I make it a point never to like a slave, and I fucking sure don't have any respect for you. Here your status is no more than one of the dogs or one of the animals out in the barn. Your only value to us is the fact that you have an attractive, usable body. And like the rest of our animals, you will be fed and watered, kept in good physical condition, kept reasonably clean and allowed to use the toilets when necessary. In return, you're going to be used hard. Especially during the first few days while you're new and fresh. You're going to be kept chained in a variety of different positions, usually with your legs or knees forced wide apart. Your pussy and asshole is going to get a real workout, especially your asshole because I'm into anal sex. Also, both of those holes are going to be subjected to a lot of use with some rather large dildos among other things. And it goes without saying that there's going to be a lot of oral sex. On numerous occasions you're going to be forced to suck cock and eat pussy until your jaws ache and your tongue is sore. You may not like it but you're fucking sure going to do it.

"And that's the easy part. Our fetishes and hang-ups include stringent bondage, dungeon games, a little sadism, nothing serious, but uncomfortable and sometimes painful. Just a few little hang-ups that we like to use when we're getting off on a bitch [laughs]. If you're a young teenybopper, and ignorant about fetishes and deviations, you're about to get an enlight-

ening crash course on sex ed. Who knows, you may like some of it. It happens occasionally.

"Now I've already told you that you're going to be here a month or two, maybe three, if you keep us turned on. If it's up to my lady, we'd keep you indefinitely. She says it's just as much fun and less risk. But personally, I like variety, a fresh pussy now and then to play with. We take four or five girls each year, depending on our urges and sometimes accidental encounters. Basically, I guess we are like predators; we're always looking. Occasionally some sweet little thing will be broke down on the side of the road, walking, bicycling, jogging. Anytime an opportunity like that presents itself, and it's not risky, we'll grab her.

"Variety is definitely the spice of life. Now, I'm sure you're a great little piece of ass, and you're going to be a lot of fun to play with, but I will get tired of you eventually. If I killed every bitch that we kidnapped, there'd be bodies strung all over the country. And besides, I don't like killing a girl unless it's absolutely necessary, so I've devised a safe, alternate method of disposal.

"I had plenty of bitches to practice on over the years, so I pretty well got it down pat, and I enjoy doing it. I get off on mind games. After we get completely through with you, you're gonna be drugged up real heavy with a combination of sodium pentothal and phenobarbital. They are both hypnotic drugs that will make you extremely susceptible to hypnosis, auto-hypnosis, and hypnotic suggestions. You're gonna be kept drugged a couple of days while I play with your mind. By the time I get through brainwashing you, you're not gonna remember a fucking thing about this little adventure. You won't remember this place, us, or what has happened to you. There won't be any DNA evidence because you'll be bathed, and both holes between your legs will be thoroughly flushed out. You'll be dressed, sedated, and turned loose on some country road. Bruised, sore all over, but nothing that won't heal up in a week or two. The thought of being brainwashed may not be appealing to you, but we've been doing it a long time, and it works and it's the lesser of two evils. I'm sure that you would prefer that in lieu of being strangled or having your throat cut. There are not going to be any knights in shining armor coming to rescue you. As for escaping, I'm sure you'll try to figure out a way—that's human nature—but it's hardly worth talking about here. It wouldn't be prudent on our part to have you running around in the woods screaming "Rape." It would be embarrassing, to say the least. Consequently, you're gonna be kept in an environment that's even more secure than a prison cell. A steel padlock is going to be placed around your neck. It has a long, heavy chain

that is padlocked to a ring on the floor. The collar will never be removed until you are turned loose. It's a permanent fixture.

"The hidden playroom where you are going to be kept has steel walls, floors, and ceiling. It is soundproof and has a steel door with two keyed locks. The hinges are welded on and there are two dead bolts on the outside. The room is totally escape proof, even with tools. If you are in the room alone, your wrists will be chained. There is a closed-circuit TV system wired to the main TV in the living room, so we can check on you every once in a while or just sit and watch you for the fun of it.

"Electronics is a wonderful thing. Expensive—but hell—everything in the playroom is expensive and well worth it. If everyone knew how much fun it was to keep a sex slave, half the women in America would be chained up in somebody's basement.

"Okay, let's talk about your training, the rules and the punishment. Here you are a slave, and discipline is extremely strict. You're gonna be given a set of rules. As soon as each rule is told to you, it will become law. This is what will happen if you fuck up. We use a couple of different methods of punishment. A whip is an excellent training aid, so is the electroshock machine. Anytime you get out of line, one or both will be used on your body. And I assure you, it will not be pleasant. After the first, we won't cut you any slack at all.

"Now, let's start this off right. You're a slave. I'm your master and the lady is your mistress. You will be totally docile. You will be very quiet, and you'll speak only when spoken to. Never initiate conversation. Keep your mouth shut. Do exactly what is told to you, nothing else. Obey my commands—anything less will get you beaten. If I tell you I want to be sucked off, you say, 'Yes, Master,' and open your mouth. Each time when I get ready to come, I'm going to push my penis down your throat, and keep it there until I get through squirting. I'm not going to choke you, but you need to learn to hold your breath and to swallow every bit of sperm. If I see one drop leaking out of your mouth, I'm going to punish you. It's the same with your mistress. Learn how to use your tongue.

"If during oral sex or any other time you should bite one of us, I'm going to cut you a little bit. Your teeth are serious weapons. I have been bitten and I've cut off nipples, so don't fuck around. If your mistress comes into the room and tells you to get down on the floor, you say, 'Yes, Mistress.' If she tells you to pull your knees up, you say, 'Yes, Mistress.' If she tells you to spread your knees, you say, 'Yes, Mistress,' and spread them wide apart and hold them there, so she can play with your pussy.

"Don't kick, struggle, or resist in any way. If you do, you're gonna be

in a world of hurt. For repeated rule violations, the punishments are eventually going to become harsh and even brutal, and you won't have nobody to blame but yourself.

"Now, let's discuss talking. You cannot talk. I believe that rule gets more bitches into trouble than anything else, because they can't keep their damn mouths shut. They always want to whine, beg, plead, try to talk me into turning them loose. I used to listen to it. I don't anymore. I enjoy blessed silence.

"Around here, your mouth is for sucking, not talking.

"The only time I ever want to hear you initiate speech is if you have to use the restroom. If you have to pee, say, 'Pee, Master' or 'Pee, Mistress.' You definitely need to tell us, because if you make a mess, you're going to be punished and you'll have to clean it up.

"Now, I've got to tell you, there is another side to the coin. Once in a while we get a bitch who is rebellious and won't mind. That doesn't work here. I'm sure that you realize you are on thin ice. If you should hurt either one of us, you could be in very serious trouble.

"I'm sure you want to survive this experience, but you are expendable. It's no big deal to go out and grab a replacement. It may sound harsh and cold, but if you give us too much trouble, I won't have any qualms at all about slashing your throat. I don't like killing girls, but occasionally bad things happen.

"I would really hate to have to dump that pretty little body off in a canyon somewhere to rot.

"Everything we do to a girl is designed to cause pain, not injury. No matter how painful it is, nothing we plan to do to your body will cause any permanent damage. I'm not lying to you. You're gonna be whipped lightly, for pleasure. You're gonna be shocked lightly, for pleasure.

"Most of the other nasty little things we're going to do, for the most part, will be done to your breasts, nipples, and between your legs. The lady is fortunate. She can get off anytime. She just likes to be a little sadistic with the slave once in a while.

"In my case, I could not get off with a girl unless I hurt her first. That is basically the reason I'm into rape and slavery. And that's the reason you're going to be subjected to a certain amount of pain. Mostly, what we do to a captive is stick needles in her breasts and through her nipples, through her cunt lips, through her clit—and I'm also into stretching certain things. Clamps with long nylon cords will be put in your cunt lips, so your pussy can be kept pulled open, and they're also going to be attached to your nipples. The nylon cords will be put through ceiling rings and pulled very tight to stretch your tits.

"Occasionally, your clit will also be clamped and stretched. And we're going to be using dildos. The dildos are going to be used a lot; more than anything else, and consequently, what you're going to have the most trouble with. Many of them are very long, very large in diameter, and very painful while they're being forced in. I like to use them in both holes and your mistress will use them in your pussy.

"As far as needles go, they'll always be sterilized. The clamps are going to hurt like a motherfucker, but they won't cause any permanent injury. They don't even break the skin.

"As far as dildos go, both of those holes between your legs will stretch a hell of a lot. Your pussy is designed for a baby to come out of, and we won't be using anything bigger than that. The really large ones will not be used in your butt.

"Every once in a while, we get a screamer. Some bitch that just wants to scream all the time. And that always gets on my nerves. We live in an isolated area, so screaming is usually not a problem—but it irritates the fuck out of me. If you do it habitually, I will keep a ball gag in your mouth all the time—I'll never take it out.

"Pretty soon I'm going to be asking you a bunch of questions. I have prepared a questionnaire that I will fill out with each new captive. Some of the questions are going to be embarrassing, but you should answer them truthfully. I don't want to catch you in a lie. You will be naked and you'll be strapped down to the gynecology table so you can't wiggle or squirm around. I like to keep a girl that way while she's answering questions. Before you start answering questions, two small electrical clamps will be put on your nipples. Each time a question is asked, you will respond properly. Think about what you're going to say before you say it because we're not in a hurry. Each time you fuck up, I'm gonna press a little button and send a few thousand volts of electricity through your nipples. I'm not going to hold it down to torture you, but each time you screw up, it's going to get a little bit worse.

"After you finish answering the questions, I'm going to examine you. All girls are different. I want to become very familiar with your sex organs and the size of your holes. Later that first day, you're going to be raped several times, but that's no big deal. The second day, after you get totally familiar with the rules and procedures, we're going to get down to the nitty-gritty. Things will not be very pleasant for you, but you might as well get used to it, because it's going to be like that for a while.

"Well, I believe I've told you about everything that I can. Be smart and be a survivor."

BACKGROUND NOISE

Other tapes Ray made distinguished themselves by being interrupted by the screams of slaves being tortured. Following is from one such tape where he is talking to a captive.

"I make very special adult videos. The videos sell for about a thousand dollars each and they are only sold to a very select group of collectors of sadistic erotica. I've learned over the years that there's a hell of a lot of people out there with some awful weird fantasies. I rather enjoy the work; the money's great. Our customers want a lot of wide-angle and close-up camera shots of the breasts, nipples, and sex organs being abused with a variety of instruments in a variety of ways. The action has to be real. It can't be faked. We need to actually kidnap a woman for the action scenes.

"Sometimes the movies are shot in the woods, sometimes in a boat or in the desert. Other times we shoot you in a dungeon-type room in our house. The shooting of the action scenes usually takes three or four days. We videotape a dozen or so rapes, several whippings, and several hours of abuse with a woman chained in a variety of different positions. And, if I may say so myself, we put out some pretty damn good movies.

"There is a bright side to this. Before I turn you loose, I'm going to give you a hundred dollars for your trouble. Thirty to forty percent of the movie will be where the camera zooms in for a close-up between your legs. So all you have to do is show us what you've probably already shown some other poor sucker who had to pay a lot more than a hundred bucks to catch a glimpse of the promised land. The pink hole.

"Fuck flicks are a dime a dozen. You can buy them all over the place for eight or nine dollars and ninety-five cents. Our group of clients wants to see a woman actually raped, whipped, and tortured. They like to see a woman wiggle, squirm, bite the chains, and sweat a lot. And if you don't sweat enough, we'll put baby oil on your body to simulate it. We strive to please; that's our claim to fame. I prefer to use the word 'abuse' because I don't think we actually torture a woman in our films.

"Let's go into a few types of abuse. We use damn big dildos on your two holes and they look wicked as hell. We're careful and we use them with restraint. That's necessary to create the illusion of reality. If our procedures didn't cause pain, we wouldn't have to kidnap a live woman to make these movies.

"Since these movies are into bondage, it's necessary that we tie up your tits. We attach long nylon cords to each nipple and we put on a few drops of Super Glue to bond the cord to the skin: a woman's breasts are very elastic

and they can be stretched upward like two slender cones. You're going to squeal like a stuck pig while I'm doing it, but it won't bother me at all.

"You'll also be whipped, about twenty lashes during each session. The whip has to be used hard enough to leave some good welts for the camera. I don't want to get you all bloody, so the whip strokes will be concentrated on your thighs, your butt, sex organs, belly, and tits. Even if you're gagged, the microphones will pick up the sounds. The whip is a great tool for effect.

"It never ceases to amaze me how barbaric some people can be. Our customers want to see you getting hurt. We use some gigantic dildos. To create some special effects, we pull the skin around your vagina back and then thrust in a dildo four to six inches wide at the base. On the viewing screen it looks pretty terrible. It looks like we're tearing you apart, and that's what we want the viewer to think. Our customers think that's exactly what we do to a girl when we make these movies. But that's not the way it works at all . . ."

[Abruptly, voices can be heard in the background.]

"You may be tempted to strike out, kick, bite, try to scratch me. I wouldn't do that if I were you."

[Still lots of screaming, sighing, and crying in the background.]

"Can't you all keep that bitch quiet in there? Put a gag on her or something. Fuck, I'm trying to make a tape out here. Close that damn playroom door. Anything!"

[The background screaming ceases.]

"Shit, that's better. Fuck, that bitch has got a set of lungs on her. My friend was forcing the devil's dick up her ass and she didn't like it for shit, that's for sure.

"Now, where were we?

"Just be careful what you do with your hands and feet. If you piss me off, things are gonna get a hell of a lot rougher. A woman scratched me in the face one time, and I cut her clit off. Another thing I might tell you right now is that . . ."

[Starts talking to someone in the background.]

"What? What do you all want?"

[Loud noises in the background.]

"All right, damn it, wait a minute and let me turn this damn machine off here."

[Pause.]

"Well, I'm back [laughs].

"Shit, they're like a bunch of little kids in there with a new toy. They just wanted me to show them how to use the electroshock machine. That little cunt in there is chained down and she can't be over fifteen or sixteen

years old. My friends sure are giving her a working over. Damn . . . I guess I should have made this tape when it was a little bit quieter. But you know how it goes . . . the excitement of the moment and all that shit.

"Anyhow, what I was about to tell you a while ago was that there is absolutely no way in hell that you're going to be turned loose until I'm done with you. Hell, I even picked up one little ol' bitch, seventeen or eighteen years old, that told me she had a two-week-old baby at home. And I didn't doubt it for a minute. Her pubic hair was just starting to grow back where it had been shaved off. Her pussy lips were still swollen and puffy but the really novel thing was her tits. After I had her for a few hours, her nipples started leaking milk constantly. Made a hell of a mess. Even with all her excuses, I still didn't turn her loose, and I'm sure as hell not going to turn you loose."

[Loud screaming and cries can be heard in the background.]

"Damn! That's carrying right through the walls. I don't know what they are doing to her, but it must be good. Hang on a minute, I better look in there and make sure they're not killing the little whore."

[Three voices are heard in the background: a male's, a female's and David Ray's. Their words are hard to make out.]

"Yeah, I'm back [laughs]. She's okay. One of the girls was touching a lit cigarette to her nipples. But I told her not to do it anymore. I don't particularly like that. Not because of the pain, because we're in the business of pain . . . but because cigarette burns kinda messes up a woman's appearance. And that doesn't turn me on."

THE CHURCH OF SATAN

Ray's activities were based on sadism, and he had various ways to implement his urges. One tape started with the sound of religious instrumental music and Ray's soft voice.

"Hello, bitch. I'm sure you're wondering why you've been kidnapped and what's going to happen to you. That's why this tape has been made. It saves a lot of talking. It's brief, blunt, and to the point.

"I'm a dungeon master for a local chapter of the Church of Satan, Lucifer, or the devil, to you. You have been abducted so that your body can be used during rituals, and for sexual purposes for the congregation after the meetings. Our membership is pretty small, about twenty people, mixed male and female. Our meetings are pretty much what most people imagine—the way it is depicted in the movies.

"A hidden church, black robes, pentagrams, rituals, chanting, a lot of nakedness, animal sacrifices, chicken blood, and a hell of a lot of sex afterward! The meetings get interesting and exciting, to say the least. Trying to raise the demons is important, but it is the sex that keeps the church financially afloat. The high priest likes to keep everybody fired up on sex, and for that, we like fresh meat. Every couple of months we kidnap some good-looking little bitch to use during the rituals and to be kept available for everyone to use during the orgy.

"Let me tell you what happens at the meetings. The orgy room is separate from the main church. It contains several couches, many mats on the floor, and a refreshment center. In the middle of the room is a large wooden table with leather straps on it. Prior to each meeting, you'll be taken to the church in a wooden box, naked, in chains and with your eyes taped shut—so you can't identify anybody.

"Once there, you will be strapped down on top of the table. Your arms will be chained straight out to each side and leather straps will be buckled across your upper chest, your rib cage and your belly—so you can't move. Your legs will be spread extremely wide apart because some of our members have diversified interests in, ah . . . which hole they want to use. There is a U-shaped cutout at the top of the table and it allows your head to drop right down into it. Another leather strap will be put across your forehead so you can't move, allowing your mouth and throat to be available for sex.

"Dental jaw blocks will be installed in your mouth so that you can't bite anybody during oral sex. When your mouth is wide open, members will just shove their dicks down your throat and hump your face until they come. After the meeting is over in the church, every one will move into the orgy room, take their robes off [laughs]. Now everybody is fucking naked! And they'll surround the table. You're definitely going to be the center of attention, especially at the first meeting when you're the new girl.

"Everybody is going to want to feel you up and try you out. Anyway, the high priest will move to the bottom of the table with a large wooden box that contains the dildo—what we call the devil's dick. The tip is small, so it'll start in the vagina easy but the thing is tapered. It widens enormously at the base to about three inches thick, and the whole thing is pretty close to twelve inches long. It's a real pussy stretcher.

"Once it starts to go in, the high priest will chant:

The Devil fucks!
The Devil fucks!
The Devil fucks!

"A half a dozen people will help hold your body still while the high priest forces the dick up all the way inside you. There will be a sudden blast of pain between your legs and it's not unusual at all for a girl to pass out while this is being done.

"Next the high priest will rape you. After he gets through, your body will be available for everybody's use. They'll take turns using you in various ways, and during the course of the evening, most of them will come back for seconds and thirds. You'll probably be raped forty to fifty times.

"The next morning, after everybody goes home, I'll take you back to the dungeon, wash the sperm out of your body, and clean you up. I'll give you a bath and let you build your strength up so we can do it all over again [laughs]. You're gonna be used for three or four meetings. By then, a captive is pretty well worn out and everybody's tired of fucking with her. Remember, your body is the property of the Church of Satan. The church is going to have you one night every two weeks and I've got you the rest of the time. Now, the dungeon belongs to the church, and it's very well equipped. They spent a ton of money buying all sorts of specialized equipment, about anything I asked for. They even gave me medical supplies to patch up girls in case the high priest tears some slut's pussy with a big dildo, and that doesn't happen too often. One of my duties is to prestretch a girl's vagina so the dildo won't tear it. There have been a few occasions when we've kidnapped a bitch and had to take her to a meeting that same evening. Usually when that happens, the devil's dick tears the fuck out of her vagina. Then I have to patch her up afterward.

"A few years ago, there was a certain period of time that we didn't do that. During that time there were instances where the fellows caused so much vaginal damage that the girl hemorrhaged and sometimes didn't survive. And it caused some problems within the congregation. Nobody likes watching a girl bleed to death. Well, now you know what this is all about. You're not exactly a sacrificial virgin. I don't imagine you're a virgin anyway. Virgins are pretty hard to come by. During the years that I've been dungeon master, for variety we sometimes snatch some pretty young girls . . . thirteen, fourteen years old, and even with that, we've only had two virgins.

"Well, so much for that, but know now how you're going to serve the church. Now let's talk about how you're going to serve me.

"It is within my power to make your stay in the dungeon reasonably easy or a living hell. There are going to be some rules, and whether you like them or not, you will learn to obey them. You're going to find that I don't have any patience at all with pretty little girls that forget and make mistakes.

"Crying is acceptable, as long as you're not too loud about it. Most of

the time I expect you to keep your mouth shut. You need to tell me, however, when you have to use the restroom, because if you make a mess, whether it be a piss or a crap, you're going to be forced to lick it up.

"Don't bite. There are no second chances. If you bite, I cut.

"As far as kicking goes, I really don't have a set punishment for that. If you should hurt me with your feet, the punishment shall be whatever I decide. That's not fair, but that's life.

"When the church is done with you, the high priest will advise me when you are to be released and I will initiate a process that will take about two days. You're going to be injected with a combination of drugs and then brainwashed until you don't remember the church, me, this place, or any fucking thing about what's happened to you. After the hypnosis has taken effect, you'll be taken near some town and turned loose.

"Everything will heal up in two or three weeks. It will probably take just a little longer for your vagina to shrink back to normal size, but, ah [laughs] . . . that too will come to pass.

"Now this is the beginning of a very trying ordeal for you. This experience is going to be very traumatic. The nights when you are taken to the church are going to be the worst by far. Each time you are going to experience about ten hours of pure hell.

"Satan is a harsh taskmaster."

BREAKING IN CAPTIVES

Ray also had written instructions on how new captives should be handled, or demoralized, when they were first captured. Following are guidelines for members of Ray's satanic cult. Some of his instructions were written in pen, but the list that follows was neatly typed.

PSYCHOLOGICAL AND PHYSICAL PROCEDURES
INITIAL HANDLING OF A CAPTIVE
PERSONAL FETISH

1. The new female captive should be gagged and blindfolded with wrists and ankles chained.
2. Move her into the Recreation Room. Place her body under the suspension chains.
3. Stand her up under the chains and lock her wrists well above her head.

4. Place the neck chain around her neck and lock it in place. IT IS PERMANENT.
5. Clip her leg irons to the floor chains.
6. Use scissors to slowly remove her dress, blouse or sweater. Cut and remove the bra.
7. Fondle and abuse her breasts, nipples, and upper part of her body.
8. Keep her blindfolded to increase disorientation. Use verbal abuse. (Dumb Bitch, Slut etc.)
9. Slowly unzip, open, and remove the lower clothing. Cut or rip the panties off.
10. Fondle and abuse her sex organs. Continue the verbal abuse.
11. Attach the overhead suspension straps to her body. Ankles, waist, hips, and upper chest.
12. Remove the leg irons and tighten the ankle straps, pulling her legs upward, until the middle part of her body is horizontal. (THE ANKLE STRAPS WILL FORCE HER LEGS WIDE APART.)
13. Tighten and adjust the waist, hip, and chest straps until the middle of her body is straight. Clip the short floor chain to the bottom ring on the waist belt, so she cannot jerk or lift her body upward.
14. At this point, the captive is suspended at a convenient height, immobilized and fully exposed. She is very uncomfortable, disoriented, and probably terrified. Don't cut her any slack. Continue a lot of verbal and physical abuse . . . *Keep her mentally off balance.*
15. Play with her sex organs. (Vagina or anus.) Force large dildos deep into both holes. Use clamps, needles, or other devices on her tits and sex organs. (Clit and cunt lips.) Whip her and use Electro-shock.
16. *Don't give her time to collect her thoughts.* Use her body aggressively, during the first hour or two. She will sweat, struggle a lot, and exhaust herself. Particularly if the Electroshock machine is used extensively.
17. Intensify her fear. Tell her how she is going to be kept as a Sex Slave. Describe, in detail, how she will be continuously raped and tortured. Work on her mind, as well as her body.
18. Keep her body suspended two or three hours, then roll the Gynecology Bench directly beneath her. Lower her body down on the bench. Release one arm or leg at a time, and secure it to the bench, until she is strapped down. Buckle all the straps on her body, until she is totally immobilized, feet in the stirrups, and knees forced wide apart.

NOTE: THE SHOCK VALUE OF DISORIENTATION, PLUS CON-
TINUOUS VERBAL AND PHYSICAL ABUSE, DURING THE FIRST
FEW HOURS OF CONFINEMENT WILL HAVE A GREAT INFLU-
ENCE ON HOW DOCILE AND SUBDUED THE CAPTIVE WILL
BE DURING THE REMAINING PERIOD OF CAPTIVITY. IF IT IS
DONE PROPERLY SHE WELL BE INTIMIDATED AND MUCH
EASIER TO HANDLE.

Material from Jim Fielder, *Slow Death* (New York: Pinnacle Books, 2003).
Courtesy of the Kensington Publishing Corp. Photo courtesy of New
Mexico Department of Corrections.

16.

GARY RIDGWAY

BACKGROUND

In the early 1980s in a seedy downtown area of Seattle, Washington, women, mostly teenagers, working as prostitutes started to disappear. On July 15, 1981, two boys discovered the body of one of these women near the Green River. Investigators determined that the victim, Wendy Lee Coffield, sixteen, had been strangled.

Then the bodies of other women started to turn up, also in the Green River, on its banks, or nearby. The press got wind of it, and someone dubbed the murderer the "Green River Killer." Bodies continued to show up, and before too long panic had gone through the ranks of the prostitutes working the strip like a fire through dry brush. They started to vet potential johns or made sure they were never defenseless against a possible attack.

But it soon also became apparent that the killer was cunning and found ways to lure women into his clutches.

In King County, of which Seattle is a part and where all the murders occurred, a considerable task force was formed but they were unable to snare the killer. In fact, as it turned out, the killer escaped detection for almost twenty years, a period during which he was to admit later, in a plea deal that would keep him off death row (he got life without parole), to having strangled forty-eight females to death, the vast majority teenagers. This earned him the rank as one of the most prolific serial killers in US history.

Gary Ridgway

The perpetrator turned out to be an average-sized but powerful man employed as a truck painter in the Kenworth manufacturing plant in Renton, Washington, whose home was not far from the area where prostitutes plied their trade.

During extensive interviews with Gary Ridgway, police, psychiatrists, and others questioned him extensively. Following are the questions by investigators and his answers that sum up how Ridgway operated, followed by a Q & A between Ridgway and Dave Reichert, the head of the Green River task force, who hated Ridgway so much it brought him to tears. Reichert also partnered with Bob Keppel in questioning Ted Bundy to try to glean insight on how the Green River Killer operated (see chapter 2).

RIDGWAY INTERROGATIONS

Q. Were the killings planned?
A. When I get in the truck, when I'm driving and, I might pick up a woman, I wanna be in the mood to kill. I . . . I don't have the mood, ah, like I don't get her in the truck and drive down the road and all of a sudden, you know, I jump on her and start chokin' her, no. But I always . . . I always had it in my mind to kill them.

Q. Did any of the women ever ask you whether you were the Green River Killer?

A. All the time. They's always ask. Even the ones I didn't kill.

Q. How did you answer?

A. No, I'm not. Uh, do I look like the Green River Killer? [Ridgway was 5'10" and weighed 155]. And they say no, you don't. They always thought it was a big, tall guy, about six foot. So, 6'3", 185 pounds, or somethin' like that.

Q. A lot of women were nervous once word got out about the Green River Killer. How did you calm a woman down so you were able to lure her into your truck?

A. I would . . . talk to her about . . . anything she was nervous about. And think, you know, she thinks, oh, this guy cares, and which I, I didn't. I just wanted to uh, get her in the vehicle and eventually kill her. Another way was I opened up my wallet and there would be my ID and a picture of my son on one side, uh, you know, behind my ID. And they'd see that and then would uh, lower any big defenses. And just, you know, also see kids' toys in the, on the dash.

Q. We understand that you would pick up some women even if you knew conditions were not right for killing her, such as there being witnesses around or their pimp was there, that you saw a "date" (having sex) with them as investing in the future.

A. Yeah, to get 'em used to me in case I see one of 'em at a time [alone].

Q. How did you feel when you didn't capture a woman you wanted to kill?

A. . . . The next one I'm gonna do everything I can to sweet talk her. . . . I'm gonna talk her into getting in so I can . . . kill the bitch, kill the one I didn't get a chance to kill today, I'm gonna strangle her head . . . strangle her neck so it breaks.

Q. I understand that there was a difference the way you treated young women and older women.

A. I talked to them (the young) before I had sex with them, and she'd say typically, "I've only done this a few times before." I mean if she's thirteen or fourteen years old, you figure that's true. If you get one that's twenty and twenty-five that talks the slang and everything and they say "I've only done this a few times," they probably got an arrest record and they're lying.

Q. You were very shook up when you missed a kill, right, so how did you hide your rage when you picked up the next woman?

A. I'd be in the mood right to get her [the next potential victim] in the car

and choke her. But I had to calm down to . . . so I wouldn't look like I was, you know, scared and shaking. I'd have to bring in on the side that I just got arrested a couple of weeks ago for prostitution and [tell her], "You can see I'm a little bit nervous."

Q. How did you normally strangle someone? In the truck when you were under the canopy with her? We understand that the key was you telling them that you could only get excited having sex "doggie style."

A. After I got behind them, I would climax and usually the woman would raise her head because, you know, the guy's through, I can get dressed. When she raised her head up, I would wrap my right arm around her or put something around her neck and choke her.

Q. What if they didn't raise their head?

A. I'd tell 'em there's a car coming, so guess what, she lifts up her head like that. She's not thinking anything of it. Her hands are down normal and it's my time to wrap my arm around her neck and to choke her and not . . . get in the way of her mouth. I got bit in the hand with a mouth one time. But it's my idea to get her head up so I could get a clear shot of her neck to kill her.

Q. You also employed a con if they struggled. You said that if they stopped struggling, you'd release them.

A. Yeah. But I wasn't gonna let her go. It was just my way of lying to her to keep her from fighting. She stopped fighting and I just kept on chokin'.

Q. What did the women say to you so you would not kill them? Some would say, "Don't kill me," "I'm too young to die," or "I've got family I'm taking care of," "I've got a daughter at home," "I don't want to die."

Q. Did you ever stop?

A. No.

Q. How did you physically handle it if they struggled?

A. I'd wrap my legs around them, sometimes I'd roll over and be on the bottom chokin' 'em.

Q. Anything else to finish them off?

A. Sometimes, if there was room, I'd stand on their throats.

Q. How long did a strangling take?

A. Not more than two minutes.

Q. Did you have sex with the dead bodies? Could you tell us about such an experience?

A. That would be a . . . uh, that would be a good day, an evening or after I got off work and go have sex with her. And that'd last for one or two days till I couldn't . . . till the flies came. And I'd bury 'em and cover

'em up. Um, then I'd look for another. Sometimes I killed one, one day, and I killed one the next day.

Q. We understand that on one occasion you drove to the woods where you had killed a woman with your young son in the car and he fell asleep and you went into the woods and had sex with the woman. Weren't you afraid of him waking up?

A. No. He was a hard sleeper.

Q. How many bodies did you have sex with out of the fifty or sixty women you killed?

A. Ten.

Q. And why did you have sex with the dead?

A. Well, for one thing you'd have to pay for it and she was already dead. And (sometimes) I spent hours looking, looking, and looking for other women to kill and a lot of gas and everything, and didn't find anyone.

Q. At one point you found it less satisfying to have sex with the dead, right? Why?

A. It was hard to get a hard-on with a cold body.

Q. Can you tell me why many of the bodies were found with their legs spread wide. Were they posed?

A. I had to open their legs so I could have sex, and I left 'em that way.

Q. You put rocks in the vagina of a couple of your victims. Why?

A. They were there.

Q. Most of your victims were strangled in your house—in your bedroom. You obviously preferred to take the women to your house because they feel more secure.

A. Yes. They look around and everything, they're getting more secure as you go. They look in the bedrooms, nobody's in there, nothin's, you know, there's my son's room, hey, this guy has a son, he's not gonna hurt anybody. His name's written on the door and it's empty and it's got his bunk bed there, toys on the floor . . .

Q. And you'd also invite them to use the bathroom before sex because you knew dying made people incontinent.

A. I didn't want them to shit in the bed.

Q. We understand that you'd use the same killing method on a bed in your bedroom as outdoors. Put your arm around their neck and also wrap your legs around them if they squirmed. And that sometimes to finish them off you stood on their neck?

A. Yes.

Q. You don't remember many of the faces or names of your victims, do you? But you do remember where you dumped them. Why?

A. So I could have sex with them.

Q. How did you get rid of the women you killed in your house?

A. The girl is in the bedroom and then I'd pull her off the bed on to the rug and grab her by the feet and drag her around the corner so it was easy on the plastic 'cause it slid so easy and I could wrap . . . wrap the plastic around her and take her out that way.

Q. And you would back up your truck close to the back door of the house, open the tailgate, and load the body into the back and close the canopy. And unscrew the light by the window in this kitchen door during this process.

A. Yes.

Q. And you stripped the body of clothing so no evidence would be clinging to it, right?

A. Yes.

Q. How about valuables?

A. They die. I take their jewelry.

Q. We understand that you left a lot of jewelry in the women's bathroom at Kenworth, where you worked.

A. And my favorite thing was maybe if someone's walking around with a piece of that jewelry that they found in the bathroom.

Q. We understand you had high regard for the bodies. What did a body mean to you?

A. She meant, she meant that, uh, um, a beautiful person that was my property, my . . . uh, possession. Someone only I knew and, I missed when they were found where I lost 'em.

Q. It really bothered you when they found the bodies. That in the beginning of killing you took steps so they couldn't be found. That you held one to the bottom of the river and weighted [her].

A. You had already found two of 'em by then. And she . . . I wasn't going to let this other one get away.

Q. You had a dream about controlling one body, right? Tell me about it please.

A. I had control of her when I killed her and I had control over her if she hasn't already been found, I'd have control over her where she was still in my possession.

Q. We understand that you took some bodies out of state, to Oregon.

A. That was to throw off the task force, 'cause the . . . bodies were already being found and I didn't want any more to be found.

Q. Why did you bury only a few of the bodies?

A. I buried the ones in areas where I was going to have fresh kills. I don't

want the dates to smell decomposing bodies, like in South Airport, and lead to them being found.

Q. You liked to hide bodies in sloped areas that were remote, right, where a person casually walking by would not discover them? How did you do this?

A. I'd have one hand on her leg while using the tree for stable, to keep me stable. Wrap my arm around a tree and pull her down . . . uh . . . go to another place and a . . . grab a bush and hold on to it, while I am pulling her down.

Q. Did you ever get hurt doing this?

A. If I got hurt, like pulling her because of her weight, and it bothered me, I'd just blame it on work so State Industrial paid for it.

Q. Why did you dump bodies far apart?

A. For one thing I didn't want anyone seeing me going to the same site more than once and uh, the reason why I put 'em so far apart is because if I wanted to go back, there wouldn't be any smell. Then [if] I could uh, take 'em and drop 'em in the bottomless mineshaft, uh, uh, every, every one of 'em, and I could'a had uh, then I would have a, uh, much clearer mind at, at, at killing more women, not spending the time finding locations was the, was a big burden [that] took the time away from killin'.

Q. When you killed outdoors, you seemed to place bodies next to physical objects visible from a distance—large trees, guardrails, hills, large fallen logs—which served as landmarks.

A. So I won't forget where they . . . where they are. So, I've done it before and, ah, just easy. When . . . if I drive by and think somebody's been, you know, found 'em, then that way I would stay away from them.

Q. You avoided detection for twenty years. How did you feel about that?

A. Well, I was in a way a little bit proud of not being caught by things like removing the clothes. Not leaving anything . . . any fingerprints on it, using gloves. Not bragging about it. Not talking about it.

Q. I was wondering how you think about yourself. Now say we have a scale, say of one to five, and five being the worst possible evil person that could have done this kind of thing.

A. Uh-huh, yes.

Q. Where do you wanna fall on the scale?

A. I'd say a three.

Q. Three?

A. Uh-huh, yes. For one thing is, ah, I killed 'em, I didn't torture 'em. They went fast. I'm sorry for doing it but, um, it just I wasn't killin' a person, I was killin' a prostitute, I killed a lot of bad people for society.

Q. Do you think of yourself as different from other people? I mean, is anything missing from you?
A. Yeah. That caring thing.

The dialogue below is between Gary Ridgway (GR) and Sheriff Dave
Reichert (SHF).

SHF: Okay.
GR: Good afternoon.
SHF: How ya' doin'?
GR: Pretty good.
SHF: Yeah? So, we talked quite a long time ago.
GR: Um-hm, yes, we did.
SHF: It's been a while.
GR: Um-hm, yes.
SHF: How long do you think it's been?
GR: Five weeks, six weeks. Maybe a little more.
SHF: Yeah, prob'ly longer than that.
GR: Um-hm, yes.
SHF: How long do you think you've been here?
GR: Well, on uh, the thirteenth, it was uh, six . . . six weeks . . . six
months.
SHF: Six months?
GR: Thirteenth of uh, December, yes. Came in here on the thirteenth,
Friday the thirteenth, June, I think it was. Yeah, June, I think.
SHF: Friday the thirteenth?
GR: Friday the thirteenth.
SHF: Boy, that's a . . . kind of ironic, isn't it?
GR: Um-hm, yes.
SHF: You think that's significant at all?
GR: I'm not superstitious.
SHF: It's just a coincidence.
GR: No, just a coincidence.
SHF: You're not superstitious?
GR: No.
SHF: No? Six months.
GR: Um-hm, yes.
SHF: How do you think the last six months have gone?
GR: I think they've been gone, goin' real good.
SHF: Do ya?

GR: Yeah.

SHF: Why?

GR: I know because one thing is the number of, I think we started out, you know, we got halfway through it and maybe was only like fifty-six to fifty-seven [bodies], now we're up to seventy-one, which I think is a real improvement.

SHF: Seventy-one?

GR: Um-hm, yes.

SHF: Do we have names for all of those people now, or?

GR: Hm, no, not all of 'em, no.

SHF: 'Cause you pled guilty to forty-eight, right?

GR: Forty-eight, yes.

SHF: I was there that day.

GR: Um-hm, yes. And there's six sites they found bodies, uh, locations, and the rest of 'em, they haven't found bodies or were still pending on my information of where I picked the, uh, lady up, where I killed her, uh, what I put in a lady's vagina, or . . . and uh, where I picked up another woman. Uh, I don't remember where [crosstalk, couple words].

SHF: Why do ya think that they're not able to find 'em?

GR: I think a lot of 'em are uh, way far out and the animals got most of 'em 'cause . . .

SHF: Are they doin' a good job searchin' you think, or did, do you think the detectives . . .

GR: I think they've got a good job, but . . .

SHF: . . . are just . . .

GR: I, no, I think they've done the best they can.

SHF: Do ya?

GR: But th-they're gonna have to do like they did . . . well, well, for instance, uh, April. I thought it was McGinness where, out Leisure Time . . .

SHF: Yeah. Do you think we should call the FBI in, maybe, 'cause they have search techniques that maybe we not, may not [crosstalk, couple words].

GR: Well, I wish they had somethin' that would pick up bones, uh, you know, they could just take a Geiger counter and do that.

SHF: Yeah. Do you think the FBI could find 'em?

GR: I don't know. Uh, if we had the . . . the funds to do it, yes.

SHF: Yeah.

GR: I think they could do, I'd think they would help.

SHF: Or maybe they need better direction?

GR: Not maybe better direction.

SHF: Or . . .

GR: Uh, 'cause some of 'em I couldn't find, like six of 'em I couldn't find. Uh, they were prob'ly put in there during the winter when the leaves are down and that makes a difference in going out during the summer. But they have to . . .

SHF: What is some of the, what are some of the good things that you've seen over the last six months since we have had you here since June 13? What are some of the good things you think have happened while you've been here?

GR: Well, the good things are that you know, sometimes like every week we'd, we'd find an extra body, which is what I'm in here for. An extra body or a, um, a site that uh . . .

SHF: What do you mean by an extra body?

GR: An extra body that I didn't account for. The . . .

SHF: So we'd find a, we'd find somebody's remains. That was a good thing.

GR: You find somebody's remains, or you uh, uh, yes, you found somebody's remains.

SHF: Why was that a good thing in your . . .

GR: 'Cause that's . . .

SHF: . . . in your point of view?

GR: 'Cause that's what uh, it, it takes sometimes visual things to, to, to, for me to locate spots, and when they took me out on places, that helped a lot in [crosstalk].

SHF: So why was that a good thing, though, to find a bone, or to find a human . . .

GR: To find it because that's . . .

SHF: . . . remains?

GR: . . . because it gets one, uh, for, for me, and for society, and for you guys, you have a, one more . . .

SHF: Why is it good for you?

GR: It's because it takes the pressure off me, uh . . .

SHF: Pressure for what?

GR: Pressure on my shoulders of havin' a, how, the, the women I killed, get release. It takes a lot of pressure off my chest, cause I'm getting it off my chest.

SHF: I don't understand.

GR: Well, because . . .

SHF: What pressure?

GR: . . . they're, they've uh, it, it bothers me to have all these women inside my, uh, self, and uh, to me get 'em out. I kinda, you know, in one way I celebrate that I found another site, another person or at least a site. But because of the many years, uh, it is, it was really hard on uh, animals and stuff on, on the sites, on the, on the bodies.

SHF: So it was a good thing for you because it relieves some pressure.

GR: Relieves me the pressure, but also gives the, some families recognition of who, who killed 'em—me. And tryin' to figure out who was uh, who was where . . .

SHF: So one of the things you were trying to do was to help the families when you did this?

GR: When, help the families a lot.

SHF: Is that what you wanted to do?

GR: Yeah. Help the families, uh . . .

SHF: Wouldn't it have been better not to kill 'em at all?

GR: At the time when I was killing really heavy, it didn't uh, it didn't bother me at all. I didn't have a, I didn't have a heart.

SHF: No, I know that. Yeah. But all of a sudden now you wanna help the families.

GR: Yes.

SHF: Does it have anything to do with the fact that you're saving your own life?

GR: No, it doesn't. It doesn't . . . it, it doesn't, uh, have anything to do with myself. I prob'ly would've, at the end of the trial we went through, and I prob'ly would've coughed up the body . . . up the bodies then. But doing it earlier because of people coming forward to me, not because of myself, saving myself, but 'cause of them. They want . . .

SHF: A lot of people think that, though.

GR: Oh, I [unintelligible].

SHF: [Unintelligible] The only reason you're doing this is to save your own life, not, not to . . .

GR: Well . . .

SHF: . . . for the families.

GR: Well, I look at it this way, that, that if by giving it, that gets me the, 'cause I, all the way through, all, all when I got arrested, I had a big knot on my chest and I couldn't sleep. I couldn't . . . because of, of all the, the . . .

SHF: So the day you got arrested, you felt like you had a knot in your chest?

GR: I had a knot in my chest because I, I, I put it all off.

SHF: Because you got caught.

GR: Because, not . . . well, because I got caught, but also because of uh, it's my time . . . thinkin' about it, it's my time to give these bodies up and I was, I was fighting myself inside—should I give 'em up or should I . . . or should I, I not. And I was waiting . . .

SHF: You would've never turned yourself in, though . . .

GR: No, I would not have.

SHF: . . . if we'd not have caught you.

GR: No. But uh, like I said, in those uh, letters that I mailed in to, one letter to the . . . I would have communicated that way through and give the bodies up—but without givin' myself up.

SHF: But you only wrote the one letter.

GR: I only wrote the one letter.

SHF: And you didn't sign your name to it.

GR: No, I didn't, and I wouldn't . . .

SHF: So we didn't know who it was from.

GR: No. And even the FBI didn't think it was from that, but . . .

SHF: Yeah.

GR: . . . if I would had come, if I would of had communication between you the same way as more letters through the mail, I would of coughed 'em up earlier and you would of had more . . .

SHF: But you didn't wanna do that because you didn't wanna get caught.

GR: Yeah, I . . . but I could, I could do that where I wouldn't get caught with, 'cause you know, lickin' the letter, I didn't lick the letter. I typed it, used gloves. I don't, there's no . . . I don't think there's any way . . .

SHF: Why didn't you lick the letter?

GR: Because I just, I just didn't. I didn't lick the letter and that's why, sometimes like I cut the fingernails off of some of the ladies that scratched me.

SHF: Yeah. But why didn't you lick the letter?

GR: I don't, don't know. Um, maybe they get saliva off . . .

SHF: What were you thinkin'?

GR: . . . of it or some'n.

SHF: Saliva?

GR: Um-hm, yes.

SHF: And what would that do?

GR: You could link it to me.

SHF: How?

GR: Uh, I don't know. But uh, I was just t-tr-tryin' to be more cautious about it. But I would've gone . . .

SHF: So what was your, what were you thinking, though, back then? You didn't lick the letter because . . .

GR: Because I thought maybe they'd get some saliva off it or some'n like that.

SHF: And, and what would that do? And . . .

GR: They could prob'ly trace it if they found . . .

SHF: . . . how could they do that?

GR: If they, later on if uh, they got blood from me or some'n from a victim or some'n, they could trace it to that one. And maybe later on get uh, so find that I am what, O-positive, or whatever it is, A-negative, whatever it is.

SHF: There's millions of people that are O-positive though.

GR: Yeah, I know. Yeah, I know, but . . .

SHF: Right?

GR: . . . if I would of got caught, that would be, narrow it down to the Green River Killer, is . . .

SHF: Uh-huh.

GR: . . . certain, certain uh . . .

SHF: So you were pretty smart about that kind of stuff.

GR: Um-hm, yes, I was . . .

SHF: Right.

GR: . . . smart about typing, and uh, uh, taking pictures of the women I threw the . . . away, with the camera . . .

SHF: Um-hm.

GR: . . . and then later on tore up the pictures.

SHF: Hm. So that's one good thing.

GR: But . . . that's, that's one good thing, is . . .

SHF: What was that again, the one good thing?

GR: That was letting the, giving the bodies up—both times—either back in that time or new, so it'd take the pressure off of me, and also give relief to the families. And . . .

SHF: So the finding of, finding a set of remains that we hadn't known about, was a good thing because that family then would know that their daughter was . . .

GR: That, that family would know.

SHF: . . . killed and that you were the killer.

GR: That I was the killer, yes.

SHF: Yes.

GR: And back . . .

SHF: What's another good thing?

GR: Another thing is because of, uh, one thing, I wasn't really too worried about goin', goin' to prison and death sentence. I, if I would of, I would of gave those things up knowing I already had the death sentence [unintelligible word, crosstalk].

SHF: You weren't worried about dying?

GR: Not really, because . . .

SHF: Most people are.

GR: Because, uh, one thing, I'm, I'm worried about dying a little bit, but uh, another thing is I don't want to, um, it's gonna take ten to twelve years and by that time I prob'ly would of, you know, died of a heart attack or some'n in, in prison.

SHF: Oh, you'll only be what, in ten years, sixty-five?

GR: Well, I read a lot of those, I read a lot of those books, and some of the guys only lasted about ten years.

SHF: In prison?

GR: Um-hm, yes.

SHF: Why is that?

GR: Oh, ones I read, most of 'em died just of heart attacks, you know, uh . . .

SHF: How about at the hands of other inmates?

GR: Uh, only because they were taken out of protective custody . . .

SHF: Yeah.

GR: . . . that they put in for.

SHF: So are you gonna be in protective custody?

GR: I, I thought maybe I'd be workin', but I guess if you're in protective custody, you don't work.

SHF: Right. So . . .

GR: I'll, I'll prob'ly be in protective custody.

SHF: Yeah. Does that concern you at all?

GR: Well, it's not, it concerns me a little bit but it also, too, it gives me that chance if you guys find some'n, you come to me and I can—hey, I'm already in there for life imprisonment . . .

SHF: Right.

GR: . . . and if you find some'n that links me to a, a body they found that I can say yes, that's, that's, that's . . . that's uh, one of mine. Uh, I, you know, welcome the, the, the police to come in there and talk to me in, in prison because . . .

SHF: Why?

GR: . . . of that one—to get 'em off my shoulder and get out of me, out of me.

SHF: Isn't, it's not because that you're gonna, you're gonna be in that cell by yourself twenty-three hours a day and you won't have anybody to talk to?

GR: No, I . . .

SHF: I mean, isn't that part of it, that you want people to come by and at least have people to speak to?

GR: Not really. It's uh, it's because of the getting it off my shoulders because there's a lot of 'em out there, that we go for a week and all of a sudden they show me a picture and another one pops up.

SHF: Hm.

GR: And that, it, it, I'm happy to give it up. But there's a lot of those things is, is it, it comes down to is only ten people I know out there [unintelligible], I know exactly where I picked 'em up. The rest of 'em I don't and that's what hurts me.

SHF: Yeah. Why does it hurt ya?

GR: Oh, because they don't believe me. The . . .

SHF: Who doesn't believe you?

GR: . . . the task force and, and you know, everybody that's in here. Pick up a woman someplace and then I, I kill her. Well, I picked up three or four hundred of 'em, so my uh . . .

SHF: Why do you think they don't believe ya?

GR: Because it's some'n that I should know.

SHF: Yeah.

GR: I should know about the woman, but . . .

SHF: But, so you should know it. I agree with that.

GR: Um-hm, yes.

SHF: But isn't there another reason too?

GR: There's a big reason, is because of some so many I picked up. There's a [crosstalk].

SHF: That's two reasons. What's the, there's another reason too that people don't believe ya.

GR: Oh, because they think I'm uh, holding it back or uh, it's so gruesome that uh, about the woman that I did some'n to, it's . . .

SHF: Yeah, that's three. We've known that . . .

GR: That's three.

SHF: . . . yeah, you're, that you . . .

GR: And when . . .

SHF: . . . [unintelligible] things back. What else? Why wouldn't people believe you?

GR: They think I'm maybe trying to, uh, bring the score up in one way. You know, more body count when . . .

SHF: Um-hm, yes. Right.

GR: . . . when that's, some people count bodies that aren't theirs.

SHF: Why would you do that, bring up the body count?

GR: That wouldn't be what I wanted.

SHF: Why would someone do that?

GR: They get notability of, but none of this stuff is gonna be going on . . .

SHF: Notoriety?

GR: No . . . no . . . you know, that's give them a, a more body count than what they normally have.

SHF: And so they, they would just do that—become famous?

GR: They'd do it to become famous, but not me.

SHF: Who's done that? Do you know anybody that's done that?

GR: I, I don't know. Maybe Bundy, I don't know.

SHF: Bundy?

GR: Uh, yeah. But uh, with me, I wanna, there's so many things that I know about the cases, uh, like no scratch marks on the back and these things here.

SHF: Um-hm, yes.

GR: That they know. But . . .

SHF: These are decomposed bodies, so how would we know that?

GR: Well, some . . . you know, the one in the street wasn't.

SHF: Oh, the one on the street, yeah.

GR: This is the one on the street.

SHF: What about other, another reason why people won't believe you, why the task force detectives don't believe you?

GR: Why, is maybe because uh, um, maybe they think they're hol-holding some'n back, you know.

SHF: You already said that one.

GR: Oh. Um . . .

SHF: It's hard to remember, isn't it?

GR: It's hard to remember.

SHF: Maybe, maybe because you've been lyin' a little bit here and there?

GR: No, it's not that.

SHF: You haven't lied this whole six months that you've been with us?

GR: I've been lyin' the first part, but during the end I haven't been lyin'. It's, it's . . .

SHF: But see, that's what happens though, right?

GR: Um-hm, yes.

SHF: It's like raisin' your children, they lie to you and then you expect, they expect you to believe 'em the next time and you have a tough time. Right?

GR: It, it is.

SHF: So they're, they're prob'ly strugglin' because you've lied once and so . . .

GR: Um-hm, yes. And the thing is . . .

SHF: But you haven't lied. When's the last time you lied you think?

GR: I don't know. Uh, I, I been putting a lot a' stuff on the task force, not, not lyin'.

SHF: And . . .

GR: Uh, of, uh, of . . .

SHF: Now let's see, now see, okay, we had one good thing and that was findin' the human remains. What was the second good thing again?

GR: Getting it off my chest and getting the families to recognize the . . .

SHF: So that's that one. [Unintelligible.] What's the third good thing over the, the past six months? Is there another good thing?

GR: Um, I don't know what it is.

SHF: [Crosstalk, unintelligible word.]

GR: Uh, other than they took the death penalty off. That's all, but . . .

SHF: Um . . .

GR: Uh, we went . . .

SHF: That's a pretty big thing. I mean, I would think, right?

GR: That's a . . . pretty big thing, but uh, still, you know, it was the pre-pressure going into court, but I felt a lot less pressure afterwards.

SHF: You did a good job by the way, that day.

GR: Um-hm, thank you.

SHF: Yeah. That was prob'ly a lot of stress for you.

GR: Um-hm, yes.

SHF: Right?

GR: Um-hm, yes.

SHF: Were you, what were you worried about that day?

GR: Uh, mostly worried about you know, if I had chains on like before, of trippin' over myself, uh, makin' a fool of myself.

SHF: Yeah. You wanted to walk in there and be dignified in, in the way you presented your guilty pleas and [crosstalk unintelligible word].

GR: Uh, I didn't wanna uh, you know, break down and cry too much, and, and uh . . .

SHF: Did you feel like you were gonna do that?

GR: Several times, yes.

SHF: Why?

GR: Because through, through the points there was a lot of women that I killed there and certain of 'em st-stood out more . . .

SHF: Oh, the families?

GR: The families. And you know, in the background thinkin' somebody's gonna yell some'n or say some'n.

SHF: Yeah. Certain stood, certain stood out? Which . . .

GR: Certain, certain . . .

SHF: . . . which ones were those . . .

GR: Uh . . .

SHF: . . . that you were worried about that kinda brought some emotion to you? What were, which ones were those that day?

GR: Um, Abernathy.

SHF: Hm.

GR: Um, Naon.

SHF: Naon?

GR: Na-Naon.

SHF: Yeah.

GR: Uh, oh, it's . . . you know, um, let's see, and a couple other ones that was in there.

SHF: Do you remember their names?

GR: Um, well, the Mayham [sic], uh, because . . .

SHF: Meehan?

GR: Me-Meeham [sic], yeah.

SHF: Um-hm, yes.

GR: Um, and then not getting the ones that I did uh, kill, uh, Dottie, I think her name is.

SHF: Um-hm, yes.

GR: Uh, I call her the camper lady. The . . .

SHF: Now why did Abernathy strike some emotion with you that day?

GR: Uh, be-because, I don't . . . and uh, the one on Christmas Eve, uh, well, Jovina [sic, Jovita] Boulevard.

SHF: Right. Brockmann?

GR: Brockmann.

SHF: Um-hm, yes.

GR: Because uh, she was on Matthew's birthday.

SHF: Yeah.

GR: And New . . .

SHF: Matthew, your son?

GR: Um-hm, yes. And he, he was, she was uh, one of the ones I, I knew from almost front to the end, uh, where I picked her up . . .

SHF: Um-hm, yes.

GR: . . . where I killed her. But uh, it wasn't that I, I had to be told where she was.

SHF: What about Aber . . . uh, Abernathy?

GR: Abernathy?

SHF: Yeah, what about her? You said that, that's the first name you mentioned. Why does that . . .

GR: Well, it's, that was because that was uh, Matthew's birthday and uh . . .

SHF: Oh, okay. I thought you said Brockmann was on Matthew's birthday.

GR: No, uh, Brockmann was Christmas.

SHF: Oh, Brockmann's . . .

GR: Uh . . .

SHF: . . . Christmas, okay. So Abernathy, so these are dates that are important. Abernathy was on your son's birthday and that's why that kinda strikes some emotion with you?

GR: Um-hm, yes.

SHF: And then Naon was . . . ?

GR: Was Naon, was uh, the one I put a rock in her . . . um, just, just a beautiful, uh, young woman.

SHF: Yeah. Meehan.

GR: Meehan, uh, knowing now what I didn't know back then that she was pregnant. I, I didn't.

SHF: Yeah.

GR: So uh, that, that bothered me.

SHF: And Brockmann was on Christmas.

GR: Chr . . . Brockmann's on Christmas.

SHF: So, so you thought you might get emotional when those four names were read.

GR: Those, and other ones, yeah. I did get a little bit . . .

SHF: Yeah.

GR: . . . but I kept it back.

SHF: What other ones?

GR: Um, well, uh, the ones that weren't counted. Um, like uh, Keli.

SHF: McGinness?

GR: McGinness.

SHF: Um-hm, yes.

GR: Uh, April, which would . . . no, I think April was . . .

SHF: April Buttram?

GR: . . . was, but . . .

SHF: Yup.

GR: There was a, a, uh, the ones that weren't counted was, was I wanted, um, accountability for 'em, but we, we never found the bodies on those.

SHF: So you were a little nervous goin' into the courtroom?

GR: Yes.

SHF: 'Cause you thought you might hear some things from the family, there might be some shouting or there, or you were afraid you might fall and trip over the chain or some'n.

GR: Yeah, trip over the chains or some'n. That's why they took the chains off.

SHF: Uh-huh, yes.

GR: And um, everything went according to what the lawy . . . lawyer said, you know, the, what was gon . . . gon . . .

SHF: Um-hm, yes.

GR: And we went over [unintelligible couple words, crosstalk].

SHF: So you were, you were pleased with the way the hearing went that day?

GR: I think it went real good, yes.

SHF: Um-hm, yes. So uh, what do you think Thursday's gonna bring then? That's gonna be a [crosstalk, unintelligible word].

GR: Oh, I've read some, I've read some of the letters. I think there's uh, gonna be mixed emotions, but I think there's gonna be a, a lot of angry uh, families out there and it's gonna last a couple hours, uh, s- . . . five, six hours.

SHF: It'll last . . . yeah, could last all day.

GR: Yeah. I think we'll prob'ly go for uh, recess for lunch and come back.

SHF: Um-hm, yes.

GR: There's a lot of people wanna, wanna talk.

SHF: What do, what, what letters have you read? What do you mean?

GR: Just the ones that they went to the judge. They had some letters to go to the judge and uh, some of 'em I think might even been addressed to me.

SHF: Some families . . .

GR: Some families.

SHF: . . . have written the judge?

GR: Yes.

SHF: And, and you've been able to read those?

GR: Um-hm, yes.

SHF: What, what some of the letters say?

GR: Uh, some of 'em, uh, you know, called me a, you know, the evil and the devil, you know, and, and uh, Satan.

SHF: Um-hm, yes.

GR: Then he also called me uh . . .

SHF: What do you think about that?

GR: What I think about that?

SHF: Yeah.

GR: I think it's, I think it's true. Yeah, it . . . is.

SHF: You are, you are the devil?

GR: I've got, had the devil in me when I did it. And . . .

SHF: You are evil? Some people have described you as pure evil.

GR: And, yeah. Yeah. That's what he said in the notes, yeah.

SHF: Yeah.

GR: And lack of love, lack of uh, uh, in control.

SHF: Yeah.

GR: Um, didn't have remorse.

SHF: And you still don't have remorse.

GR: I, I have m . . . re-remorse.

SHF: You do?

GR: Yeah. Remorse for, for killin' those.

SHF: What does, what does that mean?

GR: Well, it means sadness in my heart, um, means um, sorry I killed these women. Uh . . .

SHF: What are you gonna do when they, when they get up and start to speak to you? And there will be a lot of anger, I can guarantee. What are you gonna do?

GR: There'll be a lot of anger, and prob'ly . . . I'm gonna prob'ly, I gotta take it in and uh, and be ready to answer whatever questions they have.

SHF: I don't think you're gonna be able to have a dialogue. I think they're gonna be able to talk to you. You may have a statement that you might present, I understand.

GR: Um-hm, yes.

SHF: But you're, I don't think you'll be allowed to talk back and forth.

GR: I, I . . .

SHF: It could be, but your attorneys may know better than that, but I don't think that'll be allowed.

GR: Then . . .

SHF: So you're just gonna have to sit there.

GR: I'm just gonna have to sit there. It would be nice to uh, answer their questions.

SHF: They prob'ly, any answer you gave them they wouldn't care about, don't you think?

GR: I, I think they would. I think they . . .

SHF: Well, what if somebody killed your son?

GR: I'd be ornery and, and mad about it.

SHF: Um-hm, yes. Would it matter what they said to ya, explaining why?

GR: It'd matter a little bit, but you know . . .

SHF: I killed your son because I'm evil.

GR: Evil, bad uh . . .

SHF: So please understand that, and thank you very much.

GR: Uh, it would . . .

SHF: Sorry, but I just had to do it because I'm the devil and I'm evil.

GR: Uh . . .

SHF: 'Cause they're not gonna wanna hear that . . .

GR: Uh, they won't.

SHF: . . . crap.

GR: Jus . . . but uh, it's not that. Uh, I thought they would be asking questions of, 'cause uh, I think there's one of the letters somewhere he said in the paper or some'n like that, that they were, they wanted to know why I killed their daughter or, or sister.

SHF: Yeah, why did ya?

GR: I had, I had . . .

SHF: I'd like to have an answer to that.

GR: . . . a craving to kill these women and . . .

SHF: Why?

GR: 'Cause they were prostitutes and um . . .

SHF: But why?

GR: Oh, just, jus', uh, just, just mad at 'em and wanted to kill 'em.

SHF: Why? Why were you mad at 'em?

GR: Oh, because of, uh, I wanted to be in control. I wanted to be in control and, and . . .

SHF: You can control things without killing people.

GR: I know, I know you can, but I . . . in that . . .

SHF: So why did you kill, that's the, and that's the million-dollar question, right? A lot of people askin' why . . .

GR: Well, be . . . because they were, they were . . .

SHF: . . . in the hell did he do it?

GR: Because they were . . .

SHF: Why did he do it?

GR: . . . uh, prostitutes, and I killed 'em because of, I wanted to kill 'em.

SHF: Why did you wanna kill 'em?

GR: Oh, I was mad at uh, women and prostitutes and . . .

SHF: Why?

GR: Oh, because I didn't uh, ju . . . uh, didn't wanna pay for sex and didn't want to uh, I was havin' all kinds of problems and, with my ex-wife.

SHF: All kinds, so you got all kinds of excuses why. Right?

GR: Um-hm, yes.

SHF: And they are excuses, aren't they, 'cause there's no r- . . . there's no reason that you'd give that could justify what you did.

GR: No.

SHF: No.

GR: There isn't, other, other than you killed 'em.

SHF: You killed 'em.

GR: Um-hm, yes.

SHF: You took somebody else's life.

GR: Um-hm, yes.

SHF: More than once.

GR: Um-hm, yes.

SHF: Yeah. But really they were garbage anyway, you've said that all along, how much they didn't mean anything to ya.

GR: I said, you know, that . . . at the time, yes. At the time, and, and then uh, I slowly taper . . . tapered off.

SHF: But today they, they, they have meaning for ya.

GR: They had meaning for me now. It's [unintelligible crosstalk].

SHF: So if you could go back right now, the things that you know and, and the change that's taken place in you, you would not do what you did. You still . . .

GR: I think I'd have to go all the way back to when I was uh, young and uh . . .

SHF: When you first stabbed the . . .

GR: When I first stabbed that boy.

SHF: . . . little boy.

GR: Uh, before that when I was prob'ly, should of went to that uh, I was supposed to go to Woodside, uh, Alternative School for retarded people.

SHF: Right. Um-hm, yes.

GR: And I think that would'a helped. Uh . . .

SHF: But you're not retarded.

GR: At the time I was, yeah. I, I couldn't . . .

SHF: So you don't, you, you don't change. I mean you're not retarded. You might have a learning disability but . . .

GR: I already had . . . at the time I had a really . . .

SHF: So did I.

GR: I had a really bad one and I didn't uh, I had to work . . . it took me years.

SHF: See what happened. You ended up being the serial killer and I ended up being the sheriff. What, what, what happened? We grew up in the same south end of the King County community here. How come you're the serial killer and I'm the sheriff? Some'n had to happen.

GR: Uh, uh, I chose to be a serial killer, I guess. That's all I, all I can say.

SHF: When did you do that? When did you decide to do, to be the serial killer?

GR: I thought it was in the, in the '80s. But everybody says it's gotta be in the '60s and, and the '70s that I killed. Uh . . .

SHF: Well, you know that's true though, too. You're just trying to, I mean you know it's true and you killed in the '60s or the '70s, but you just don't remember . . .

GR: I don't know of any.

SHF: . . . but you just don't remember.

GR: Uh, I don't remember killing anybody in the '60s and '70s. I had a, a lot of [unintelligible words].

SHF: But you stabbed somebody.

GR: I stabbed one boy, yes.

SHF: Right. So you didn't just stop there and go, Oh, that was interesting, and then in 1982, killed Wendy Coffield?

GR: No, I, I killed uh . . .

SHF: That certainly didn't make sense.

GR: No, I, I killed a lady in '8- . . . uh, '80 to '81.

SHF: Yeah, I remember you talked about . . . you know, I watched uh, almost three months of these interviews.

GR: Um-hm, yes.

SHF: I was sittin' in the other room there kinda watchin' things.

GR: Um-hm, yes.

SHF: So . . .

GR: Yeah, that, I, you know, that, that's what your job is to, to watch.

SHF: Yeah. Yeah. Uh, so what's another good thing in the last six months?

GR: Last six months? Well, the trial went okay. The uh, uh, after that I think I found another couple, at least one more body, I think. Yeah, at least one.

SHF: After the plea?

GR: After the plea, yes.

SHF: I don't think there's been any other remains found after the plea.

GR: Oh, not any re-re- . . . uh, yes. You had uh, not uh, the one at 18 . . . 188 . . . 178th and uh . . .

SHF: 188th and Military.

GR: Yes.

SHF: Goocher? Kurran?

GR: I don't know. Uh, well, 188th . . .

SHF: Yeah, [unintelligible word].

GR: Yeah, that one of the f- . . . the stuff in her vagina, the washing out her vagina, and I forget what I put into her. That was Kurran. But there was one at 178th and I-5, we just talked about . . .

SHF: Oh, yeah?

GR: . . . two days ago.

SHF: Um-hm, yes.

GR: And I can't remember . . .

SHF: But we didn't find anything there. Right?

GR: No. You found a, you found a body there back in . . .

SHF: I mean after the plea, there's not been any other remains found.

GR: No, I don't think so.

SHF: Right. You know, we were kinda lookin' forward to another six months, you know, that we saw the plea date uh, coming . . .

GR: Um-hm, yes.

SHF: . . . and now it's gone. The judge gave us six months to continue to talk but . . .

GR: Um-hm, yes.

SHF: . . . but in the last, since the plea hearing, and I've talked to the, the detectives and uh, from what they're tellin' me is that you, you've uh, just totally shut down in giving them any real information. It's been all a bunch of bullshit.

GR: They're, I, I th- . . . I think most of the, is because where there's . . . there's no more uh, bodies. We got up to s- . . . in the sixties and then we, it's kinda tapered off.

SHF: Well, they tend to believe that since you've pled guilty and you're about to be sentenced to life in prison, that there's no more incentive for you to talk or to be honest with them about . . .

GR: No, it's not that. It's, it's uh . . .

SHF: Why would you tell anything now?

GR: Why? I gotta be, be [unintelligible].

SHF: Because you're already, I mean you're already goin' . . .

GR: Uh . . .

SHF: We can't prove those though. You're already goin' to prison for life, so why would you even, why would you talk to us at all?

GR: Because I, I wanna, I wanna get all these things out, and I wanna make sure that all . . .

SHF: Haven't you had a nice place to stay back there?

GR: I had a nice place to stay, but you know, I wanted to make sure everything's, uh, uh, everything's done before I leave.

SHF: So you never mentioned the, the . . . I, I don't think, you never really mentioned that one of the good things is that you're not goin', you're not going to be put to death.

GR: Yeah, I know that. But there's still that chance . . .

SHF: That's not the important piece for you.

GR: There's a real important one because uh, there's one in 2000.

SHF: Do you wanna live?

GR: I wanna live and get this out of me, yes.

SHF: But even after that, I mean do you have a desire to continue to live . . .

GR: Yes.

SHF: . . . in this world? Why?

GR: Well, in case I find any other b-bodies that, that I [unintelligible].

SHF: How you gonna do that in prison?

GR: Th . . . uh, thinkin' about it. Uh, some'n be in the news, some'n, read some'n about it. Uh . . .

SHF: And some'n would jog your memory?

GR: Yeah, if they'd find a . . .

SHF: And then, and then what will you do?

GR: I'd get in touch with the lawyers and talk, talk, you know, because yeah, I'll prob'ly get the paper over there or somebody will, and I'll get information to my lawyers if there's some'n comes up. If it's one of mine, it, you know, the, they're, I still have that one in 2001 that's supposed to be, that one of the jewelry I can't, I don't remember killing her. That's still . . .

SHF: So, so you would be . . .

GR: . . . is gonna be on my mind so I think, I think maybe possibly next year they, it's possible because I didn't tell 'em where I kill her, how I kill her, and because the jewelry ended up at work, that I might get charged again.

SHF: But we're not gonna drive over there just, you know, on, and get . . . and get more bologna. You know? More bullshit.

GR: No, you're not.

SHF: We wanna come and visit ya, we want to know that you've really got something . . .

GR: Correct.

SHF: . . . substantial to share, right?

GR: Correct.

SHF: Right. So . . .

GR: If some'n comes up on these other ones, what I put in the vagina, what, where I locate, where I found the body, I don't have to . . . Those are already, I don't have to have you guys come over. This would be one I already said I did kill. I'd say to Mark or Todd by letter or phone that I found, I just realize where I uh, put the lady in the baseball uniform . . . where I found her. And I wouldn't have to have them come over. It'd be just a word from me to them . . .

SHF: Hm. But what's the . . .

GR: . . . and go over there . . .

SHF: . . . good things that, would you say that one of the good things that's happened here is that you've made some uh, relationships. You've built some relationships with some people over the past six months?

GR: The, the guards and stuff, yeah, and . . .

SHF: The guards?

GR: . . . and guards and . . .

SHF: What about the detectives that have come in and, and visited?

GR: I've built a, a, it was a, it was the touchy uh, up-an'-down feelings with 'em, you know, because we've been through uh, hell together, all of us.

SHF: Yeah.

GR: You know, my . . .

SHF: What do you mean by that, you've been through hell together?

GR: Yeah, because of me givin', first comin' in here and lyin' all this time, and then, and then comin' out with the different personality. The, the uh, uh . . .

SHF: It's been intense in here sometimes.

GR: It's been tense in here, yes.

SHF: Right. Because they want the truth from ya.

GR: They want . . .

SHF: . . . it's been hard to drag that out of you.

GR: It's n-not the truth, but some of the things I just don't think it's, you know, like I told 'em before, there's some of the things that I didn't think that anything, some things didn't uh, come out because I didn't think some of it didn't matter, or I put the . . .

SHF: But you let us be the judge of that.

GR: . . . [unintelligible] on it.

SHF: Don't you think?

GR: Yes.

222   **I, MONSTER**

SHF: Or at least think we should be the judge of that?

GR: Um-hm, yes.

SHF: Yeah.

GR: And it takes me sometimes to go back in my room and come back the next day and [unintelligible word].

SHF: Right. I've wa—I've watched that. Have you, the detectives that come in, uh, so you'd be willing to talk to them even though it's been kinda rocky at times, that you know, you'd be willing to talk to any of those detectives if they came . . .

GR: Um-hm, yes.

SHF: . . . to uh, to where you end up?

GR: Um-hm, yes.

SHF: And be honest with them?

GR: Be honest with 'em, yes.

SHF: Um-hm, yes.

GR: There, there will be some, there will be some . . . cases that'll come up that they need to talk to me about.

SHF: There'll be a lot of people that wanna come and talk to you.

GR: Um-hm, yes. And there'll be a lot of people.

SHF: Who do you think will, might, might wanna come and visit with you?

GR: I think uh, uh, Pierce County might come. Uh, Snohomish . . .

SHF: Pierce County Sheriffs, Snohomish County Sheriff's Office?

GR: [Mumble] yeah.

SHF: Yup.

GR: And I can talk to them, and . . .

SHF: Why would they come?

GR: Oh, because uh, uh, you know, they might have some bodies down there they wanna ask questions about.

SHF: Yeah.

GR: And I'm, I'm willing to talk to any of 'em. That's fine with me.

SHF: Right. Why would you think they might have some bodies up there?

GR: Oh, because they've, you know, I've read, read things in the paper about bodies down there and . . .

SHF: Have you had access to newspapers here while you've been here?

GR: A few of 'em here and there, but mostly I had the newspaper at the jail for uh, three months, so I got a chance . . . and then there always was one floating around. I'd be uh, first on the list with mine. I read my articles, take out my articles, throw 'em out.

SHF: Oh, so you were kinda savin' your, your articles?

GR: I jus' didn't want any other inmates to read 'em.

SHF: Did you put that, did you save, do you still have those?

GR: No, I threw 'em in the garbage. I didn't, I didn't . . .

SHF: You didn't save those?

GR: No, I just tore 'em out because I didn't want the inmates reading oh, Ridgway's doin' this . . .

SHF: Oh, oh . . .

GR: . . . and Ridgway's doin' that.

SHF: I see.

GR: And I gave it to Burns and he'd take his ad out.

SHF: Oh.

GR: Threw 'em in the garbage, uh, and then 'cause . . .

SHF: Are you gettin' fan mail yet?

GR: I don't, uh, I got some mail, but I don't remember what it was from. Uh . . .

SHF: You know what I mean, don't you, fa-fan mail . . .

GR: Yeah, I mean fan mail and . . .

SHF: . . . because you're pretty famous right now.

GR: Um-hm, yes. And everybody wants, I've read one I think or two things, but that's about it.

SHF: It kinda made me famous too. Did you know that?

GR: Um-hm, yes.

SHF: You did?

GR: Yeah, I, uh, read articles in the, in the jail about it when I was in jail.

SHF: Yeah. But even after the plea, you know, it's got . . . the detectives are pretty famous too.

GR: Um-hm, yes, detectives are pretty famous. Uh, I can overhear some of the times when they were in, we went to make the plea that they were contacted by the uh, some of 'em were contacted by the news media and . . .

SHF: Um-hm, yes.

GR: . . . and they gave statements. I don't know what it, what it was, but I just overheard 'em.

SHF: So you'd be willing to talk to the Snohomish, Pierce County detectives if they came through and they worked through your lawyers?

GR: Yes, definitely. Um-hm, yes.

SHF: Um-hm, yes. What about other, other people who you think might [crosstalk, couple words].

GR: I think maybe San Diego would be fine to have 'em come up. Um . . .

SHF: San Diego?

GR: San Diego because, you know, 'cause my ex-wife was down in San Diego.

SHF: Yeah.

GR: The news also said uh, when I got arrested I, you know, pulled out some of the articles that said uh, it's just like a mirror image of what's happened down in, in San Diego, some reporters.

SHF: Oh, yeah, that was a long time ago, yeah.

GR: Um-hm, yes. In '82.

SHF: Yeah, I think they solved most of those cases.

GR: And so they might still wanna come up and talk to me.

SHF: Hm. So what are some bad things that have happened in the last six months here?

GR: Uh, just a little, you know, confron- . . . uh, sometimes with some of the detectives havin' uh, uh, not . . . tryin' to get information that I don't have to give 'em, you know? Uh . . .

SHF: What happened?

GR: Uh, they leave angry. Sometimes they leave angry.

SHF: They leave angry?

GR: Yeah.

SHF: Did you blame 'em? Could you blame 'em?

GR: No, I don't blame 'em because I don't.

SHF: Did you ever leave here angry?

GR: Uh, prob'ly a little bit, but not much.

SHF: How'd you, how did you show your anger?

GR: I didn't show it.

SHF: Right.

GR: No.

SHF: Why not?

GR: 'Cause I try to hold back my anger.

SHF: Why?

GR: Uh, because it doesn't do me any good, you know. I go back to my . . . and I can't sleep. I can't.

SHF: Yeah. So that's one bad thing. You got the, you got the detectives frustrated so they got . . .

GR: Uh, I got . . .

SHF: Are you kinda proud about that though?

GR: I'm not proud. I'm proud in the little ways because they don't believe me.

SHF: Yeah. Why?

GR: And especially with the, like the last three cases, that there's always some'n missing, li-like Ware.

SHF: What, why were you proud? Why are you proud?

GR: Because they don't, because they don't believe me.

SHF: Yeah.

GR: And I'm givin' 'em what the, my paper says . . .

SHF: What they want?

GR: . . . is to give all information about victims. And I give it to 'em and it, and it's . . . and every one was, every person up on that list and every, almost every person up on that list there, there's always some'n I haven't given 'em.

SHF: Why would that make you proud?

GR: Because they don't believe me. Because . . .

SHF: So you've been, you kinda tricked 'em?

GR: Not, not tricked 'em, no. Not make, it's not make me proud, it's because they don't, they don't believe me. It's not proud, but I, I've already told 'em that out of all the seventy women, only about ten of 'em I know where I picked 'em up and, and that is a big thing. I picked up four hundred, five hundred women, some'n like . . .

SHF: What, what are some other bad things?

GR: Uh, some of the things that I did to the women. I don't remember, like you know, posing 'em and posing for, for me . . .

SHF: Within the last, just in the last six months, during your stay here.

GR: Just little things that come up, that I, I don't remember what I did with the bodies and when it, when it comes up it, it uh, backfires on me. Not backfires, but you know, it . . . I don't remember where it is, and I put some'n in a, in a woman's vagina. Uh, you know, and . . .

SHF: So it's bad you couldn't remember.

GR: I couldn't remember it, yeah.

SHF: What about your stay here though? How was your, how was your stay?

GR: My stay has been real, real good here.

SHF: Well . . .

GR: They tr-treat me really good. Uh, uh, they, they treat me r-really good. Um, it's been, it's been real good.

SHF: That's gonna change, you know?

GR: Oh, I know it's gonna change. I know . . .

SHF: How do you think it's gonna change?

GR: Well, I'm gonna go back to jail and it's gonna be a, kind of a meeting before I go to the prison, and prison. I gotta go down to um, Shelton for uh, six weeks or a month or whatever it's supposed to be, and then go over to W- . . . uh, Walla Walla or whatever. And it's gonna be uh, it's gonna be uh, back noisy and rough and . . .

SHF: Yeah.

GR: Um-hm, yes.

SHF: There's some tough characters in that joint.

GR: Um-hm, yes.

SHF: You're not worried about that?

GR: In some ways I'm not, no. I'm, I'm gettin' worried about it, yes, but there's uh . . .

SHF: How you gonna handle twenty-three hours in the cell every day for the rest of your life?

GR: Uh, I'll prob'ly read. Uh . . .

SHF: That's a lot of books.

GR: Um-hm, yes. I . . . I had like seven or eight books in my room the, brand-new books and I haven't even read. They'll have to go all the way home and I'll order some more.

SHF: You know you're not gonna get the same kind of treatment there as you, as you got here?

GR: No. It's gonna be a lot less treatment here, there than here—than even in jail.

SHF: Um-hm, yes. That doesn't bother you?

GR: No. Uh, I get a . . .

SHF: 'Cause we know [unintelligible crosstalk].

GR: . . . I got to . . .

SHF: I'm gonna go back to this again. We, we've been together now, you've been here for six months.

GR: Um-hm, yes.

SHF: Nearly six months, and after the plea we thought we were lookin' forward to another six months of us talking if you could continue to provide us with information that we could verify.

GR: Um-hm, yes.

SHF: And what's happened is you've not done that and so the, the sentencing date now has been moved up. So what that means is for you is that you'll no longer be housed here.

GR: Um-hm, yes.

SHF: After Thursday, you're gone.

GR: Right.

SHF: You're out of here.

GR: I know that.

SHF: And you're on your way to prison. You could've had another five months here, staying here, talking to the detectives, uh, if you had continued to provide information, accurate information that we could verify and, and uh, and use. But you've not done that. Why not?

GR: It's because . . . why? Because I've ran out of . . .

SHF: No, I don't want . . . no.

GR: No.

SHF: Why not? You know that when we first put this together . . .

GR: Um-hm, yes.

SHF: . . . and we heard that you were going to make an agreement, what we heard were numbers up to sixty, and now it's sixty to seventy.

GR: Seventy-one. Seventy-one.

SHF: So, and, and I've heard you say in some of the interviews early on that, well, maybe it's only thirty, could be forty. Then it went to fifty to sixty, from the fifty, sixty in the early days. Now it's up to sixty, seventy, now it's seventy-one. Now you know an exact number. And my point is, Gary, what are we supposed to believe? I mean you've gone from thirty to sixty-one, you plead guilty to forty-eight, we know there's more than forty-eight. You know there's more . . .

GR: Um-hm, yes.

SHF: . . . than forty-eight.

GR: Yes.

SHF: You've given us the number seventy-one.

GR: Yes.

SHF: If you had continued to provide us with accurate information, you would be staying here continuing to help us in this place that has, it's a much better facility than where you're about to head.

GR: Correct.

SHF: Now, I'm the sheriff. You know that.

GR: Um-hm, yes.

SHF: I was a detective back in the '80s, uh, and, and working this case, and you know that too. This is an important case to me. Sentencing is happening on Thursday.

GR: Um-hm, yes.

SHF: The sheriff has certain things that he can and can't do. There's some, uh, power that I do have. I'm not sure I can get the sentencing date changed. But if you were to start to talk to us today or tomorrow and you gave us information that is absolutely accurate information, we may be able to keep you here longer and talk before you go off to prison. Eventually you'll go to prison.

GR: Um-hm, yes.

SHF: But you could have another five months here, but you've got to provide us with that accurate information. And uh, I'm under, my understanding is that you're not willing to do that. That the information that you're giving is the same old, you know, round the mulberry bush kind of stuff. You know what that means? You're runnin' us in circles.

GR: Yeah, running in circles, but it is, it is . . .

SHF: We're tired of that.

GR: It is true about those, like I only remember about ten women uh, that, I picked up like four, maybe five hundred women.

SHF: Yeah.

GR: Only know ten women where, that are on the list and of where I picked 'em up. And that's one of the things, where I killed the, uh, I put the woman in the street, I don't remember where. I figured she was alive.

SHF: Well . . .

GR: There's other ones like that, I don't remember what I put in their vaginas. I know I killed 'em. I don't know where. And, and I think, I, I'm thinkin' right down to . . .

SHF: See, you and I had quite a talk. You remember the talk we had? It was over, it wasn't a, a full three days, but it was over a three-day period . . .

GR: Um-hm, yes.

SHF: . . . that you and I talked?

GR: Um-hm, yes.

SHF: And uh, uh, you remember what we talked about?

GR: Yes.

SHF: What?

GR: You, you wanted me to see if I could give you a, a, a, a fresh um, uh, body somewhere, and I couldn't.

SHF: That was one.

GR: One.

SHF: I said tell me that one thing, right?

GR: Um-hm, yes.

SHF: Okay. You never called me back, so I imagine that that didn't happen.

GR: That happened later, but not then.

SHF: Um-hm, yes.

GR: I don't know what, what, what, how many I had at the time when I talked to ya, but it's gone up.

SHF: What else did we talk about?

GR: We talked about um, you know, a little bit about uh, uh, me goin' to ja—prison, and uh . . .

SHF: Right.

GR: . . . about the p-people down there.

SHF: And we talked, there was some cases that we talked about. We talked about the, the Kurran case, and . . .

GR: The Kurran case. What I, what I put in the . . .
SHF: What you put inside her.
GR: Um-hm, yes.
SHF: And we went on with that discussion for quite some time.
GR: Yes, we did.
SHF: And you denied, denied, and denied having any involvement in that.
GR: I did deny, yeah.
SHF: And you denied putting anything in anyone's vagina. You denied using knives and that kind of, those kinds of instruments or tools.
GR: Um-hm, yes.
SHF: But now you're saying you did Kurran. See how, what are we supposed to believe?
GR: Um-hm, yes. Well, after seein' the site and after . . .
SHF: 'Cause you lied to me that day.
GR: I th-I thou- . . . and I told you I thought, I told you I thought she was shot, and she was in the parking lot by the motel behind, on the . . .
SHF: And Agisheff was supposedly shot, right? And you said you didn't do her.
GR: I didn't do her, no.
SHF: And then we talked about the lady behind the Fred Meyer who had her . . .
GR: Yeah.
SHF: . . . skull bashed in.
GR: Skull, yeah.
SHF: And that's where you hid your condoms, right?
GR: Yeah.
SHF: And you said you didn't do her.
GR: I didn't do her, no.
SHF: And I don't believe that. But what am I . . .
GR: Uh . . .
SHF: . . . supposed to believe? See, and that's the one thing.
GR: Uh . . .
SHF: . . . that you, you've not been able to uh, especially since you pled guilty to forty-eight, uh, do you think you've changed . . .
GR: I think I . . .
SHF: . . . in the last six months?
GR: Yeah, I've changed.
SHF: What, what has changed?
GR: Been open up on all the, the women I killed.
SHF: Not all of 'em.

GR: All, every one I could remember.

SHF: 'Cause, 'cause [crosstalk, unintelligible] only been, but, we've only been able to plea guilty to forty-eight.

GR: We pled guilty to f-forty-eight, but I showed you uh, on maps about where other women were.

SHF: Um-hm, yes.

GR: And there is no, no bodies because of the animals takin' 'em away. And when you did, took you about a week or so to find uh, just two bones. And that one there, remember on that one especially that the, we went over it and I thought it was, there was uh, it was clear-cut and I said there was bushes in here or some'n like that. And uh, they showed me a picture a month or two before it was taken.

SHF: Yeah, I know. I remember all that, yeah.

GR: And I denied, uh, that uh, I thought I went through brush to get there, but that also was the same thing [crosstalk, unintelligible].

SHF: But it hasn't changed.

GR: Have I changed?

SHF: Since the, yeah, in the six months that you've been here.

GR: I've changed a lot, yes.

SHF: Yeah. In, in what way?

GR: I've given up seventy-one, uh, bodies.

SHF: Well, we don't see it that way.

GR: I, all I can do is give you what I agreed on. I agreed on givin' up the bodies. If they're not there . . .

SHF: Do you think you changed after the plea?

GR: No. I been still trying to figure out any more.

SHF: What, what has changed for you after you pled guilty to forty-eight murders? What's changed for you?

GR: Well, they took the death penalty off.

SHF: Yeah. No, what . . . you, for you personally?

GR: And for me . . .

SHF: Your . . .

GR: I've been trying to figure out where more bodies are. And by them showing me pictures or going out some place, that helps a lot, and I'm still . . . number one is that woman with the jewelry in 2001 that I can't figure out where she is. That's . . .

SHF: So after the plea though, I'm told that you, that you've changed a little bit. People in here have noticed a change in your, uh, in your behavior, in the way you act.

GR: Well, uh . . .

SHF: I can kinda see it.

GR: Well, the . . .

SHF: I see a change in you from the, the last time that you and I talked [crosstalk, unintelligible].

GR: There, there is a, there is a change. I'm, I'm . . .

SHF: What's the change?

GR: I'm upset because, not . . .

SHF: You're upset?

GR: I'm upset about that I can't remember where I picked up those women and what I put in their vaginas. And, and still . . .

SHF: So that's the change? What's the change? I, I, I see a change in, in you today as I talk to you right now. There's some'n different about you.

GR: I'm nervous about that, that uncharged, that, that jewelry . . . they, and that's what bothers me. I'm, I'm afraid . . .

SHF: Why?

GR: . . . because when I go through the court here, go through all the sentencing, next year sometime they'll bring me back in to charge me with one count of first-degree murder of some lady in 2001.

SHF: And then what?

GR: We're gonna go right back to court to, I don't know . . .

SHF: And you could be . . .

GR: Could be, could be, uh . . .

SHF: . . . could be put to death for that.

GR: Could be the death, yeah.

SHF: So that bothers you.

GR: That bothers me. And it's, it's, it's hangin' over my sh-shoulder, ev-every bit of the day.

SHF: But I, I've noticed a, a change in you, and I've only—from the last time that you and I talked, I mean I've only been here now oh, maybe about an hour . . . talking to you.

GR: Uh, I don't, I don't know what it is. [Unintelligible.]

SHF: You, you seem a lot more cocky to me, a little more . . .

GR: I'm, I'm, I'm gonna be cocky because of the, the three that I can't find out where, and they're, they uh, things about them that . . .

SHF: Do you, you know what that means, cocky?

GR: Yeah, it means that, uh, it means that I'm . . .

SHF: You've got an attitude.

GR: . . . bolder.

SHF: Bolder, yeah. You got an attitude about you.

GR: Um-hm, yes.

SHF: I think so. Do you, you . . .

GR: It might be a little bit of an attitude about the ones I can't . . . and I

don't wanna take credit for it, but they're not, you know, they don't uh, I, I would at least . . . I'd at least have 'em say well, you're number one suspect of that cr-crime.

SHF: Um-hm, yes.

GR: We have nobody else, and I wanna make sure they know that yes, I did it. You're . . . and it's a waste of their time to try to put it on another person.

SHF: Yeah.

GR: That is my woman I killed. I don't know the information. I don't know information on, on uh, the, the river victims. I don't know where I picked 'em up—where I killed any of them. I could guess. There's six, fi- . . . six, actually six.

SHF: Um-hm.

GR: The one over at Cottonwood Park as I'd call, uh, uh, the cluster.

SHF: Right. Right.

GR: I don't know where I killed . . .

SHF: Winston.

GR: . . . any of 'em. Winston.

SHF: Yeah.

GR: It doesn't, and it's the same thing, I don't know where I killed the baseball lady. I don't know where I killed the woman in the street.

SHF: Right.

GR: And I'm not, uh, I'm cocky about that 'cause I wanna take credit for it—even if they'd come up and say, you're number one suspect, and that. You say it but we're, we got a problem here. So, and uh, seventy-one is what I've come up with.

SHF: Maybe you're inflating your numbers because you wanna be known as . . .

GR: No.

SHF: . . . the most . . . no?

GR: No.

SHF: The only way that would happen, you know, that you'd be known as the most prolific would be for us to prove those others . . .

GR: Um-hm, yes.

SHF: . . . above the forty-eight. So if we had something from you that could give us seventy-one, I mean, there's no one that can touch that number, but you would have to give us accurate information again for us to follow up on that we could actually prove that you are the one who committed those crimes. We can't take your word for it.

GR: Um-hm, yes.

SHF: That is not how, uh, we do business.

GR: I know it.

SHF: That's not how the King County Sheriff's Office works.

GR: Um-hm, yes.

SHF: So I mean you, it's possible you could stay here a longer time and continue to talk to us, but not if you don't give us the, the stuff we need 'cause I mean I could, I could go talk to some people today and see if we can get that handled.

GR: Um-hm, yes.

SHF: But I'm not gonna do that if you're gonna contin- . . . 'cause my detectives are frustrated. They've talked to 'em, or since the plea . . .

GR: Um-hm, yes.

SHF: In fact they're more than frustra-frustrated. They're pissed. They're PISSED. They're tired of your crap. They're tired of your bullshit. They're tired of your lies. They're tired of your attitude now since the plea because you've not been cooperative. You, the cockiness, the sense is, is that you're walkin' around, you're thinkin' uh, "I did what I needed to do. I told only that information that I, that I needed to tell, and I have all these other secrets hidden deep inside me, which we know you do, and uh, and I'm not gonna tell those." And of course one of those you and I have talked about, uh, and you didn't mention it because it's a very, very sore subject for you, and that is the, the souvenirs. And man, I'll tell ya, if, if you really wanted to gain some, some credibility, let us know where that is and we'll go get it.

GR: There, there, there won't be any souvenirs. I told you where they were.

SHF: I know what you said. I know what you said.

GR: And uh, I [crosstalk] it out at . . .

SHF: But I don't believe it.

GR: Yeah.

SHF: I don't believe you for a second.

GR: Um-hm, yes. Well, like I said . . .

SHF: You got souvenirs and I'm gonna find 'em.

GR: Like I said . . .

SHF: You don't remember, I don't know if you, did you see *Manhunt Live* back when we did that documentary?

GR: No. I di-don't think . . .

SHF: You remember the, the Patrick Duffy, I think it was 1988 maybe . . .

GR: Um-hm, yes.

SHF: Two hour, you mentioned it I know in one of your interviews that we did a two-hour . . .

GR: I think somebody had a, Duffy [unintelligible].

SHF: Yeah, you're . . .

GR: But I don't know if I saw it.

SHF: At, well, at the end of that I . . . I looked into the TV camera and they tur- . . . they ended the program this way and I said, "Whoever you are, Green River Killer, we will catch you, just believe that. We will catch you." Whether you saw it or not . . .

GR: Um-hm, yes.

SHF: . . . I meant it then and guess what . . .

GR: You caught me.

SHF: . . . and here you are, right?

GR: Um-hm, yes.

SHF: Well, I'm tellin' you today that we're gonna find those souvenirs because we have a lot of searches to do yet.

GR: Yes, you do.

SHF: And we're gonna find those things. You know, we're x-raying some homes, and then we're doin' some other things too.

GR: Yeah, like I s- . . . like I told you before . . .

SHF: If I find those ext- . . . if I find those souvenirs and there's other bodies in there, I'm gonna come back.

GR: You, you, like I told you . . .

SHF: You think this is funny?

GR: No. I, I think this is, is, it's ridiculous for you . . . that, that house over on 288th where I killed, 218th where I killed . . .

SHF: Yeah.

GR: . . . a lot of the women.

SHF: Right?

GR: That house is up for sale, so you can have it.

SHF: But I don't want it.

GR: Yeah. There could be, there [unintelligible] . . .

SHF: I don't want it. Do you want it?

GR: No, I don't want it.

SHF: Why don't you want it? You're not gonna be livin' in it.

GR: Because they're building a freeway there and it's gonna be up for sale.

SHF: Oh, really.

GR: The neighbors told my wife, my . . .

SHF: Oh.

GR: And, and then you can, you can tear apart the other houses and you will not find not one shred of any jewelry or any clothes.

SHF: Um-hm, yes.

GR: And uh, that's a, a quote . . . a, a major quote.

SHF: That's a major quote?

GR: Major quote that you wo-won't find any jewelry, no, nothin' of, of anybody's.

SHF: Not there.

GR: It's not there because it's not anywhere. It's down at Kenworth, and at uh, at those sites where I told you.

SHF: The photographs you took at, at the river of Mills, Chapman, and Hinds.

GR: Yes, I tore. Yes, th- . . . four of 'em.

SHF: I know you said you, you tore 'em up, yeah.

GR: Tore 'em up, yes.

SHF: And the, and the notes that . . .

GR: You won't find 'em.

SHF: . . . the notes that you took . . .

GR: When, when you, when you . . .

SHF: . . . I won't find 'em.

GR: You won't find 'em. When you come, when get through with your x-rays, you know, you, uh, and everything—there'd prob'ly be a note in the paper and, and uh, I'll, I'll uh, hear about it 'cause you, you won't—they'll come up with zero. There's n-nothin' you can find. There's not, not in any parks. It's not in anyplace else. That's where I put 'em. That's, it's still possessions. I know where they're at. They were given away at Kenworth in the bathrooms and stuff.

SHF: Oh, yeah, I heard that story.

GR: And that's where uh, that's where you'll find 'em and the, and the four sites I told you about. And you will not find any photographs. You won't find any. I think you might find at, at the time even you were out lookin', you might'a found a tore-up uh, driver's license in the, in the road.

SHF: Um-hm, yes.

GR: And on, on the way out to 410 or down the hill . . . uh, maybe possibly one piece could be still around there someplace. But I don't, I don't think nothing—be swept up by the sweepers by now.

SHF: So you're pretty much in a, in . . .

GR: I'm, I'm a 100 percent, I'm a 100 percent sure that you're not gonna find anything.

SHF: Um-hm, yes.

GR: And no f- . . . none of those because they're no, no longer there. They're in the spots where I told you, and at Kenworth.

SHF: They're not in the spots where you talked about because we went out and searched there.

GR: Because they were, they were easy for them, they . . . uh, uh, be picked up and they're under cement now. One of 'em is.

SHF: One of 'em is, yeah.

GR: Um-hm, yes.

SHF: But the other areas we searched, there was nothing there.

GR: There was nothing because it was, it was out in the open. Was by that uh, a-a-a ha- . . . a half a block away, less than half a block away from, from where I killed uh, Kurran—or put her body there.

SHF: Um-hm, yes.

GR: Was right up the street from there. They're all, they, all this stuff comes together.

SHF: [Crosstalk, few words] Well, just continue to . . .

GR: Yeah.

SHF: . . . keep on workin' on that because I don't believe you.

GR: Um-hm, yes. Yeah, you, you won't find anything.

SHF: Yeah. Are you mad at me?

GR: No, I'm not. I'm . . .

SHF: Why not?

GR: . . . I'm a little bit upset about you still goin' back to the jewelry, but . . .

SHF: Why?

GR: Because that's a major thing you want, that you want the jewelry to . . .

SHF: No, I don't really care about the jewelry.

GR: N- . . . but they're . . . I'm, like I'm tellin', I don't know . . .

SHF: [Crosstalk, a word.]

GR: They got pissed off when I told 'em the places and they were not, they were very upset when they didn't find any.

SHF: Right. Yeah, they should'a been.

GR: They should'a been.

SHF: Yeah.

GR: That's when I put it down there and I, I didn't go back. I just put it down there and, and left it.

SHF: Uh-huh, yes.

GR: And there's places I knew, I drove by and see 'em. Always remember 'em. They were in my possession. I don't, I didn't care if they were, if somebody found 'em.

SHF: Okay. So you don't have, right now today, you don't have anything new to tell us right, right now.

GR: Other than, other than, I don't know if I get a chance to talk to the one on 180 . . . 178th.

SHF: No. But know what's gonna happen right now? I'm the last person you're gonna talk to.

GR: Um-hm, yes.

SHF: This is it right now.

GR: Okay.

SHF: Nobody's talkin' to you today, nobody's gonna talk to you tomorrow . . .

GR: Um-hm, yes.

SHF: Uh, we'll see ya in, in court on Thursday, and then you're gone.

GR: Um-hm, yes.

SHF: That's, that's what's gonna happen. That's why I'm here today.

GR: Um-hm, yes.

SHF: To, to bring this to, this interview process is, is ended.

GR: Yeah, whi-which it should of been.

SHF: We're done talkin'.

GR: Yeah.

SHF: You're not gonna be talkin' to Tom, not gonna be talkin' to Sue.

GR: Um-hm, yes.

SHF: You're not gonna be talkin' to Randy, not gonna be talkin' to Jon or any of the other, any of the other detectives.

GR: Um-hm, yes.

SHF: Period.

GR: Right.

SHF: And you're gonna follow the directions and instructions of those security guys just as you have been over the past, uh . . .

GR: Um-hm, yes.

SHF: . . . six months.

GR: Um-hm, yes.

SHF: When they tell ya to jump, you jump.

GR: Um-hm, yes.

SHF: You might as well practice that because that's what's gonna happen in prison. When they tell ya it's time to go to, it's time to eat, you stand up and you take your food and you eat. When it's time to turn your plate in, you turn your plate in, you sit back down and you wait for the next meal. When they tell ya it's time to take a shower, you take a shower. When it's time to go out in the yard, then you go out in the yard. When it's time to come back, they put you back in your cell.

GR: Um-hm, yes.

SHF: When it's time to go to sleep they turn out your light. When it's time to wake up, they turn the light back on again. That's, that's your life for the next whatever.

GR: Um-hm, yes.

SHF: That's it, period. It ends today.

GR: Um-hm, yes.

SHF: So all the, the perks that you've enjoyed here, uh, will no longer exist.

GR: I know that. I know that. I've already talked to the . . .

SHF: So . . .

GR: . . . people from prison. They already told me what, what's gonna happen.

SHF: Um-hm, yes.

GR: They were a little bit, uh, more, more of a, a harsher than, you know, they were more on, yeah, uh, for somebody like me, I'd keep your back to the wall and uh . . .

SHF: Why is that?

GR: Oh, because of, I got pro- . . . I got a lot of emories [sic] in there, prob'ly a, a . . .

SHF: Enemies.

GR: Ene- . . . I'll have a lot more enemies in there.

SHF: Why?

GR: Well, 'cause of the number of women I killed, plus a lot of people don't like guys killin' women. There are a lot of pimps.

SHF: You're not gonna be a very popular person.

GR: No, I won't be any popular at all.

SHF: Somebody may try to take your life is what you're sayin' to me.

GR: Um-hm, yes.

SHF: So that's another worry that you have.

GR: I have anoth- . . . yeah, I have that worry. Plus I have the [unintelligible word] . . .

SHF: You think Judith will . . .

GR: No, I don't think she'll come by.

SHF: . . . come to visit ya?

GR: No.

SHF: No? Why not?

GR: Because she's starting a new life.

SHF: She is? How, what do you mean? I don't know any about, anything that she . . .

GR: Ah, I think she's seein' somebody else.

SHF: Oh.

GR: She needs somebody else.

SHF: Uh-huh. Yes. Did she get a divorce?

GR: No, not yet.

SHF: Is that what she's . . . oh.

GR: It, it's in the process.

SHF: Yeah.

GR: Um, and then she doesn't, I don't wanna have her any more pain of it.

SHF: So if she did come to visit you, would you see her? You would?

GR: Um-hm. Yes.

SHF: But you don't think she'll, she'll stop by?

GR: No.

SHF: Think your son, Matthew, will be there?

GR: Eventually, yeah.

SHF: Come to see ya?

GR: Eventually he'll stop by.

SHF: Really?

GR: I think he will.

SHF: You know all these tapes, all these interviews that we've done will be released to the news media.

GR: Um-hm. Oh, yeah, I definitely.

SHF: You know that? Do you remember some of the parts where you talked about if your son was a witness, that you'd kill your son? What do you think he's gonna do when he sees that?

GR: Uh, I think he's gonna be upset.

SHF: You think he's gonna come and . . . do you think he's comin' to visit ya?

GR: I don't know. He prob'ly might.

SHF: After he knows you'd kill him?

GR: You know [crosstalk, word].

SHF: I heard, I've heard some, and there are some . . .

GR: You . . . that's, yeah, I said a lot of things that's . . .

SHF: . . . you think, you said you'd kill your son if he was a witness.

GR: It's, there was a, uh, there, there mi- . . . I, yeah, but I had . . . I had . . .

SHF: That's pure evil.

GR: I had [unintelligible word]. That's evil, but hey, I had a witness. I had the guy in that raft. Why didn't I kill him in the boat, the guy that called you guys.

SHF: Well, you had, you'd of had to swim out in the middle of the river.

GR: No, I would of called him over and, and, and if I wanted to kill him . . .

SHF: Well, I, I think you chose women because they're weak and you're

not uh, you're, essentially you're a coward. I don't think you're gonna go after a man.

GR: Oh, I could've.

SHF: I don't think so.

GR: I could have.

SHF: Yeah. You wouldn't have though. What if he would of killed you? That's prob'ly what you were thinking.

GR: I don't know. It . . .

SHF: You, you chose weak, young women because you're a coward.

GR: Uh, not, no . . .

SHF: You're ev- . . . you're pure evil, and you're a coward.

GR: I'm uh, pure evil, and they . . . they satisfied my sex habit for—guys wouldn't do that. I wouldn't, I wouldn't, uh, have sex with a guy.

SHF: There's male prostitutes out there.

GR: There's prob'ly a lot of male prostitutes, but that's not what I was into.

SHF: Yeah. But you would not have killed the, the guy in the raft.

GR: Prob'ly not, no.

SHF: No.

GR: Just like I wouldn't kill my son.

SHF: But a nine-year-old boy, eight-year-old boy, you could of killed. He's weak too. If that . . .

GR: He's weak, but I wouldn't. It's, it's . . .

SHF: But you said you would.

GR: Yeah, but I was also . . .

SHF: More than once.

GR: I was also, uh . . .

SHF: Why would you come, he would come to visit you after you said that? You're not gonna have, Judith isn't gonna come to visit ya.

GR: No.

SHF: Matthew's not gonna come to visit you.

GR: I don't . . . hard, hard to tell.

SHF: Do you care?

GR: Not really. It's uh . . .

SHF: If it . . .

GR: It's, they, if they don't wanna come, they don't have to come.

SHF: So it really doesn't matter.

GR: No. I did this, you know, now I gotta live with what I did.

SHF: Um-hm. Yes. What does that mean?

GR: I killed all these women. Now I've gotta suffer for what I did.

SHF: And how are you gonna suffer?
GR: Oh, bein', being in prison.
SHF: That's suffering?
GR: That's suffering, yeah.
SHF: The pain, uh, the pain that you put these families through?
GR: It's suffering because I'll be by myself . . .
SHF: It's, it doesn't even come, no . . .
GR: No, it doesn't come anywhere . . .
SHF: No, no.
GR: . . . close to it.
SHF: I don't feel sorry for you.
GR: I don't . . .
SHF: You're, I mean is that what you're . . .
GR: . . . think most people don't . . .
SHF: Nobody's gonna . . .
GR: Nobody's gonna feel sorry for me, no.
SHF: No, no way. You took, you took the lives of forty-eight women. You
   snuffed 'em out. More than forty-eight women.
GR: Seventy-one, yes.
SHF: Right. You killed 'em all, Ridgway. You killed 'em all.
GR: Um-hm. Yes, I did.
SHF: And you think you're gonna suffer by sittin' in a cell for twenty-three
   hours?
GR: I'm not gonna suffer as much as the women that I killed, no.
SHF: I guess not.
GR: They're, they're dead. That's, and it's, and . . .
SHF: Right. And what you did to them before you killed 'em . . .
GR: I choked 'em [crosstalk].
SHF: That's even worse to think . . .
GR: Yeah.
SHF: . . . think about.
GR: They, they died [crosstalk, unintelligible].
SHF: Ah, you did more than that. We know you did more than that. You
   didn't just choke 'em to death.
GR: I choked 'em . . .
SHF: There were things that you did that you don't wanna tell us about.
GR: N-no. The, that's, that's . . .
SHF: Things that are too horrible to even imagine.
GR: . . . that is, that is, that is what you think.
SHF: That's what I know.

GR: That is not what you know. When I put the tourniquets on their neck and I had to put their clothes on, the tourniquet slipped a lot of times and I really reeked on 'em. That's why there's tugs so far to their necks. No, I did not revive them and have sex with 'em or, or do any damage to 'em, no. I killed 'em. I put tourniquets on because I was not confident. That's why on a couple of 'em they had places where I had the uh, piece of wood or some'n jus' lodged in their back of their heads to keep them from, the tourniquet from movin'.

SHF: You're a coward. You choked 'em from behind. You choked young innocent women from behind, sixteen-year-old girls. You got behind 'em, you choked 'em, and you're, you're a, you're an evil, murdering, monstrous, cowardly man.

GR: Yeah, I am.

SHF: That's, that's basically it. And you did things to those women. You did things to those women before you strangled 'em.

GR: Hm, I had sex with 'em, that's all.

SHF: It would be important for us to know, but you chose not . . .

GR: No.

SHF: . . . to share that information with us.

GR: Because there is no-, nothin' to share. That . . .

SHF: I believe there is.

GR: There is . . .

SHF: You're lyin' again.

GR: No. There, there . . .

SHF: Then wh-why, why would we believe . . .

GR: The, the, the thing that I did to them was . . .

SHF: . . . you, Ridgway? Why would we believe you?

GR: The major thing was when I choked 'em . . .

SHF: What?

GR: . . . is when they died slow. I could count to sixty and they're dead. They [unintelligible, crosstalk].

SHF: What do you mean they, what do you mean, they died slow? You . . .

GR: They died slow because I was chokin' 'em. It's, there's got [sic] much air in their system. They're gonna die within fifty or sixty seconds.

SHF: Well, now you're a scientist?

GR: I think I read that in the, in . . .

SHF: What do you mean?

GR: . . . in that book of uh . . .

SHF: So you counted to sixty?

GR: I counted to sixty sometimes, yeah. Fifty, sixty—around.

SHF: What's the highest you've ever counted?

GR: I couldn't tell ya. I, I don't know. I read that in a book of uh, a, a book of . . .

SHF: So you kinda choked 'em and then you'd release it a little bit, and then you'd choke 'em a little bit . . .

GR: No, that's what . . .

SHF: . . . and release 'em, then you'd release 'em a li-

GR: . . . that's what your story is.

SHF: And then you'd choke 'em . . .

GR: No.

SHF: . . . a little bit, then you'd release 'em.

GR: No, I didn't.

SHF: Then you'd count and you'd kinda laugh.

GR: No, I . . .

SHF: Think it was funny.

GR: I choked 'em all the way, and I did know when to stop chokin' 'em.

SHF: What [unintelligible].

GR: I got tired. They were, they were dead, then I put a tourniquet around their neck on some of 'em.

SHF: You got tired?

GR: I got tired of chok-

SHF: Chokin' a sixteen-year-old girl?

GR: Yeah, sometimes. Then I'd put a tourniquet on. A lot of 'em I didn't.

SHF: See what I mean about . . .

GR: And after, after uh, when I got scratched with uh . . .

SHF: Malvar?

GR: . . . Malvar, I had to use a tourniquet because my arms were all uh, scratched up and uh, had acid on 'em.

SHF: You don't mean tourniquet, do you?

GR: It's what, a tourniquet's what I used.

SHF: Tourniquet?

GR: Wh-

SHF: What's a, what is a tourniquet?

GR: Tour-, tied as far as I could and put some'n through their knot. At home it was usually a ruler, and twisted it.

SHF: Oh. I hadn't, I hadn't heard the ruler piece. Is that just some'n you come . . .

GR: Ruler is what I used at home, and . . .

SHF: Have you told the detectives that, that you used a ruler . . .

GR: That's what I used. I don't know if I . . .

SHF: . . . to tighten up the tourniquet?

GR: . . . tur . . . told 'em or not. At, out in the woods it was a, a . . . when I did it out in the woods a few times, it was just a stick—Lovvorn.

SHF: So you choked 'em with your arm, but then you didn't get 'em all the way so then you'd put on a tourniquet.

GR: I did a tourniquet on uh, well, uh, socks around uh, because I was leaving when I did . . .

SHF: Lovvorn.

GR: . . . Lovvorn.

SHF: Um-hm, yes. Did . . .

GR: But most other ones, just with my arm. Christensen and [crosstalk, unintelligible] ones . . .

SHF: So you're gonna be known as a rapist too, you know, when you go to prison.

GR: I'll prob'ly be known as a rapist. Uh, there all, be all kinds . . .

SHF: Are you a rapist?

GR: No, I'm not.

SHF: But didn't you rape these, these girls?

GR: I had sex with 'em for money.

SHF: Isn't that rape?

GR: No. It's r- . . . it's robbery. It'd be robbery. They were for sex. I gave 'em . . .

SHF: Yeah, but you took . . . they didn't get paid. They died.

GR: Yeah, that's right. They, I took all this . . .

SHF: It's rape, but it's rape and murder.

GR: It's rape and murder, and rape and . . .

SHF: Rapists are the lowest on the totem pole when it comes to prison population. Did you know that?

GR: I know that.

SHF: So you're, you'll be known as a rapist and a murderer.

GR: I'll be known as the uh, Green River Killer that killed 'em for the money.

SHF: They don't give a shit about that. They . . . uh, you think those guys in prison give a shit about you as the Green River Killer?

GR: No, they don't.

SHF: That doesn't mean anything to 'em.

GR: They don't mean anything to 'em.

SHF: No. You're gonna be a rapist. You'll be a rapist and a murderer.

GR: Uh, I'll be a, a r- . . . I guess I'd be a rapist-murderer.

SHF: Yup. And you are.

GR: Um-hm, yes. I murdered 'em for uh, because I didn't wanna pay for sex.

SHF: But you're also a rapist. Is that so hard to say, yeah, I raped 'em.

GR: Technically I did it for murder, for money and for . . . no, I wouldn't be a rapist.

SHF: Not technically, no. You, you took the money away from 'em.

GR: That'd be robbery then.

SHF: Yeah, then you raped 'em.

GR: No. I, I paid 'em for sex. I killed 'em, and after I killed 'em I took their money—so that'd be robbery.

SHF: Well, when you, when you pay for sex . . .

GR: But when, when people . . .

SHF: . . . though, people leave with their money, then that's prostitution. But when you give 'em money and then you have sex with 'em and take their money away from 'em . . .

GR: That's [unintelligible, crosstalk word].

SHF: . . . and kill 'em, it's rape, robbery, and murder.

GR: Then it's rape, robbery, and murder—however, however [crosstalk word] . . .

SHF: So you're a rapist.

GR: . . . they wanna . . .

SHF: In fact we have a couple of cases where the women survived who were raped that we think you're responsible for.

GR: I don't think so [crosstalk].

SHF: I think Nancy McAllister came in and talked to you about one of those, didn't she, a rape case, and you, you got pretty upset with her. Detective McAllister?

GR: Uh, yeah, but . . . no, I wasn't upset because I [crosstalk].

SHF: You, you prob'ly did that.

GR: No, I didn't.

SHF: See, that's what I'm sayin'. You won't . . .

GR: I made a list 'a the ones . . .

SHF: . . . you won't talk about those cases.

GR: . . . I made a list of every one.

SHF: You aren't givin' us accurate information. That's pretty much it, isn't it?

GR: The ones I gave you is really accurate. I gave you, uh . . .

SHF: Forty-eight.

GR: . . . the forty-eight. And I gave you the one at uh, cro- . . . uh, not the cross street, but . . .

SHF: Right now, give me some'n we can go out right now and we can collect some bones and we can put, we can tie you right now, this second.

GR: There won't be any.

SHF: You can't, exactly. That's exactly my point.

GR: But I can tell ya where I . . . where I, where I had sex with ones . . .

SHF: You can lead us . . .

GR: . . . and there's no bodies . . .

SHF: Yeah.

GR: . . . because they were, I've already told . . .

SHF: So you're on your way, okay?

GR: I, I . . .

SHF: Uh, I, I can't do, what you're tellin' me right now, I can't do anything to change this sentencing date and keep you here for six more months. I can't do it.

GR: I, I don't think it'd be, it'd be a waste of time because I don't [crosstalk unintelligible] . . .

SHF: Yeah, that's what I think.

GR: Yeah, because there's no, there is no more. I don't remember any more.

SHF: Well, I . . .

GR: And I'm, I'm honest with ya. I don't remember any more.

SHF: I hope, Ridgway, that for your sake, that you have told us everything that you know because . . .

GR: Yeah.

SHF: . . . because you know what the, what the outcome will be.

GR: Yeah, I know there'll be another tr- . . .

SHF: When people come back . . .

GR: And, and I'll go back to trial just . . .

SHF: . . . and charge you with another case.

GR: . . . which I figure's gonna be one after the first year. I think I'll be goin' back in because of that one.

SHF: Right. And you could be facin' the death penalty then.

GR: Yes.

SHF: And you know that.

GR: I know that.

SHF: Okay. Well, this is it. It's uh, I'm not gonna say it's been a pleasure because it hasn't.

GR: Um-hm, yes.

SHF: Uh, I don't like you. I don't like what you did, and no one likes you or likes what you did for that matter. You don't even like you . . .

GR: Um-hm, yes.
SHF: . . . for what you did.
GR: Right.
SHF: Right?
GR: Um-hm, yes.
SHF: So uh, this will end the interview process. There'll be no one else in to talk to you, and uh, we'll see ya in court, uh, in court on Thursday.
GR: Okay.
SHF: Uh, but, we always have left a door open to you and we continue to do that. If you uh, have some revelation, uh, please call your attorneys and, uh, and they'll get a hold of us and we'd be happy to come back and, and visit with you.
GR: Hm . . .
SHF: But only if it's gonna be productive.
GR: Um-hm, yes.
SHF: Does that sound okay to you?
GR: That sounds okay.
SHF: All right.

Material above is from a weeks-long interrogation transcript by King County, Washington, police officers and other law enforcement officials. Photo courtesy of King County Police Department.

Arthur Shawcross

17.

ARTHUR SHAWCROSS

BACKGROUND

Arthur Shawcross was born in Maine in 1945, but his family moved to Watertown, New York, near the Canadian border. While the real truth about his childhood is uncertain, he spoke of a turbulent family life and of being sexually abused by an aunt at the age of nine. He had sex with his younger sister and had his first homosexual encounter at age eleven.

In 1967 he joined the army and served a one-year tour of duty in Vietnam. He related horrendous stories of murder and mutilation in the jungles and villages. He would claim a combat kill of thirty-nine enemies, but records showed that his unit saw little if any combat.

Once out of the service he became a serial arsonist and was eventually arrested for trying to break into a service station. He would serve two years of a five-year sentence for this.

In May of 1972, the killing began. His first victim was a ten-year-old boy whom he lured into the woods on the promise of going fishing. His second victim was an eight-year-old girl whom he lured to a deserted area while showing her a new bicycle. Both children were strangled and the girl had been sexually assaulted.

Eyewitnesses had seen Shawcross with the children and he was arrested. He confessed to both murders, but in a plea-bargain deal he was charged with only one count of manslaughter. He would serve fourteen

249

and a half years of a twenty-five-year sentence. He was released early because he was a model prisoner. Authorities thought he had reformed and could safely return to society as a productive citizen.

Upon his parole, he found it difficult to find a permanent residence. When newspapers or townspeople found out about his past, there would be an uproar and he would have to move on. In an effort to settle him somewhere, the parole board made the monumentally bad decision to cover his trail and seal his records from any further investigation. This allowed him to finally settle in Rochester, New York, an upstate community situated on the Genesee River.

About a year after he got out of prison, the bodies of murdered prostitutes began showing up, usually dumped in the Genesee Gorge area. The women had all been asphyxiated and sometimes mutilated. As the body count kept rising and the same MO was seen over and over, Rochester police realized they were dealing with a serial killer. An intense manhunt began.

One winter day the police got a lucky break. A helicopter pilot spotted a body splayed out on the ice below on a river. Shawcross was then seen urinating outside his car, which was still parked on the bridge. He was followed and questioned. In the face of mounting evidence, Shawcross finally admitted to ten murders.

A DAY IN VIETNAM

Arthur Shawcross was interviewed many times by police, psychiatrists, and law enforcement personnel. Here is what he had to say about one experience he had when he was in the service in Vietnam.

"Yeah, I go out there and came across a woman—[and] a girl was putting an AK-47 on the side of a coop and I shot her, tied-gagged her, took her up where I had a clear view of the area, tied her to a tree.

"I didn't have nothing to eat that day, and I took a big chunk of the hip of the girl. . . . I took off all the skin and took a piece of green bamboo and I ran it up inside the bone and I roasted it on the fire. . . . After it cooked down, it was almost like eating coal-broiled pork, the consistency of a dry roast beef. I was just in the mood, that's all. After I was done eating it—it didn't taste that bad—I took the body and carried it down through the jungle area where I knew there was a big anthill and laid it on the anthill, went back to the tree, and was sitting there sharpening the machete and eating that meat. The other girl had the sweat running off of

her. I untied her hands and tied her on the ground and raped her. . . . And I cut her throat, took her head up where the house was and put that head on a stick right in front of the house."

A SHAWCROSS VICTIM

"The next one was June Cicero," Shawcross told one psychiatrist. "She flagged me down. And she was pretty high-strung, and she got in the car, and we were driving out 31 somewhere, and—right at the moment I can't think. I can't remember, ya know? I just remember where I put her, and it was snowing, and snowplows were on the road, and I pulled up by this place, this culvert area, just pushed her out of the car, and she went over the guardrail. And what clothes that were still in the car, I put at a Salvation Army box on Manitou and 104.

"And I think about two, three days went by. I went back, and I had— I cut her, cut the vagina right out of her, bone and—bone and all. And I was driving around with that somewhere out there, and I ate that, too."

Material from Jack Olsen, *The Misbegotten Son* (New York: Delacorte Press, 1993). Photo courtesy of author.

Peter Sutcliffe

18.

PETER SUTCLIFFE

BACKGROUND

Peter Sutcliffe was born in Bingley, England. Considered the brightest of his parents' six children, he was also timid and something of a mama's boy who was bullied at school. He spent hours in the bathroom preening himself in the mirror. He was devastated when he learned that his mother had been having an affair with a policeman. Sutcliffe worshipped her and was traumatized by the event.

Prostitutes were his primary victims. His MO would be to cave their skulls in with a hammer, and then repeatedly stab and slash the dead body.

He stabbed one victim more than fifty times and gouged her back with a sharpened screwdriver. One veteran detective commented that after having seen the savagery of the attack, he was left "numb with horror."

All of England was in an uproar over these gruesome crimes, and the manhunt that was mobilized was the biggest ever seen in Britain. It involved 304 full-time officers who interviewed 175,000 people. He was interviewed several times himself but was always released.

During one period of his five-year reign of terror, someone claiming to be the killer sent a cassette tape and letters to the police. It turned out to be a cruel hoax that allowed Sutcliffe to kill three more women while the police concentrated on the misinformation. The hoaxer was never caught.

Sutcliffe was caught by luck. One evening the police spotted a prostitute getting into his car. She would surely have been his next victim. In the

course of being questioned about soliciting a prostitute, the police discovered he had false license plates on the car. Brought in for further questioning, he finally admitted to the attacks.

At his trial, he made claims that he had heard the voice of God telling him to rid the world of prostitutes. Several psychiatrists also stated that he was a paranoid schizophrenic, but despite his insanity defense, he was found guilty on thirteen counts of murder and sentenced to life in prison.

I thought "God, what have I done?" . . . I realized I would be in serious trouble. I thought the best way out of the mess was to make sure she could not tell anybody.

Killing prostitutes had become an obsession with me. I could not stop myself. It was like a drug.

The women I killed were filth-bastard prostitutes who were littering the streets. I was just cleaning up the place a bit.

THE MURDER OF HIS FIRST VICTIM, WILMA McCANN

(In Leeds at night.)

"I saw this woman thumbing a lift. I stopped and asked her how far she was going and she said, 'Not far, thanks for stopping' and jumped in. I was in quite a good mood and just before we set off she asked if I wanted to do business. I didn't know what she meant and asked her to explain and, it seemed to me, a scornful tone came into her voice. She said: 'Bloody hell, do I have to spell it out!' as though it were a challenge. My reaction was to go with her.

"I parked near a field and we sat there for a minute. All of a sudden, her tone changed and she said, 'Well, what are we waiting for! Let's get on with it.' Before we started, she said, 'It costs a fiver.' I was a bit surprised. I was expecting to be a bit romantic. I couldn't have intercourse at a moment's notice, I had to be aroused. She said, 'I am going. It's going to take you all fucking day. You are fucking useless.' I felt myself seething with rage. I wanted to hit her. I told her to hang on a minute and not to go off like that. She said, 'Oh you can manage it now, can you?!' I said, 'Can we do it on the grass!' This was my idea to start hitting her.

"She stormed off up the field. I had a hammer in the tool box and I

followed her up the field. I had the hammer in my right hand and put my coat on the grass. She sat down on the coat and unfastened her trousers and said, 'Come on, get it over with.' I said, 'Don't worry, I will.' I then hit her with the hammer on the top of the head. She made a lot of noise and kept on making noise so I hit her again. I hit her once or twice and she started making a moaning noise. I felt, 'God what have I done!' I knew I had gone too far.

"I sat in the car and could see her arm moving. I was in a numb panic. I half expected her to get up and realized I would be in serious trouble. I felt (it best) to make sure she couldn't tell anyone. I would stab her in places like her lungs and throat. I was in a blind panic when I was stabbing her, just to make sure she would not tell anybody. I can't remember driving back. I thought I was bound to get caught. I looked over my clothing before I went into the house, then I went straight upstairs to the bathroom, washed my hands and went to bed. I carried on as normal, living with my wife. After that first time I developed and played up a hatred for prostitutes in order to justify within myself a reason why I had attacked and killed Wilma McCann."

Material from http://www.brainyquote.com/quotes/quotes/p/petersutc l227798.html (accessed July 23, 2010) and first-day trial transcript, Tuesday, May 5, 1981, Central Criminal Court, London. Photo courtesy of Dewsbury Police Station.

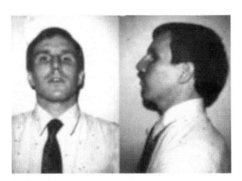

Michael Swango

19.

MICHAEL SWANGO

BACKGROUND

Dr. Michael Swango's intercontinental murder spree lasted from 1983 to 1987. Good looking, blond, blue-eyed and affable, openly supportive of his superiors, he was often well liked and appreciated by fellow professionals. He was aware of his charisma and used it to cover his suspicious maneuvers and his chronic lies. The nurses knew he was up to no good, but doctors paid no attention until the suspicious deaths started piling up. When the FBI finally caught him, he explained how he loved the "sweet, husky, close smell of indoor homicide. [These murders were] the only way I have of reminding myself that I'm still alive."

In 1982, while Swango was studying to become a doctor, his father, Virgil, a retired colonel, died. Though he was adored by his mother, Muriel, Swango was never close to his father, but he did show up at the funeral, and perhaps knowing that he would like it, his mother gave her son a memento of his father's, a scrapbook bulging with stories. The general theme was mayhem: assassinations, disasters, and mass killings. When Swango, who had started his own book of mayhem, found out, he beamed with boyish pride. Said Swango, "Hell, I guess Dad wasn't such a bad guy after all."

Perhaps a little competitive with his father after that, Swango scoured libraries and other outlets to gather more stories and photos. At one point one of his medical colleagues was forced to ask him why he had such a ghoulish hobby.

Swango's answer was scary: "If I'm ever accused of murder," he responded, "this will prove I'm mentally unstable."

DOUBLE O SWANGO

Fellow med students were surprised by his attitude toward death, which was bizarre to say the least. For one thing, he was fixated on critically ill patients, holding death watches for them. And when they died he did something that, in retrospect, is hard to believe he got away with. Swango would write "DIED" across their chests in huge letters.

Swango had a ready answer for one of his interns who asked how he could be so cold about death.

"Hey," he said, "death happens."

But with Swango it happened much more than with other medical personnel and earned him the nickname "Double O Swango."

But still, no one really looked beneath the surface to determine what was really going on. One of the coldest things he did was when he was a medical student at Ohio State University to a patient named Anna Mae Popko. He gave her a shot to elevate her blood pressure. Anna's mother had wondered why he wanted her to leave the room. But she did—she was forced out—and later Swango returned with what seemed like a triumphant smirk and said, "She's dead now. You can go look at her."

WHAT TURNS HIM ON

In the mid-1980s, Swango became a medical corpsman in his hometown of Quincy, Massachusetts, working at Blessing Hospital with fellow emergency corpsmen Mark Krzystofczyk, Jim Daniels, Brent Unmisig, and others, including Lonnie Long, who captained the group. They thought Swango was not a threat of any kind, just a guy with a bizarre sense of humor. But it got creepy when he would champion poison as the best way to kill someone, or gleefully told his fellow medics that he loved being a doctor because "It gives me an opportunity to come out of the emergency room with a hard-on to tell some parents that their kid has just died."

KIDS ON FIRE

Swango once described a fantasy he had that those who listened couldn't believe. "It's like this," he began. "Picture a school bus crammed with kids smashing head-on with a trailer truck loaded down with gasoline. We're summoned. We get there in a jiffy just as another gasoline truck rams the bus. Up in flames it goes! Kids are hurled through the air, everywhere, on telephone poles, on the street, especially along an old barbed wire fence along the road. All burning."

JUST A GREAT GUY

Reporter John Stossel, who became personally interested in the alleged crimes of Swango, sought an interview with him in prison for the investigative television program *20/20*. Swango agreed to talk and what resulted was rapid-fire dialogue. Stossel questioned Swango about the poisons in his Quincy apartment, about his internship in Ohio, and about his reaction to the mess he found himself in. Throughout, Swango insisted he was innocent, resenting the monster figure that press had made him out to be. Said he, "I did not do these things. It is simply beyond my—well, beyond the sort of person I am to even think about doing something like that."

SWANGO THE CRIME WRITER

Swango was always a voracious reader who liked nothing better than reading detective and police books, and he often concocted stories that he would tell to one of his girlfriends, Joanna Daly. All she thought oftentimes was that they sounded sick and sordid.

Then one day, excited and ebullient, he told her a plot that he was entranced by: "Someone is in town," he began, "and there's a serial killer at large. Then someone else kills in the same way. Everyone thinks this person is the serial killer—but they're wrong! They relax, and ten years go by. Then the serial killer kills again—just for fun." Daly, whom he later poisoned, didn't know what he was talking about.

I LOVE BUNDY

While being a physician and a murderer in Zimbabwe, Africa, Swango learned that there was going to be a miniseries on Ted Bundy. He asked his girlfriend to tape it because he "loved" Bundy.

"You mean you loved the show," Daly said.

"No, I love Bundy," he said. "He was a genius."

In addition to Bundy, he esteemed charismatic religious leader Jim Jones, whose followers committed suicide by his orders in Guyana in 1978. In a very real sense, one key to Swango's personality was that he loved death more than life—other peoples' deaths, that is.

Material from Joseph Geringer, "Doctor of Death," http://www.trutv.com/library/crime/serial_killers/weird/swango/index_1.html (accessed July 26, 2010) and James B. Stewart, *Blind Eye: How the Medical Establishment Let a Doctor Get Away with Murder* (New York: Simon & Schuster, 1999).

20.

AILEEN WUORNOS

BACKGROUND

Aileen Wuornos

Aileen Wuornos is undoubtedly the most famous female serial killer. She was born in the Midwest. By the time she was fourteen, she was working as a prostitute. She had developed a profound hatred of men, and in 1992 in Florida, she started picking them up, leading them into the woods ostensibly for sex, and then shot them to death. She claimed that they tried to rape her, but this didn't hold water. All told, she murdered seven men and died from lethal injection. Ironically, it was not a man but a woman, her lesbian lover, Tyria Moore, who set her up to be arrested by taping incriminating telephone conversations. Charlize Theron gave an Academy Award–winning performance as Wuornos in the motion picture *Monster*. When Wuornos was convicted, she screamed at the jury: "I'm innocent! I was raped! Scumbags of America, get raped!"

I'm a serial killer. I would kill again.

I need to die for the killing of those people.

I really got tired of it all. I was angry about the johns.

I robbed them, and I killed them as cold as ice, and I would do it again, and I know I would kill another person because I've hated humans for a long time.

I wanted to clear all the lies and let the truth come out. I have hate crawling through my system.

I'm one who seriously hates human life and would kill again.

My main concern is if this composer has been made aware of the fact that I've come clean in all of my cases. I killed in pure hate, robbing along the way. So if this person hasn't, then I'd sure appreciate it if someone would inform him or her of it.

I'm a good person inside, but when I get drunk, I just don't know. It's just . . . when I get drunk, don't mess the fuck with me.

I wanted to confess to you that Richard Mallory did violently rape me as I've told you. But these others did not, only began to start to.

I'm only here for that concealed weapons charge in '86 and a traffic ticket, and I tell you what, man, I read the newspaper, and I wasn't one of those little suspects.

—From a phone conversation with Tyria Moore

Just go ahead and let them know what you need to know, what they want to know or anything, and I will cover for you, because you're innocent. I'm not going to let you go to jail. Listen, if I have to confess, I will.

—From a conversation with Tyria

I know, and they wanted to hang me. And that's cool, because maybe, man, I deserve it. I just want to get this over with.

—When asked if she realized she was talking to cops

I hope your wife and children get raped in the ass!

—What she told assistant state attorney Ric Ridgeway

Motherfucker.

—What she called Judge Thomas Sawaya
after he gave her three more death sentences

I'm one who seriously hates human life and would kill again.

—What she wrote in a letter to the Florida Supreme Court

I'd just like to say I'm sailing with the Rock and I'll be back like Independence Day with Jesus, June 6, like the movie, big mothership and all. I'll be back.

—Wuornos from the execution chamber.
The Rock is a biblical reference to Jesus.

Material from http://www.brainyquote.com/quotes/authors/a/aileen _wuornos.html (accessed July 26, 2010) and Serial Killer Database, used by permission of Joshua Henderson. Photo courtesy of Florida Department of Corrections.